HITLER'S HEROINE
HANNA REITSCH

SOPHIE JACKSON

The
History
Press

First published 2014

The History Press
The Mill, Brimscombe Port
Stroud, Gloucestershire, GL5 2QG
www.thehistorypress.co.uk

British Library Cataloguing in Publication Data.
A catalogue record for this book is available from the British Library.

ISBN 978 0 7509 5297 2

Typesetting and origination by The History Press and Printed in Malta by Melita Press
Production managed by Jellyfish

CONTENTS

INTRODUCTION

On the movie screen a petite Hanna Reitsch stares up with naïve wonder at the ranting man she has come to adore and idolise. Hitler rages in fury at Himmler's betrayal before calming himself and revealing his final (and nonsensical) plan to save Berlin. Eyes wide in admiration, her voice a mere whisper, Hanna looks up. 'I kneel down to your genius and before the altar of our fatherland,' she says.

This sycophantic, sickening Hanna – cringe-worthy as she worships the man who has destroyed Germany – is very different from the confident, cocky aviatrix who struts across a different movie screen towards a modified V1 flying bomb. A death trap for previous pilots, the rocket plane stands with its cockpit open awaiting her. 'There's no point in your taking unnecessary risks.' Hanna is told as she strides to the plane, 'We've lost four pilots already.' 'I've got to find out why these damn crates won't fly,' she replies calmly.

The first Hanna appears in a German movie produced in 2004, *Der Untergang (Downfall)*, played by the actress Anna Thalbach. The second Hanna appears in the British movie *Operation Crossbow*, produced in 1965, played by the German actress Barbara Rütting. Hanna is central to neither of these movies, but performs as part of a side-story. In *Downfall* she barely makes two scenes, in *Operation Crossbow* she features early on and then vanishes once she has tested the V1 successfully (it was *Operation Crossbow* that invented the myth that Hanna test flew V1s to find out why they were missing their targets). Yet the two performances are diametrically opposed to each other. The sycophantic, almost idiotic

Hanna against the cool, self-assured, controlled Hanna. More than most characters of the Nazi regime she has become parodied to extremes, either viewed as a stupid girl who believed in Nazism or as a heroine of female flying. Even her name sparks controversy, far more than conversations involving other Nazi followers, such as Hans Baur, Hitler's pilot. Over and over again Hanna is either derided and scorned or discussed in overly sympathetic and apologetic tones. Neither attitude does her justice, nor do they represent the real Hanna.

Delving through the myths, the propaganda, the hatred and the adoration, the real Hanna surfaces as a pale flicker of light; as a woman who wanted to make her mark at a time when the only people with power were Nazis. She has been called politically naïve; that is perhaps rather generous. Others have labelled her a hardened Nazi, which is perhaps too harsh.

Time has allowed historians to gain perspective. It has enabled more and more academic analysis of the realities behind the horrors of Nazism. Interest is now being paid to what is sometimes called 'the ordinary Nazi'. The man or woman in the street who believed in National Socialism but not in the extermination of the Jews, who recognised the good Hitler had done for Germany – saving it from poverty, increasing employment, rejuvenating its cities and towns – and found it hard to level this with stories of persecution, cruelty and death. Much was hidden; much was not.

Some years ago, a Russian friend explained her own complicated views on Communism. When she was a child Communism had seemed the greatest thing imaginable. She was from a poor family, yet Communism enabled her to have ballet lessons, nurtured her potential and gave her hope. Only after coming to Britain as an adult did she begin to learn of its dark side. She started to study this 'other' Communism and realised that the society she had treasured for the opportunities it had given her was built on such secret cruelty, misery and corruption – it was almost unbelievable. It was impossible to reconcile this view with her own memories. Her happy childhood was now overshadowed by the knowledge that that happiness had been bought by murder and violence.

She is no different to the disillusioned National Socialist who had been spoiled by a system that was now turned on its head and exposed as brutal, desperate and barbarous. Culling people's perceptions and memories, especially happy ones, is not easy. It is even harder when those people are suffering the shock and poverty of post-war Germany. Should it surprise any of us that those people might hark back to better times, when Hitler first came to power? Germany was torn to shreds, divided by concrete and guns and left to suffer like a wounded animal after 1945. During Hanna's lifetime that suffering seemed unremitting, she did not live to see the destruction of the Berlin Wall or the flourishing of modern Germany. She saw only devastation – is it so hard to imagine that bitterness and sadness made her think of her glory days when Nazism was young?

In a recent interview the 80-year-old daughter of Rudolph Höss, notorious commandant of Auschwitz, defended her father as 'the nicest man in the world' because to her he was, and in comparing that personal image with one paraded to her by the enemy, no matter how true, the reality was impossible to accept.

Hanna had a similar view of Hitler. Always looking for a father figure in her life, she made Hitler her ultimate paternal guide. Affectionate and generous to her, kind and ready to promote her dreams, he was everything a girl could want. Joining this with his post-war image of villainy and corruption was difficult for her. She was disillusioned, hurt and very frightened. She was a girl without a father figure to support her (her own father sadly committed suicide, as did her other male mentor, von Greim). Yet Hanna did deny Hitler. It hurt her and she wished it to remain quiet, but she did tell Americans of his apparent mental collapse and the horror and the shame she felt after learning what had really gone on. She had plans to prevent Nazism resurfacing in Germany, she had hopes to build a brighter future; for this she was smashed down and abused.

Hanna has been harshly treated by many over the years, while her supporters have gone to the opposite extreme, glossing over her mistakes and making the matter worse. Somewhere between the two views lies the real Hanna, the woman who pioneered flying for women, who for many remains the greatest of test pilots. Who spoke her mind and often suffered for it. Hanna did not want pity; she just wanted to fly, that was all she ever wanted. She made bad choices, but no more so than other men and women within the Hitler regime who have been treated with generosity by history.

Why has Hanna drawn so much criticism? Why was she laughed at and shunned? What made her the villain of the piece when her actions within Nazism were very minor? Within Hanna's story jostle an assortment of characters who had done far more to aid Hitler; from the man who created the V2 rocket, to the pilot who never lost his Nazi leanings. Hanna was no Nazi, but she was no innocent either. The story of the real Hanna is only slowly emerging and must compete with tall tales told about her exploits and cruel words spoken by one-time friends. This volume focuses on the person behind the label of Nazi Aviatrix, and naturally must delve most deeply into her involvement with Hitler during the war. This is not an apology for Hanna, nor a character assassination, but an attempt to portray a complicated person impartially. Along the way Hanna's story exposes what life was really like for a woman with dreams in the Germany of the 1920s and 1930s.

THE HANNA REITSCH
WHO'S WHO

Wernher von Braun: 1912–77

After the war von Braun gave himself up to the Americans and was taken to the United States under the secret Operation Paperclip. Von Braun worked on the United States Army Intermediate Range Ballistic Missile programme until it was incorporated by NASA. He then served as a director at the Marshall Space Flight Centre and was chief architect of the Saturn V launch vehicle used on the Apollo spacecraft for the moon landing. Despite his former allegiance to the Nazi Party, von Braun was readily adopted by the Americans, largely because of his skills as a rocket scientist. In 1975 he was awarded the National Medal of Science. Von Braun died in 1977 aged 65, from pancreatic cancer, leaving behind his wife Marie Luise (married 1947), two daughters and a son.

Otto Skorzeny: 1908–75

Skorzeny was born in Vienna and joined the Austrian Nazi Party in 1931. He was known for being charismatic and was easily identified by the dramatic duelling scar on his cheek. A bit player in the 1938 Anschluss (when he prevented the Austrian president from being shot by local Nazis), he was already a member of the SA (Sturmabteilung) when he tried to join the Luftwaffe in 1939. Deemed too tall and too old (6ft 4in and aged 31), he instead joined Hitler's bodyguard regiment, the Leibstandarte SS

Adolf Hitler. Skorzeny impressed his superiors not only with his design skills – he had been a civil engineer pre-war – but with his courage and skill in battles on the Eastern Front. In December 1942 he was hit by shrapnel in the back of the head, but refused all medical treatment aside from a few aspirins, a bandage and a glass of schnapps. The wound quickly worsened and he ended up being rushed to Vienna for treatment.

Skorzeny was most famous for his rescue of Mussolini and his part in putting down the rebellion caused by the July 1944 plot on Hitler's life. In 1947 he was tried as a war criminal for ordering his men to dress in discarded American soldiers' uniforms during the Battle of the Bulge. The trial descended into farce when former SOE (Special Operations Executive) agent Forest Yeo-Thomas told the court that he and other operatives had worn German uniform to get behind enemy lines. To convict Skorzeny would expose the Allies' own agents to possible court proceedings. He escaped conviction, but was detained in an internment camp awaiting the decision of a denazification court. In 1948 Skorzeny escaped the camp and went into hiding. He was reported in various countries over the next few years, sometimes working for their intelligence agencies. He helped countless former SS men escape Germany.

He died from lung cancer in Madrid in 1975.

Wolf Hirth: 1900–59

Hirth was a renowned glider and sailplane designer; his brother Hellmuth founded the Hirth Aircraft Engine Manufacturing Company. Hirth was born in Stuttgart and took up gliding as a young man, gaining his licence in 1920. He lost a leg in a motorcycle accident in 1924, but continued to fly with a prosthetic leg. Hirth founded a company with Martin Schempp in 1935, officially becoming a partner in 1938. They manufactured gliders, their first design intended to rival the famous Grunau Baby. During the war the company made assembly parts for the Me 323 and Me 109, along with other aircraft. Immediately post-war the company had to switch to making furniture and wooden components for industry, only switching back to gliders in 1951. In 1956 Hirth was elected president of the German Aero-Club. Three years later he was flying an aerobatic glider when he suffered a heart attack. He died in the subsequent crash.

Heini Dittmar: 1911–60

Dittmar was inspired by his elder brother Edgar to begin gliding and took up an apprenticeship at the German Institute for Gliding (DFS). He went on to build his own glider, *Kondor*, which he used during the Rhön soaring competitions of 1932. Throughout the 1930s and 1940s he both worked with and competed against Hanna Reitsch. He had once been besotted with her, but after she spurned his advances he began to perceive her as a rival. Post-war, Dittmar continued to work as a test pilot. He died while testing a light aircraft of his own design in 1960, when the plane crashed.

Peter Riedel: 1905–98

Riedel had a troubled childhood; his father, a Lutheran pastor and a theology professor, suffered frequent bouts of mental illness and his mother committed suicide. He spent some of his childhood with his uncle. In 1920 Riedel attended one of the soaring competitions on the Wasserkuppe and took part in it in a home-built glider. From then on he always attended the competitions while also acting as a commercial pilot. In 1936 he began working for an American airline and was approached by the German Military Attaché and offered a post in Washington DC. Riedel gathered intelligence on the US and forwarded it to Germany.

When America entered the war, Riedel and other Germans were interned and ultimately deported back to Germany. Riedel's American wife went with him. For a time he worked for Heinkel as an engineer, then he was offered a diplomatic posting in Sweden. Once on neutral territory he began to learn the truth about the Nazi regime and was horrified to think he was working for these people. He tried to strike a deal with the American OSS (Office of Strategic Services), but was denounced by a co-worker and recalled to Berlin. Knowing his fate would be brutal if he returned to his homeland, Riedel went into hiding and remained out of sight until the end of the war.

Post-war, Riedel was arrested as an illegal alien in Sweden. He managed to escape and fled to Venezuela, eventually being joined by his wife Helen. For a few years they lived and worked in Canada and South

Africa, until settling in the US, where Riedel flew for TWA and Pan Am. After his retirement Riedel devoted his time to writing the definitive history of gliding in pre-war Germany and shortly before his death his biography was published.

Captain Eric Brown: 1919–present

Former Royal Navy officer and test pilot Eric Brown is said to have flown more different types of aircraft than anyone else in history – 487, to be precise. He first flew as a boy with his father and developed a passion for aircraft. Attending the 1936 Olympics, he met the First World War ace Ernst Udet, who offered to take him up in a plane. Brown eagerly accepted and during their flight Udet told him he must learn to fly. Brown was in Germany just before the war and was arrested by the SS at the outbreak of hostilities, though fortunately he was merely escorted to the Swedish border. Back in the UK, he joined the Royal Navy Volunteer Reserve as a Fleet Air Arm pilot.

He served on the first escort carrier, HMS *Audacity*, before spending time as a test pilot. In 1943 he flew with the Royal Canadian Air Force, as well as with Fighter Command, before returning to test work. After the war he was employed testing captured German planes, including the infamous Me 163, to gain vital knowledge. He was able to fly a captured Fw 190 and gave his opinion:

> The stalling speed of the Fw 190A-4 in clear configuration was 127mph and the stall came suddenly and without warning, the port wing dropping so violently that the aircraft almost inverted itself. In fact, if the German fighter was pulled in a g-stall in a tight turn, it would flick out on to the opposite bank and an incipient spin was the inevitable outcome if the pilot did not have his wits about him.

With his good grasp of the German language, he was also useful for interviewing German pilots such as Hanna Reitsch.

During the Korean War, Brown was seconded as an Exchange Officer to the United States Naval Test Pilot School and flew a variety of US aircraft. In 1957 he returned to Germany as Chief of British Naval

Mission to Germany with the remit of re-establishing German naval flying, separate from the Luftwaffe (under which it had fallen during the Nazi years). He retired from the navy in 1970.

Brown has written several books on aviation through the years, as well as numerous articles, and is considered one of the best authorities for the comparison of British and German wartime aircraft.

Mathias Wieman: 1902–69

Though Wieman wanted to become an aircraft designer as a young man, he found himself instead pursuing an acting career. He started on stage in the 1920s as a member of the Holtorf-Truppe theatre group, working alongside other well-known German actors, including Marlene Dietrich. Towards the end of the 1920s he moved into silent movies and was most active in the 1930s, performing in *The Man without a Name, Queen of Atlantis, The Countess of Monte Cristo* and *The Rider of the White Horse*.

During the war Wieman fell out of favour with the Nazi regime, with Goebbels in particular, which greatly reduced his ability to land acting roles. Though he did star in some films, his glory days were past. After the 1944 attempt on Hitler's life, he and his wife helped the family of one of the failed plotters.

Post-war, Wieman found more work, largely in support roles, but also producing LPs of classic stories accompanied by orchestral music. He moved to Switzerland with his wife, where he died in 1969 from lung cancer.

Hugh Trevor-Roper: 1914–2003

English historian and professor of Modern History at Oxford, Hugh Trevor-Roper was born in Northumberland and studied history at Oxford. He is most famous for his bestselling book *The Last Days of Hitler*, which was much inspired by his work as an intelligence officer and designed to refute the rumours circulating that Hitler had escaped death in the bunker.

During the war Trevor-Roper served as an officer in the Radio Security Service of the Secret Intelligence Service, and in the interception of messages from the German intelligence service, the Abwehr. Trevor-Roper held a low opinion of many of his pre-war commissioned colleagues, but felt those agents employed after 1939 were of much better calibre.

Though not his first book, *The Last Days of Hitler* made his name as a top-rate historian. The book was internationally acclaimed (though for a long time it could not be sold legally in Russia) and even earned him a death threat. His lively, humorous and intelligent style made the book something of a historical classic.

Trevor-Roper was not opposed to criticising other historians or offering alternative opinions on history, particularly such subjects as the English Civil War and the origins of the Second World War. He successfully discredited the work of Sir Edmund Backhouse on Chinese history, causing the history of China as known in the West to be heavily revised. More controversially, he stated that Africa did not have a history prior to the Europeans, as there was nothing but darkness in terms of documentation before the arrival of the latter. This has caused great debate as to what actually constitutes 'history' in societies without a literary tradition.

In 1983 Trevor-Roper was notoriously involved in authenticating 'Hitler's Diaries', later shown to be fakes. Though this led to many jokes in the press, it did not ruin his academic career, and he continued to write and publish. Trevor-Roper died of cancer in 2003. Five previously unpublished books and collections were issued posthumously.

Hans Baur: 1897–1993

Hans Baur was born in Bavaria and flew during the First World War. He joined the Nazi Party in 1926 and first flew Hitler in 1932 during the general elections. Hitler felt confident in Baur's hands, especially as he helped him to avoid airsickness, and wanted to be flown by Baur exclusively. Baur was given the rank of colonel and sent to command Hitler's personal squadron. In 1934 he was promoted to head of the newly formed *Regierungsstaffel* and was charged with organising flights for Hitler's cabinet members and generals. He had eight planes under his command, but Hitler always flew in his personal plane with the tail number D-2600.

Baur became a friend of Hitler, able to talk to him freely and even offer advice. Though Baur refused to be converted to vegetarianism, Hitler invited him to the Reich Chancellery for his favourite meal of pork and dumplings on his fortieth birthday. Hitler was also best man at Baur's marriage to his second wife. In 1939 Baur persuaded Hitler to change his personal plane to a modified Focke-Wulf Condor, but the number D-2600 was retained.

In 1944 Baur was promoted to major-general, and in 1945 to lieutenant general. He was with Hitler in the bunker and had devised an escape plan for the Führer, which Hitler refused. Baur was not present at Hitler's suicide, but witnessed the bodies being burned. He then attempted to flee Berlin with others, but was shot in the leg and captured by the Russians. He spent ten years in Soviet captivity, ultimately losing his injured leg and enduring torture, starvation and interrogation. For many years the Soviets wanted to know where he had helped Hitler escape to, much to Baur's frustration. He finally returned to West Germany in 1957 and started work on a book about his experiences during his time with Hitler. His second wife had died during his imprisonment; he went on to marry a third time.

Baur managed to skirt most of the controversy that affected other survivors of the Third Reich, possibly because he was absent for so long from his home country. He continued to live in Bavaria, where he died in 1993.

Robert Ritter von Greim: 1892–1945

Son of a police captain, von Greim joined the Imperial German Army in 1911 before transferring to the German Air Service in 1915. Two months later, he scored his first victory and went on to fly over the Somme. He ended the war with twenty-eight victories and had earned himself the title of Knight (Ritter). Between the wars, von Greim trained in law and spent time teaching flying in China, before joining the Nazi Party and participating in the 1923 putsch. In 1933 he was asked by Göring to help rebuild the German Air Force and in 1938 he assumed command of the Luftwaffe department of research.

Von Greim was involved in the invasion of Poland, the invasion of Norway, the Battle of Britain and Operation Barbarossa. In 1942 his only son was listed as missing and thought dead. In fact, he had been shot down by a Spitfire and spent the rest of the war a POW in the US.

Von Greim committed suicide in 1945 rather than be used by the Americans as a witness against other Nazis at the Nuremburg trials.

Jawaharlal Nehru: 1889–1964

Nehru was the son of a wealthy barrister who was also a key figure in the struggle for Indian independence. He was sent to study at Trinity College, Cambridge in 1907 and spent a great deal of his spare time studying politics. He returned to India in 1912 intending to settle down as a barrister, but the rising tensions in India and the continuing struggle for independence distracted him and he was soon involved in the movement.

The First World War drew mixed feelings from Nehru. His comrades were celebrating Britain's fall, but he found it hard to side with the Germans. He ended up volunteering for the St John's Ambulance. Nehru was now known for his political motivations and spent much of the next few years in and out of prison. He also spent a great deal of time with Gandhi.

During the Second World War he had again mixed feelings, but initially backed the British. When continuing protests at British rule in India were ignored, he started to feel less sympathetic. Though not impeding the war effort, Nehru and Gandhi did not help it with their displays of civil disobedience. Strains were placed on their friendship as the latter was adamantly against compromise with the British, even when Japan was threatening India's borders. Nehru was less inclined to go against the Allies, but chose to side with Gandhi. India had become very divided and internal disputes were common, and would affect politics in the country for years to come.

Post-war, the British withdrew from parts of the subcontinent and Nehru became Prime Minister of India. Gandhi was assassinated shortly after. Nehru was a good political leader who promoted peace, but the many tensions within India meant his life was also endangered on more than one occasion. He survived these attempts, but the toll of power aged him and ravaged his health. Nehru died of a heart attack in 1964.

Indira Gandhi *née* Nehru: 1917–84

Indira had an unhappy childhood with her mother often ill and her father in prison. The only child of the future Indian prime minister, she retained the family fascination for learning and eventually studied history at Oxford University. She was plagued by ill health and was being treated in Switzerland in 1940 when the dangerous encroachments on Europe by the Nazis caused her to retreat to India.

Indira married Feroze Gandhi and in the 1950s acted as her father's personal assistant. After his death she initially turned down the role of prime minister, but later accepted in 1966. India was still riven by internal tensions, and Indira had to battle these while raising two sons and enduring the criticism of US president Richard Nixon. Everything came to a head in 1977, when Indira was arrested and put on trial for allegedly plotting to kill all the opposition leaders who were at that time in prison. The trial backfired on her accusers and she gained a great deal of sympathy from the Indian people.

She was back in power in 1984 when she was shot by two of her own bodyguards just before she was due to give an interview to British actor Peter Ustinov. She died several hours later having been riddled with thirty bullets.

Kwame Nkrumah: 1909–72

Born on the Gold Coast, Nkrumah had trained and worked as a teacher before sailing to England and subsequently America to study. He read books on politics and became fascinated by Marxism and communism.

Nkrumah returned to Africa in 1947 and sought the independence of his country. The British withdrew from the Gold Coast, now Ghana, in 1951 leaving Nkrumah in charge. As president, Nkrumah had positive and negative points, the latter outweighing the former and he was regularly vilified in the British press. He became increasingly despotic and paranoid until a military coup was effected in 1966, while he was on a trip abroad. Persuaded of the futility of returning to Ghana, Nkrumah lived out his final years in exile writing books on his ideology and ousting from power.

He died of skin cancer in 1972, and is still remembered fondly by some in Africa. In 2000 he was voted Africa's man of the millennium and in 2009 a Founders' Day was created as a statutory holiday to commemorate his birth.

1

BORN TO FLY

Hanna Reitsch will fly the helicopter! screamed every poster in Berlin as the International Automobile Exhibition welcomed guests and journalists to the Deutschlandhalle. Within the large hall a petite woman with swept-back dark hair sat inside a machine that was to make history. No one had flown a helicopter like this before; in fact, no one had flown a viable helicopter before. This was a true first and Hanna realised the glory and responsibility placed upon her to fly the machine safely within a confined space.

There was little time to note the circus performers dressed in colourful garb and practising their somersaults and tricks on the side lines, nor the way the hall had been decked out to look like an African village as Hanna settled herself in the helicopter. With her slightly prominent chin, bulbous nose and hair hidden by a flying cap, few probably realised the person about to perform a miracle was a woman. Indeed, Hanna had only been due to fly on the first night, until her fellow male pilot had accidentally upset Herr Göring. In any case, no one was really looking; the real interest was not the pilot but the strange machine with double propellers facing into the air, giving the hybrid appearance of an aeroplane crossed with an ordinary household fan.

Hanna had practised for hours for this moment. The controls were sensitive and awkward, very little was needed to move the helicopter in a given direction and that was a danger: a slight miscalculation and Hanna could sweep into the audience, decapitating and maiming dozens in the process. The skill required made her tense, it also irritated her that this gargantuan feat was being performed as part of a spectacle for a mildly curious crowd. But if Germany wished to prove it was the first to build a successful helicopter, then this was how it had to be done. No one would take it seriously otherwise.

Hanna rose slowly, the propellers kicking up the sand and dirt on the floor and blowing off people's hats. She climbed to a safe height, eye-level with the upper spectators, concentrating solely on the finely balanced controls, her brow lined with effort. Carefully she edged the machine forward, then gently turned. The helicopter moved with grace, belying the intense strain placed on the pilot to keep it steady. Moving back across the hall for one last turn, Hanna began her descent with relief. Another performance over, another crowd going home uninjured and the helicopter had demonstrated itself perfectly.

By now Hanna knew her display would not bring a standing ovation. The crowd was curious, but soon bored with the helicopter. What did it do but hover? How could that compare with the swooping aeroplanes they had seen before? Or the fast cars they had come to observe? The helicopter was an anti-climax, rather dull in fact: few really understood its potential at that moment.

But Hanna climbed out of her machine beaming her wide, enthusiastic smile. Never happier than when in the air, she was rightly proud of her achievements and those of Germany. She was elated to be standing on the verge of a new era in which Germany would prove itself a nation of inventors, engineers and geniuses. In February 1938, in the circus atmosphere of the Deutschlandhalle, anything seemed possible. The future looked full of hope. How little Hanna knew. How soon would this world of wonder plunge into war, taking her, the helicopter and the German flying community down a path of self-destruction from which Hanna would never recover. She beamed at the audience, and dreamed.

On a stormy night in March 1912, two years before Germany marched itself into the First World War, a screaming Hanna was brought into the world in Hirschberg, Silesia. Emy Reitsch stared at the scrawny bundle in her arms. On other dark nights she had had pangs of foreboding that she would not survive giving birth to another child, but here she was with her new daughter in her arms, alive and well. But that foreboding would always linger with her and project itself onto Hanna – Hanna was now the one who was always worried about and deemed fragile. Hanna was the one Emy would dread dying, as if this tiny baby were as delicate as glass. In contrast, Hanna would throw herself into more and more dangerous situations, as if defying over and over again that strange prediction of her mother.

Hanna was born into a reasonably well-off family. Her father was an eye doctor, her mother the daughter of a widowed Austrian aristocrat. Hanna was only the second child, her brother Kurt was 2 at the time of her birth. She would eventually be followed by a sister, Heidi.

Hirschberg was a beautiful city. Situated in a valley and almost entirely surrounded by mountains, Hirschberg had existed since 1108 and had a population of around 20,000 at the time of Hanna's birth. The grand C.K. Norwid Theatre with its golden towers had opened ceremoniously in 1904 and the National History Museum opened to the public in 1909. A tram network opened in 1897 was already an integral part of city life by 1912. One thing in particular would come to delight Hanna: the natural heights around Hirschberg provided ideal opportunities for gliding, not to mention hiking, a popular pursuit of the Reitsch family. From a religious perspective, the city had a sixteenth-century chapel and a fifteenth-century basilica. Emy Reitsch had Catholic roots, but her husband was Protestant and she would raise her daughter on a mixture of the two, endowing Hanna with a complicated spiritual outlook.

The Reitsch family viewed themselves as German, or technically Prussian, with a deeply patriotic connection to Berlin. But Hirschberg was originally Polish, and there were still many among the population who felt more closely connected to Poland than Germany. The tensions between the two states did not make for easy living, but a form of harmony existed, even if it was fragile.

The problem was that Silesia had a complex history; originally part of Poland, it had become part of the Habsburg monarchy's territory in the sixteenth century, effectively making it Austrian, though parts remained in Polish hands. With the renunciation of King Ferdinand I in 1538, Silesia had become part of Brandenburg. All these minor border changes paled in comparison with the upheaval caused by Frederick the Great of Prussia in 1742 when he invaded and took control of most of Silesia.

His interest was unsurprising; Silesia had thriving iron ore and coal mining industries. State-driven incentives, including the first modern blast furnace in a German ironworks in 1753, helped industry to flourish. Incentives for migrant workers encouraged them to join Silesia's linen industry, which expanded rapidly under the protection of beneficial tariffs and import bans.

Invading Silesia itself had proved remarkably easy for Frederick (as it would almost 200 years later, when Hitler chose to invade the parts of Silesia that had fallen into Polish hands after the First World War). A long thumb-shaped piece of territory, with the River Oder running its length, starting in the mountains of Upper Silesia and finishing in the sea at Stettin, bisecting Brandenburg along the way, Silesia was an awkward piece of land sandwiched between various rivals. Poland sat on one side, while on the other was the kingdom of Saxony. The Saxon Elector, Frederick Augustus II, was doubling as King of Poland, so there was a natural incentive to absorb the nuisance expanse of Silesia into his kingdom.

Frederick the Great got there first, in a move some thought rash and impulsive. Whatever the case, Silesia officially became a part of Prussia. In 1871 the Prussian kingdom became part of the German Empire and Prussian leadership was supplanted by the new German emperor.

All this jostling of the state naturally tended to give its occupants a complex view of their origins and loyalties. Silesia was populated by a mix of Poles, Czechs, Germans, Prussians and those who considered themselves natural-born Silesians, not to mention the many immigrants who had been attracted to Silesia by its various thriving industries. Into this complicated historical blend of cultures Hanna Reitsch was born.

When Hanna was 6 the First World War ended and Silesia lurched into a new period of uncertainty. First there was debate within the German Republic as to whether Prussia should continue to exist at all. There was talk of boundaries being dissolved and Prussian influence being destroyed. In the end Prussia survived, though its powers were severely curtailed. Meanwhile, Poland was arguing that Upper Silesia should become part of the Second Polish Republic and in 1921 this is exactly what happened. What remained of the Prussian province of Silesia was redefined as Lower and Upper Silesia, while the small portion of territory termed Austrian Silesia, which had eluded Frederick the Great, was given to Czechoslovakia.

This was a strange time to be living in Silesia, let alone Prussia. That the Reitsch family were able to retain a strong sense of identity and a patriotic link to Germany is remarkable in itself, but the unpleasant annexing of different parts of their state, though they were unaffected, remained a lingering anxiety in their consciousness.

For Hanna, childhood continued as it had always done; she went to school, where she talked too much and was known for her larger-than-life presence and exuberance. At home she learned music and spent time with her mother, forging the close bond they retained until the latter's death. But in the wider German world trouble was rife. Berlin, once ruled by the Prussians, was in turmoil. No one was certain who was in control and there were plenty of opportunists ready to fill the gap. On 7 January 1919 leftists took over a railway administration headquarters and government troops swooped in with small arms and machine guns. While the battled raged a train full of commuters calmly travelled on an elevated viaduct over the fighting, apparently oblivious to the chaos. A witness, Harry Kessel, remarked, 'The screaming is continuous, the whole of Berlin is a bubbling witches' cauldron where forces and ideas are stirred up together.'

Revenge killings began in earnest. The Communist leaders Rosa Luxemburg and Karl Liebknecht were arrested and beaten to death by members of a cavalry guards division. Fuelled by violent hatred, the Communists launched into all-out civil war: 15,000 armed Communists and supporters took control of Berlin's police stations and rail terminals; 40,000 government and Freikorps troops had to be called in and machine guns, field artillery, mortars, flame-throwers and even aeroplanes, which had only months before been pounding Belgium and France, were now turned on the capital. When the rebellion came to an end on 16 March the dead numbered 1,200 and trust between the old leadership and the people had been destroyed forever.

Anti-Semitism in Prussia during the 1920s was as rife and virulent as anywhere else in Germany; in places it even seemed to go deeper. Branches of the German Church began spouting racist propaganda; in 1927 the Union for the German Church announced in one of its publications that Christ would 'break the neck of the Jewish-satanic snake with his iron fist'. Hanna's strong links with the Church through her mother would have brought her into contact with diverse views, including those of some Christian groups who believed that collections for mission work to the Jews should be stopped. At the General Synod of the Old Prussian Union in 1930 a vote was taken to exclude the mission to the Jews from official Church funding. The disheartened president of the Berlin mission wrote letters appealing to Church leaders to reconsider, noting his horror that so many clergymen had succumbed to anti-Semitism.

The attitudes of their superiors had to have an effect on the personal outlook of the ordinary churchgoers. Hanna was still a rather dreamy youth and the religious controversy around her failed to penetrate her consciousness deeply, but it was there nonetheless and she could hardly have been ignorant of the growing resentment towards the Jews, as she later claimed.

For Hanna, life revolved around school and the desire to fly. All she talked about was taking to the air. After the war strict limitations had been placed on Germany's flying capabilities. Powered flight was forbidden. To fill the void, aviation enthusiasts took to gliding, soon turning Germany into the greatest gliding nation. To Hanna gliding seemed everything. The mountains of Hirschberg offered the perfect place for soaring in the air and it was normal enough for Hanna to walk to school or catch a tram and see a glider swooping overhead like a bird. But such dreams were for boys, not girls. Girls got married and had children. Girls did not aspire.

But Hanna did, and when her father finally grew weary of her constant flying talk he extracted a promise – if Hanna said no more about flying then in two or three years, when she had finished school, her father would reward her with lessons at a gliding school in Grunau, not far from Hirschberg. Herr Reitsch hardly knew the error he had made. He imagined his daughter flighty, impulsive and unable to control herself. He did not recognise her iron will and determination, especially when it came to flying. Hanna kept her side of the promise, as torturous as it was for a naturally vocal child, and when she finally left school it was with her usual, enormous smile that she reminded her father of his promise.

It was now 1931. The rise of National Socialism was like a feverish virus infecting the German population. In 1928 the NSDAP (Nationalsozialistische Deutsche Arbeiterpartei) had been nothing more than a chain-rattling splinter party with only 2.6 per cent of the vote. Two years later, with the unexpected dissolution of the Reichstag, it made a triumphant rise to 18.3 per cent; 810,000 Nazi voters in 1928 had turned into 6.4 million in 1930. National Socialism was now a big threat to the other political parties and Prussia was particularly uncomfortable at seeing such a controversial splinter group making the biggest gain of any political party in German history. Nazi apologists have made a case for National Socialism seeming very innocuous in its early days, fooling innocent, if gullible, citizens into voting for a party that would later turn out so evil. But this is whitewashing history; the Prussian authorities recognised the danger in 1930 and made it illegal for any Prussian civil servant to join the NSDAP. They considered the Nazi Party anti-constitutional and preparations were even made to have it banned altogether. As history tells us, this never happened.

Instead, the Nazi Party continued to gain popularity, as did its para-military branch, the SA – despite a ban on their activities. Across Silesia membership of the SA had gone from 17,500 in December 1931 to 34,500 in 1932. As sheltered a life as Hanna led, it would be impossible to avoid all signs of the conflict within Germany. It was akin to a small revolution. SA storm troopers, identifiable by their brown shirts, would rumble into the streets after dark and seek out Communists for a fight. Soon the police and the Reichsbanner (a half-forgotten republican militia) were absorbed into the fray and all-out brawls turned streets into battlefields, with residents finding evidence of the violence the next morning in the blood on the pavements, smashed windows and the odd lost knuckle-duster. Still, in 1931 Hanna was lost in her plans to fly.

The School of Gliding in Grunau would have done little to inspire a casual observer; there was a large hangar where the gliders were kept and a small wooden building that served as a canteen and shelter during bad weather. The rest was open ground. But for Hanna riding up on her bicycle, the scene was electric. 'My heart was filled with joy,' she later recalled.

The instructor at the school was Pit van Husen, a man who would later be remembered as the greatest of glider pilots. Van Husen was strict with his pupils, for good reason. Gliding looked simple, even safe, but it was far from it. Glider pilots did die when their flimsy craft were hurled into an unexpected storm or they misjudged a landing. Hanna rarely knew fear, however, and now she was on the practice field she would not be deterred by talk of accidents. Nor would she be upset by the unpleasant stares and comments made by her fellow, all-male, students. Hanna was not welcome. Her presence was resented and openly mocked. She was a petite 5ft 5in among the lean, tall Aryans who sidled around the airfield and she endured her fair share of snide remarks that a woman should know her place and stay in the kitchen. She later claimed that she ignored these comments, but evidence from other sources suggests she was more sensitive than she cared to admit. The sneers of her fellow students stung and they spurred her to become defiant and to be the first to truly fly.

Van Husen started his students slowly, first allowing them to learn to balance the glider on the ground while he held one wing-tip, then having them perform short slides on the ground. It was during one of these that Hanna decided enough was enough – she would show these obnoxious boys what she was made of! She had completed one slide and was restless. 'Flying does not seem difficult,' she thought to herself as she sat in the glider waiting for her last slide. 'How would it be if I pulled back the stick just a fraction, without anyone noticing? Would the "crate" take me a yard or so up into the air?'

So the School of Grunau learned what the real Hanna was like. The daredevil within had taken over. The other students, wanting to spook this frail little girl who had infiltrated their class, hauled extra hard on the rope to give her a really fast slide. Hanna pulled back the stick just a few inches, and the combination sent the glider soaring. Hanna was jerked forward then back, for a moment she had no sense of what was happening, then she was looking up into blue sky. Hanna was flying!

From below a frantic Pit van Husen was shouting for her to come down. Hanna pushed the stick forward, the glider's nose dropped steeply. She didn't want to land, didn't want to come out of her bubble, and she pulled the stick back and climbed again. But then something happened, the airspeed dropped, the glider lost whatever thermal it had found and she plunged downwards. There was a crash and Hanna found herself thrown from the plane with a gang of whooping boys tearing towards her. The glider was in one piece, so was Hanna, and she stood up and laughed at the oncoming students, who were delighted to see a woman fail so dramatically. Pit van Husen was another matter. 'What did you think you were doing?' the instructor was screaming at her, bellowing in his fury and fear. 'You are a disobedient, undisciplined girl! I should never have allowed you here, you are completely unfit for flying!'

Hanna was cowed before the boys who were smirking and enjoying the performance. 'As a punishment,' continued van Husen, 'you will be grounded for three days!' Van Husen spun on his heel and stalked off. Several students followed, but a few remained. They were quietly impressed by Hanna's daring. After all, she had been the first to fly. As they helped her haul the glider back to its start point, they gave her a new nickname – Stratosphere.

Hanna cycled home more dejected than she liked to admit to herself. Her foolhardiness had stripped her of her dream to fly before she had even begun. Now she would have to ensure she stayed on van Husen's good side to avoid any further bans. It was to be far from the last time Hanna's tendency to act before she thought landed her in trouble. What Hanna could not know as she rode home, arguing with herself that she was *not* completely unfit for flying, was that Pit van Husen was working on removing her from the course altogether. After Hanna had gone, he went to report to Grunau's director, Wolf Hirth, and explained the full problem. A pioneer of gliding, Hirth was something of a god to his young students. He had a round, jovial face which, when he smiled, folded into happy creases and crumpled up his eyes. He was never happier than when flying, undeterred at having to wear both glasses and a prosthetic leg, having lost the original limb in a 1924 motorcycle accident. If anyone spotted him smoking they might have noted his unusual cigarette holder carved from the fibula of his lost leg.

Hirth had taken up gliding at the same age as Hanna, in the days just after the First World War, when gliding was all that remained of Germany's aviation industry. He had excelled at competitive gliding, particularly in annual competitions at Wasserkuppe. Nothing deterred him. Certainly not the loss of a leg. Hirth's brother, Hellmuth, had founded the Hirth Aircraft Engine Manufacturing Company and this, coupled with having a father who was an engineer, spurred Hirth to explore aircraft construction. In 1928 he attained his diploma in engineering from the Technical University of Stuttgart and over the next decade would promote gliding in almost every country across the world.

The year 1931 had brought another dramatic change in Hirth's life: he was involved in a serious crash during a gliding demonstration tour in Hungary. Sustaining major injuries, he was confined to hospital for four months and had not been long back in Germany at his training school when the reckless, headstrong Hanna landed on his doorstep. Still reeling from the effects of his own crash, van Husen's tales of Hanna's adventures were enough to make him sweat. The last thing the Grunau School needed was a fatal accident involving a girl. 'We must get rid of this girl,' Hirth told van Husen. 'We don't want any corpses.'

That night Hanna sat on her bed mulling over what she had done. Her temper was dulled by thoughts of what could have happened, how she could have been seriously hurt or worse. Van Husen's words kept ringing in her ears and it was difficult to contain tears of frustration and humiliation. It would be hard to live down the episode, especially among her fellow students. Worse, Hanna was now grounded. She had a tendency towards self-pity throughout her life, but as a teenager it was natural enough and the long hours of winter darkness were not helping. She desperately wanted to prove herself to van Husen, to everyone.

Finally, at some point in the wee hours of the night an idea struck her; she might be physically grounded, but no one could ground her mentally. She sat on the bed and wedged a walking stick between her knees as if it were the steering column in a glider. Then she imagined the finely balanced plane all around her, and practised keeping the stick perfectly upright so a wing-tip would not dip and touch the ground. In her mind the students were clustered around the bungee, she called to them, 'Heave!' They pulled. 'Double!' They pulled harder. 'Away!' They released her and Hanna was so engulfed in her fantasy she felt her body jerk as the glider started on a long ground slide. So Hanna continued for the next hour, practising ground slide after ground slide, before falling into an exhausted sleep. Hanna would fly one way or another.

Three days without flying were torture, but Hanna endured them, consoling herself with her imaginary night-time flying. Van Husen was watching her like a hawk, looking for any reason to be rid of her for good, but Hanna refused to give him such pleasure. Instead she was the perfect student and even began to form friendships with some of the boys on the course. One was a handsome student with curly blond hair and a broad smile who seemed like any other enthusiast to Hanna, even if he was a little dreamy, his mind far away out in the reaches of space. Wernher von Braun was a rocket man. As a boy in Berlin he had found himself in a police station after attempting to create the first rocket-powered child's wagon. The experiment, in the middle of fashionable

Tiergartenstrasse, had gone disastrously wrong. The six large skyrockets he had attached to his wagon had quickly gone out of control, shooting the flimsy cart violently back and forth across the street while streaks of flame flew out behind. Naturally he had scared a number of people, caused a minor panic and come close to endangering the wellbeing of several passersby. It was an inauspicious start to the career of the man who would be pivotal in the creation of the V2 rocket and jet-propelled aircraft. Sitting quietly on the grass between gliding flights, Hanna could hardly imagine the role this young, dashing man would play in her future. By 19 von Braun had his glider pilot's licence; by 21 he had a regular pilot's licence. Throughout her life Hanna would remain friends with the boy who dreamed of rockets.

But friendship at Grunau was always tainted with the mockery Hanna 'Stratosphere' earned simply for being female. She had failed and no one would let her forget it. Then luck finally fell in Hanna's favour. Another student had had a disastrous A test flight and van Husen wanted to explain the reasons why to his students. He told Hanna to sit in the empty glider to ensure it didn't move while he lectured the group. Hanna did as she was told; sitting at the controls, she envisaged herself on her bed and stared out at the sky as if about to be launched. She was so absorbed in her dreaming it was only the laughter of her fellows that roused her. Pit van Husen was amused; he should never have allowed this undertrained girl into the sky, but an odd, mischievous thought arose in his mind. 'All right, harness up!' he shouted, and before Hanna knew it she was in position to be launched into the air.

Hanna took to the skies; she focused on a spot ahead and concentrated all her energy on keeping the glider straight and true. She was in the air for less than forty seconds, but it was enough to convince her that she must spend her life flying. She landed perfectly, having unexpectedly passed the A test for gliding. It was pure chance, of course, the boys yelled. Van Husen was similarly unconvinced. 'I expect that was just luck. I can't count it for your A test,' he said. Then he paused. 'You had better try it again, straight away.' Naturally, Hanna flew perfectly and passed the test a second time.

Curiosity now overcame Wolf Hirth. Who was this girl who was in danger of fatally crashing one minute and the next passing her A test without any practical experience? Hirth had to meet her in person.

Petite Hanna was neither awe inspiring nor impressive in appearance, but then neither was Wolf Hirth. He was a little on the plump side and very ordinary looking for someone treated as a god of gliding. He liked Hanna almost instantly: she reminded him of himself. Hirth took Hanna under his personal tutelage and soon she was flying and passing her B and C tests. She impressed him so much that he allowed her the privilege of flying the school's newest glider, one normally reserved for instructors and Hirth. Hanna had permission to stay in the air as long as she pleased; she stayed there for five hours and landed to learn that she had broken the world record. For the first time Hanna's name was on the radio and Hirth was delighted – he could not have asked for better publicity for his training school.

Hanna was meant to be training as a medical student, but her head was now, quite literally, in the clouds. She could no more concentrate on her studies than she could resist the temptation to fly again – this time in a powered aircraft. She was studying medicine in Berlin and it happened that nearby was a flying school run by the German Air Mails. Based at Staaken, the school ran a course in flying sports planes and Hanna persuaded her father to pay for yet another set of lessons. By this point Herr Reitsch was despairing of his daughter achieving anything in her studies, but she swore she would stick to medicine if only he would let her learn to fly. In fact, she had plans to become a flying doctor in Africa, so she *had* to take a flying course, didn't she?

There were a few more women at Staaken than at Grunau, though female friendships would never be a priority for Hanna. In fact, for most of her life she was quite a lonely individual; her relationships were professional and often with men, but they rarely developed into anything close. At Staaken she came to know Elly Beinhorn, five years her senior, who had recently returned from flying around the world. They were friendly enough at the time, though years later Elly did not warrant a mention in Hanna's memoirs, *The Sky My Kingdom*. One person who did, however, was a young actor named Mathias Wieman, who had only recently appeared as a supporting actor in the German film *Avalanche*, '... with whom I soon formed a real flying friendship', Hanna recalled.

Not all was happiness at Staaken. The years were ticking by towards Hitler's catastrophic accession to power and the reek of politics was often in the air. Hanna was politically ignorant; in fact, politics was a topic that entirely failed to interest her. She had been raised a good German patriot and this she would remain without questioning it unduly. Honour, to her, meant loyalty, even when that loyalty was misplaced. Hanna lived partly in a world of imagination; escaping into the skies was part of that. When something penetrated that happy sphere she was shaken and uncomfortable, she would turn away and dig her head into the figurative sand. Hanna did not want to know about the world of politics. It was too complicated, too frightful and it would destroy her brave dreams of loyalty, honour and hope. These were her exact feelings when she befriended a group of workers near Staaken. Every now and then the workers would launch into arguments over politics:

> In the whole gang there were hardly two who belonged to the same party and with horror I realised how people who otherwise get on well together can become bitter and fanatical opponents as soon as politics are mentioned. It was all new to me … one day so fierce an argument developed between them that they almost came to blows. Then, depressed and thoughtful, I left them, for our happy atmosphere seemed now finally to have been destroyed.

This was Hanna's attitude throughout the war. Politics to her was something distasteful that brought out the worst in people, but she tried to retain a quiet loyalty to Germany without judgement. This unfortunately meant loyalty to Hitler and all the horrors such misplaced, foolish, honour would bring.

2

A NEW WORLD

Hanna was determined to ignore German politics because it made her uncomfortable, but politics was not ignoring Germany: 1932 saw the end of Prussian power as Reich president Paul von Hindenburg chose to collaborate with the Nazi Party and demolish the old republican system. It all led to the carefully orchestrated 'Bloody Sunday' of 17 July. The Nazis staged a provocative march in Altona, a busy harbour in the Prussian province of Holstein, riling up tempers in the working-class district with the result that eighteen were killed and 100 wounded. It was the culmination of many days of street fighting between the SA and the Communists, a bloody turf war that ruined faith in the Prussian system of government. The Prussian government was declared to have failed to keep the peace in its territory and an emergency decree deposed the Prussian minister-president Otto Braun and his ministers. It might not have been so easy had not the Prussian authorities resigned themselves to their fate, thus opening the door for Hitler's period of tyranny.

Hitler came to power in 1933 as Hanna was working with Wolf Hirth on a book concerning the theory behind flying in thermals. As much as Hanna chose to distance herself from the reality of politics in her country, she could not change the distance of her hometown from the epicentre of Nazi power. Breslau (now Wroclaw, Poland) was only an hour and a half away from Hirschberg by car and in 1932 it had become the strongest support base for the Nazis – 44 per cent of the city's vote was National Socialist. Immediately after he came to power Hitler began to persecute the city's Polish and Jewish population. Breslau had the largest Jewish community outside of Berlin, many of whom were thoroughly integrated into the city's society – not the stereotypical Eastern European Jew that propaganda sought to vilify. Fewer than half were even practising their religion, but this would not save them from the blood lust Hitler had sparked.

Jewish-Marxist books were burned in huge bonfires. Jewish businesses were boycotted and Jews were forced to give the Nazi salute to passing SA troops. Boys from the Hitler Youth (Hitlerjugend) flooded the streets, singing 'Set fire to the synagogues'. Ordinary citizens felt pressure to exclude Jewish friends from their lives. Already relationships between Jews and non-Jews were banned. Many Breslau citizens, who would otherwise have considered themselves good people, cut Jewish ties, quietly expunging Jewish friends from their lives and disowning former relationships.

The Gestapo moved in to seek out 'undesirables', and these included Communists, Social Democrats and trade unionists, along with the Poles and Jews. It was now illegal to speak Polish in public and anyone who looked Jewish was in constant danger; many were herded together and sent to concentration camps. One of these camps was Gross-Rosen, originally a satellite camp to the notorious Sachsenhausen before it became independent in 1941 and started to create its own sub-camps. One of these sub-camps was at Hirschberg, Hanna's hometown.

While specific evidence of anti-Semitism in Hirschberg is mostly unrecorded, we can infer the atmosphere of the town from examples of what was happening all around it in Silesia. With Breslau very close, the Nazi influence in the area was strong and tension was high among the various ethnic groups. Hitler whipped up resentment that had been festering away just beneath the surface. Hanna's mother complained of the Jews, blamed them for the bad that had happened to Germany. She might not have resorted to violence against them, but many of her neighbours would have. Mostly it started with bullying tactics: dead cats and pigeons thrown into Jewish gardens, the beards or hair of Jewish men being pulled on the street. This was simply an escalation of the vague anti-Semitism that had existed before Hitler. Jews had been called 'Christ killers' before 1933, only now such abuse was authorised by the state.

Name calling was one thing, but the situation was rapidly to get worse. Abuse became more violent, Germany imposed more and more restrictions on Jews and it became noticeable to the public that there was a widespread persecution of Jewish culture happening under their very noses. Yet neither Hanna nor her mother discussed the crisis spreading all across Silesia. No mention was made of the sub-camp to Gross-Rosen being built at Hirschberg. When vast numbers of people vanish, all from the same population, it has to be noticeable. Businesses were inexplicably closed; the Jewish owners disappeared. Yet still Hanna noticed nothing. Her home, her country was falling apart, but her only priority was a selfish one – getting to fly again. In fact, not even her beloved gliding escaped Hitler's grasp. After the First World War and the ban on powered flight in Germany, the only means any dictator had of building an air force of new, young pilots was to train them in gliding.

While Hanna was learning of the freedom gliding could bring her, Hitler was using the sport to further his plans for world domination. The Hitler Youth was already bringing military discipline and training to the young boys who would be future members of the Wehrmacht or SS. The Flieger-Hitlerjugend or Flying Hitler Youth was training future members of the Luftwaffe. They started by building and flying model gliders, gaining a basic grounding in the principles of flight. They moved on to a short flight in a glider, much the same as Hanna had done in her training, before progressing to longer flights and, eventually, to powered aircraft at secret airfields in Russia. By the time Hitler was ready to unveil his Luftwaffe to the world he had several units of young pilots trained in this manner, all under the pretext of healthy fun and games. Not only were they ready to fly, but their early experiences had instilled a passion and enthusiasm vital for the numerous dangerous missions they would soon be involved in.

In May 1933 Hanna was busy with the 'Grunau Baby', the very latest in training gliders and the pride and joy of Wolf Hirth. Hanna was home in Hirschberg, having just scraped through her medical examinations, by luck rather than judgement – she had spent far more time studying plane physiology than she had human. The invitation to fly the Grunau Baby was both unexpected and exciting. Hirth was interested in filming Hirschberg from the air using the Baby and saw no reason why Hanna might not try the glider. Dressed in a light summer frock and without goggles or helmet, Hanna climbed happily into the glider, little realising this was going to be one of the most frightening flights of her life. 'Try flying her blind,' Hirth said confidently as he set out to tow her into the air.

It was a beautiful day and at 1,200ft Hanna cast off, taking full control of the Baby. Beautiful as the sky was, for flying it was disappointing: there was no wind and before long Hanna was heading back to the ground. Two hundred and fifty feet above the earth Hanna prepared to land – disappointed at the false start – when her wings quivered. Was this an unexpected up-current? Hanna circled and the glider climbed a little, then it suddenly dropped. Searching for the frail up-current she had just encountered, Hanna instead came across a second, stronger one. She began to climb again, first steadily, then faster and faster until, before she knew it, she had risen to around 1,500ft in barely two and a half minutes. A more experienced pilot would have been worried by this change. Hanna did not immediately sense anything was wrong. Instead she was pleased to be rising again. Then her eyes came off the instruments and looked out into a hideous black storm cloud.

It had only formed in the last few minutes, unobserved as Hanna had obeyed Hirth's instructions to fly blind. Now she looked at it, not with fear, but with glee. 'Here, at last, was the opportunity of an experience I had been longing for, to fly through a cloud.' Was Hanna really so blind to danger? The answer is a simple yes. She was confident in her own abilities and besides: '… Wolf Hirth himself told me that as long as he has that knowledge [of flying instruments], a pilot can come to no harm.'

Hanna was now 3,600ft up and headed for the storm. She broke into the base of the cloud, catching one last glimpse of the world below before she was absorbed into the black mass and a thick layer of cloud blocked out everything. Hanna pinned her eyes to her instruments. She climbed another 20ft, and for a moment she feared hitting the nearby Riesengebirge mountain, but then she relaxed: her instruments read 5,500ft and the Riesengebirge peak is only 5,200ft. Still Hanna underestimated the danger.

Suddenly the storm erupted. Rain pelted her wings and turned into a loud hammering that overwhelmed every other sound, like an army of drummers pounding on the Baby. Worse, the windows were beginning to ice up and just beyond them Hanna could see rain and hail crashing out of the sky. Now she was afraid. Where was she? What would happen? Hanna checked the controls and they told her she was still flying true.

As fast as it began, the storm ended, but at once it was replaced by buffeting winds that tossed Hanna about in her cabin, and still she was rising! Her instruments, when she could see them, read 9,750ft! Then they just stopped. They refused to move up or down. Panicking, Hanna thumped at them, but they didn't move. They had frozen solid …

With no instruments Hanna was truly blind. Scrabbling at the control stick, she made a desperate effort to maintain normal flight, but what was normal in this dense, hellish cloud? Before she could connect her thoughts there was a new noise, a sort of high-pitched whistle, first loud then quiet. For any pilot it was a terrifying sound – the sound of a plane slipping into a stall. The noise would stop any moment and then Hanna would have a split-second to push the Baby's nose down before the glider became completely uncontrollable. The whistling ceased. Hanna thrust forward the control stick and lurched in her harness, but already it was too late. Helpless, falling forward, the blood rushing painfully into her head, Hanna was diving vertically, the Grunau Baby flipped over on its back. There was nothing to do. For an instant the Baby swung forward, but the dive continued, its speed building and building. Hanna pulled frantically at the control stick, heaving it back as hard as she could, trying to right the plane and completely unaware she was performing a series of involuntary loops. Still the glider shot downwards, Hanna hanging from her harness while the world shrieked by.

The mica windows had frosted over. A sudden claustrophobia enveloped Hanna and she smashed her fist into the plastic, forcing open a hole, so at least she could get one last look at the world. Her head spun, her brain in agony as the g-forces of the dive pummelled her. She was frozen, the rain pouring through the hole in the mica drenching her light summer dress. Her hands had turned blue. Hanna had failed the Baby and all she could do now was let go of the controls and hold a vain hope the natural stability of the plane would counter the dive. Fear had turned into panic, an overwhelming sense of terror engulfing Hanna Reitsch. She could not move a muscle. The fierce gale of air caused by the plummeting glider had forced her mouth open as she tried to clench her teeth.

Then, remarkably, the Baby started to climb again. The violent thrust from one position to another was even worse for Hanna. Her eyes felt as though they were bulging from their sockets and Hanna expected blood to spurt from her temples any moment. 'HANNA-A-' she screamed to herself, trying to get her mind out if its loop of terror. 'Ya! Ya-a! Coward!

Hang on, can't you, cowa-ar-!' The Baby flipped again, and now when Hanna dared to look up it was not sky she saw but dark brown earth. Something awoke inside her; she reached automatically for the controls and turned the glider right-side up. She was still very high in the air, ahead were the snow-covered peaks of Riesengebirge and even further away the rapidly moving storm clouds. She had been spat out by the clouds and by some chance of fate had survived her deadly plunge. The terror receded as fast as it had come. The slopes of Riesengebirge coasted by beneath her. Despite the ear-splitting dive, Hanna was still over 5,000ft up.

Picking a clear spot for a landing, Hanna came down beside a hotel-restaurant serving a ski resort on the Schneekoppe. It was evening and no one appeared to notice her land. Hanna walked into the hotel and presented a strange sight to the skiers; not only was she completely inappropriately dressed for such altitudes, but Hanna was soaked from head to foot, her hair clinging to her head and face in bedraggled dreadlocks. She placed a call to Wolf Hirth from the hotel reception. The Baby would need a tow to get her airborne again and there was a lot of explaining to do, not least because Hanna had crash-landed across the Czechoslovak border and come down in a neutral zone without permission. Germany, or rather Hitler, had been nagging at Czechoslovakian anxieties for a while (they were soon to discover with good reason). A German glider in the middle of the neutral zone was going to ring alarm bells.

Hirth could not risk landing his own powered plane on foreign soil to rescue Hanna. The best he could do was to drop a towrope and leave his student the task of recruiting skiers from the hotel to haul her up into the air. Fortunately, the hotel residents were enjoying the novelty of the unexpected plane and a number of them volunteered to pull on the Baby's starting rope. Hanna took to the air once more. Darkness was descending as Hanna traced her path back to Hirschberg. She lost sight of Hirth before long and visual landmarks vanished into the gathering night. She landed in a likely looking field. The glider had lost too much height for anything else, and she resigned herself to wait for Hirth to find her once more. This was to be just the first of many Hanna-esque adventures.

Hanna came close to losing her wings again that day in 1933, both literally (for she had come close to crashing) and metaphorically. What would the new German regime make of the daring girl who had broken frontier regulations and crash-landed in Czechoslovakia? In fact, the authorities were ecstatic – Hanna had broken a new altitude record. Who cared about a silly border infringement? Once again, Hanna was mentioned on the radio and discussed in the national press. All this would naturally go to a young woman's head and Hanna had always been one to crave attention and glory. Emy clucked around her daughter as she basked in the adulation of a fickle public. 'Remember that false pride is a sin,' Emy rebuked. Hanna was cross. Throughout her life she would find it difficult not to revel in her achievements, nor to avoid coming across as boastful when she was really only enthusiastic. If Emy was worried about her daughter's pride, her father was worried about her education. It had become all too plain that medicine did not really appeal to Hanna. Herr Reitsch would not have worried so much if there was a prospect of his eldest daughter getting married, but there had been no boyfriend during her teenage years and the man she was closest to was the middle-aged and happily married Wolf Hirth. What had become of those handsome young men Wernher von Braun and Mathias Wieman whom his daughter had once spoken of? But Hanna was not interested in the burdens of love and marriage: all she thought about was flying. Boys were very far down her list of priorities.

Throughout her life, speculation followed Hanna concerning her personal relationships. Those who dabbled in such rumours included the British test pilot Eric Brown, who once met Hanna and maintained a postal acquaintance with her, despite war coming between them. He suggested that Hanna was in a relationship with Field Marshal Ritter von Greim in the last year of the war, this being the reason she flew with him to Hitler's bunker. In reality, this seems as spurious as the suggestion (also made by Eric Brown) that Hanna committed suicide to join her lover von Greim some thirty years after his death. Brown was disillusioned with the aviatrix he once idolised and his later comments have to be taken with a good dose of salt.

Still, Hanna's life seems rather devoid of the usual love tangles most people experience. Either she was incredibly clever at keeping her relationships secret or, more likely, she had so much on her plate trying to achieve her goals as a pilot that any relationship would have got in the way. Besides, Hanna would have hated any suggestion that she had consorted with someone to afford her a better place in the aviation world.

If lovers were missing in Hanna's life, she did at least form strong bonds with a variety of men whom she came to respect and adore. Most of these men were older and Hanna thought of them as father figures, the first of these being Wolf Hirth (to some small extent Hitler too fell into this category, which was why Hanna felt a strong loyalty to him). Hanna's relationship with her own father was difficult; he was a stern, strict man, not particularly loving, unlike her mother, to whom she was especially close. Herr Reitsch was aloof and though he took Hanna with him to visit patients, he was not a loving father, nor was he good at supporting and promoting Hanna's dreams. In many ways Hanna lacked confidence and needed the constant praise and comfort of men such as Hirth to bolster her self-esteem. Her father could not give her that, so Hanna found replacements wherever she could, quite unconsciously. She even sometimes referred to them with the affectionate addition of 'father' to their name.

Hirth was also very taken with his star pupil – the girl he had once wanted to kick out of his gliding school. Only two years after she had started gliding, he invited Hanna to be an instructor. This was both a privilege and a nightmare for Hanna. How was this little slip of a girl (still only 21) supposed to teach male students, many of whom would be much older than her? 'Men do not like being taught by a girl,' Hanna said to herself. There was no point trying the usual teaching tactics of Hirth or van Husen. Instead Hanna acted as a comrade to her students, turning her lessons into discussion groups where they could run through good and bad flights, ways to improve and how to get through that all-important first A test. Hirth was dubious of her methods initially, but Hanna soon proved herself when her pupils excelled at gliding. She also earned their respect, which was extremely difficult: '… I managed to lull my pupils into forgetting that they were being instructed in the manly sport of gliding by a mere school-girl.'

It was all going so well until the last day of the course. All but one of Hanna's students had passed their C test successfully and had gone to a nearby airfield to experience their first towed flights. Hanna was left alone with her last pupil. There seemed no reason to Hanna why this young man should not pass his C test with ease: he had proved adept at gliding in his A and B tests and seemed calm and self-assured as he sat in the glider. He took off smoothly and soared in the air for a full two and a half minutes without issue. It was looking as though Hanna had successfully got all her pupils airborne as the student made his first turn according to the outline of the test. The turn was steep, but handled well. What happened next came completely out of the blue. The glider suddenly nose-dived and plunged with a horrendous crash into the ground.

Hanna couldn't move at first. Then she began to run as fast as she could towards the glider. Her pupil was dead, of course. No one could survive such a fast crash in a flimsy glider. Instead of heading to the airfield to watch her students flying, Hanna made her way to the boy's village, his house, where a poor old woman ran out crying, 'Ach, Fraulein, I already know. My son! My son is no longer!'

As the woman wept she explained that her son had had a dream the night before of crashing during the test just as he entered the turn. She had begged him not to go that morning, but he had insisted. Hanna didn't know what to make of all this. Was it premonition or under-confidence in the pupil manifesting as a nightmare? Had the memory of the dream sparked that awkward steep turn, or had the turn sparked memories of the dream and caused the fatal crash? Whatever the case, the accident shook Hanna's confidence in herself, and for many months the horror of that final flight lingered in her mind, making teaching impossible.

3

THE SOARING
DREAM

When Carl Oskar Ursinus sat on the hillside of Rhön and watched the eagles floating on the thermals in 1920 his mind was absorbed by one problem – the Treaty of Versailles. Ursinus had been obsessed with flying since the early 1900s when he began publishing a magazine on flying sports. During the First World War he had worked on the designs for the Gotha G.I biplane, which had served the German air corps well through the war years. When the war ended and the Allies had prohibited the building of powered aircraft in Germany, he was stricken. What were aviators to do now?

It was sitting on that slope, smoking his pipe, floppy hat on his head, that Ursinus turned his mind to gliding, a hitherto very neglected aspect of aviation. He recruited his friends and fellow engineers to the notion of turning Rhön, or, more specifically, the hillside of Wasserkuppe, into a gliding test ground. People donated money, time and sometimes their lives to the cause, but before many years glider pilots were making an annual pilgrimage to Wasserkuppe to test their planes and their skill. The first competitions were held as early as 1920 and Ursinus founded the RRG (Rhön-Rossitten Gesellschaft), the first gliding organisation in the world to be recognised officially. The RRG flourished throughout the 1920s. In 1924 Alexander Lippisch (later to work on the Me 163b, which Hanna would test) was recruited as head of its technical branch, a bold move by Ursinus that paid dividends. By the 1930s the Rhön soaring contests, still held at Wasserkuppe, were considered *the* place for pilots to prove their skills.

Hanna went in 1933, just as politics was sinking its dirty claws into the sport of gliding. Under National Socialism, the RRG simply could not exist. The various clubs were dismantled or absorbed under the new guise of the Hitler Youth. Though many glider enthusiasts failed to realise its significance at the time, this move would forever tarnish early German gliding with a distinct taint of Nazism.

As Hanna sat on the Wasserkuppe nervously awaiting her launch, the world of politics was distant from her mind. If she heard complaints from other flyers about the destruction of the RRG, it meant very little to her. All she was thinking about was flying and winning. It was not an auspicious time; Hanna's mind was still churning over the death of her pupil and though she had one of Hirth's Grunau Babys to fly, it was soon apparent that she was out-classed by the gliders around her. The first launch was a disaster. The Baby could not find an up-draught and Hanna landed in the valley while other gliders soared away. Her launch team came running down the slope, their disappointment plain. 'That's all right, it doesn't matter, doesn't matter a bit!' Hanna told them with a forced smile as they hurried to dismantle Baby and get her back up the slope.

The next launch was no better, nor the next or the one after. In fact, over every day of the Rhön contest Hanna did no better than a short belly flop into the valley, much to the amusement of onlookers. Hanna ignored the mockery as best she could, but was despondent to see so many of her fellow gliders making it into the air without a problem. Among them was Wolf Hirth flying his new glider *Moazagotl* and doing very well against his closest rival Peter Riedel. Another who was proving himself on his first outing was Heini Dittmar flying *Kondor*, which he had built himself. Both Riedel and Dittmar would come to be very well known to Hanna.

There seemed no rhyme or reason to the failure of Baby. Hanna blamed the out-of-date machine for her bad luck, despite another Grunau Baby achieving a flight of 60 miles. It was all very embarrassing and made worse by the malicious humour of the male contestants. At the prize-giving ceremony Hanna was given a meat mincer and set of kitchen scales as a booby prize, sending the unpleasant message that women should stay at home in the kitchen (in fact, the prize had been quite innocently donated by a manufacturer of kitchen goods and had caused the judges some consternation until they alighted on the idea of awarding it to Hanna).

Not everyone was so intent on ridiculing Hanna. Oskar Ursinus gave a speech in which he referred to Hanna's refusal to give up despite her constant defeats. 'In soaring it is not success but the spirit which counts,' he reminded his audience. Even better, however, was the response of meteorologist and 'Professor of Soaring' Walter Georgii. Georgii was organising a trip to South America to study thermals and had already recruited Wolf Hirth, Reidel and Dittmar. Now he wanted Hanna too. He liked her spirit and determination in the face of defeat and thought she would be a good addition to his team. There was only one problem: Hanna would have to raise 3,000 marks if she wanted to go with him.

Hanna was too excited about the possibility of travelling to South America to allow the opportunity to slip away just because of money. As it happened, she had recently been contacted by the German film company Ufa to act as a stunt-double in a gliding movie. Heini Dittmar and Wolf Hirth had already accepted similar offers and though she had originally turned down the invitation, she now accepted – as long as Ufa gave her the 3,000 marks she desperately needed. Ufa paid without hesitation. Hanna was surprised, but she shouldn't have been. Ufa had begun its dubious movie making in 1917, producing propaganda and public service films. It was inextricably linked with the government that had founded it and, as such, its movies were never simply pure enter-tainment. During the 1920s Ufa was known for its large range of silent movies, often thought provoking and very popular internationally, rival-ling Hollywood. One of its most famous directors was Fritz Lang, the genius behind the celebrated silent movie *Metropolis*. However, Lang was a Jew and at the rise of Nazism he left Ufa and Germany behind for America, not long before Hanna took her first steps into the movies.

Ufa came under Nazi control in 1933. That same year new laws were instigated banning the employment of artists of Jewish descent. Ufa became a compliant producer of propaganda movies under the crow-like gaze of Goebbels. Hitler paid visits to his pet studio, and movies were created to promote Nazi imagery and inspire young people. This bias was far from hidden – blatant was more like it! The studio began making movies that lionised the Hitler Youth movement and broadcast propaganda in cinemas. The film Hanna had been engaged for was no different; the plot of *Rivalen der Luft* (*Rivals of the Air*) focused on two young flyers, Karl and Christine, who both wanted to earn their gliding licence. Christine reminded Hanna very much of herself: headstrong, determined, small and eager to fly. It would not be far-fetched to imagine that the Nazi propaganda department was modelling the character on the newest aviatrix who was taking Germany by storm and proving what Aryan aviation could do. Christine and Karl are taken under the wing of gliding instructor Willi Frahm, who is soon infatuated with the young female flyer. However, Karl is also in love with Christine and a rivalry soon develops, leading up to the dramatic thunderstorm scene. During a competition at Rhön Christine (who has been forbidden to fly, and so takes off secretly) is engulfed in a storm cloud (a moment that reminded Hanna distinctly of her own experience) and Frahm flies to her rescue, nobly giving up his chance to win the contest. The climax of the story sees Christine crash-landing and realising she has fallen in love with Frahm, who wraps her in his arms. Meanwhile, Karl goes on to win the competition, apparently oblivious to his lover's fate. A win–win situation for all?

The love story was superfluous to the real message of the film, which wanted to promote an Aryan image of courage, mental strength and virility, and inspire young people to take up flying. The Luftwaffe was still under wraps, but Hitler knew he needed to inspire and train the next generation of pilots. Gliding, as has been mentioned, was ideal, and *Rivals of the Air* aimed to get as many young men interested in flying as possible, thus providing a ready stock of pilots for the war. Hanna could argue she was oblivious to this dark under-current, though Ufa's role in Nazi propaganda was hardly secret. But her association with the film's director Karl Ritter is harder to ignore. Ritter was a committed Nazi, having joined the party in the 1920s. When Hitler gained power Ritter was moved from being head of production at another company to become company director and chief of production at Ufa. One of his first films was *Hitlerjunge Quex*, which ridiculed Communism, while promoting an image of the Hitler Youth as clean-cut, organised and morally superior. Released in 1933, there was no mistaking its overt political message; Hitler, Göring and Goebbels all attended the premiere.

Ritter was unrepentant about his role in Nazi propaganda: 'The path of German films will lead without any compromise to the conclusion that every movie must stay in the service of our community, of nation and our Führer.' Ritter would go on to be rewarded by Goebbels with membership to the chamber governing the film industry, the Reichsfilmkammer, and on Hitler's fiftieth birthday he gave Ritter a professorship. Admittedly, in 1933 Nazism was still in the background for many, just another part of the turbulent post-war political scene, and Hanna, who chose to avoid politics all her life, saw nothing but an opportunity to make money and appear in a movie. That she later went on to meet with Ritter in the 1960s is another matter entirely …

In those exciting days of 1933 Hanna saw nothing but another chance to fly. She empathised with Christine and enjoyed taking part in the filming, especially the crashes:

> The crash into the lake was not easy, for the 'lake' turned out to be no more than a large-sized pool and the 'pancake' landing had to be timed with absolute precision. However, all went well and I landed plumb in the middle of the water, giving vent, in joy at my success, to a loud 'yippee!'
>
> I had clean forgotten that the cameras were recording sound as well as vision and that, instead of the 'cry of despair' which the story required, the girl would now be heard to give a yell of triumph!

Heini Dittmar was doubling for Karl and Wolf Hirth for Frahm. A strange symmetry now formed. While Hanna watched her double fall into the arms of Hirth's double, she was meanwhile being observed and adored by Heini Dittmar, who, much like Karl, was completely overshadowed by the instructor figure of Hirth. Was Hanna in love with Hirth? It is difficult to say. She certainly idolised him and saw him as a father figure. Hanna was always drawn to older men and the scenario of *Rivals of the Air* struck home to her. In any case, Dittmar was out of luck. A year older than Hanna, he was a small, wiry man with a cheeky, boyish grin and rather prominent ears. He never seemed to stop smiling, but there was a quiet reticence in his manner and he lacked the kind of commanding presence that drew Hanna in. Dittmar did not attract her and though they would remain friends she always repelled his romantic advances.

Filming came to a close with Hanna giving no thought to the role the film would play in Nazi propaganda (after the war *Rivals of the Air* would be banned by the Allies). Instead she was just glad to have her

3,000 marks and was ready for adventure in South America. She had even achieved two new world endurance records for women in her spare time while filming – one for nine hours, and the other for eleven hours and twenty minutes.

There were ice floes in the waters off Hamburg as the *Monte Pascoal* began slowly to negotiate its launch from Germany. Winter in Germany can be cruel and Hanna was more than willing to wave goodbye to her homeland for the promise of sunshine and flying in South America. It was January 1934, the *Monte Pascoal* was far from the most luxurious liner leaving harbour that cold morning, and ice floes broke on its hull as it slipped out, but for Hanna it was a dream-ship, a chance to escape from her ordinary life – her first adventure outside the fatherland. Her parents waved her off as the ship's band played '*Muss I denn, muss I denn zum Städtele hinaus*' and Hanna leaned precariously over the rail. She was a few weeks off being 22 and her excitement was almost unbearable.

Ship life suited Hanna. As might be expected of someone who loved to soar and swoop without any discomfort, she was not affected by the swell of the sea and indulged eagerly in the exotic menus and rich meals provided aboard. Hanna had always lived a restrained life and the offer of such food was almost too much to resist. When she wasn't eating she was exploring, discovering every secret nook and cranny of the ship, or avoiding Heini Dittmar, who was now making himself something of a nuisance.

Hanna would rather spend time with Peter Riedel, the overall winner at the 1933 Wasserkuppe. Riedel was seven years her senior, with a gentle, ordinary face and a quiet smile. He lacked the boyish charm of Dittmar, but that in itself attracted Hanna. She felt able to confide in him, much as she did Hirth. Hanna complained to Riedel about Dittmar's attentions, she perceived him as a brotherly figure rather than lover material. In fact, Hanna remained aloof to the possibility of romance, seeing it as a deadly ensnarement resulting in marriage. Married life, to Hanna, was akin to slavery and a complete destruction of her freedom. If she wished to fly, she must do so unfettered by male companionship and control.

Riedel remembered her as 'a flight-crazy young girl'. When they arrived in South America there was a great deal of free time and on one expedition into Rio, Riedel remarked to Hanna, 'Hanna, you are like

Joan of Arc.' He expected her to laugh. Instead she gave him a questioning look and then changed the subject. Perhaps it was too uncomfortable being compared to a woman who was martyred for her patriotism.

Rio de Janeiro is a beautiful city and it seemed Professor Walter Georgii could not have chosen a better place for his gliding research. Georgii had taken over the management of the RRG, now under Nazi control, in 1933. He had National Socialist leanings, but not to the extent of some of his colleagues. Hanna's presence on his expedition was partly due to her determination and partly for good PR. Hitler was no fool when it came to knowing how Nazism was viewed outside of Germany, and during the 1930s he would arrange various stunts and goodwill missions to improve his regime's reputation. South America had always been a hotbed for Nazism, but external pressures, not least from the US, were taking their toll. Bans on German films and other forms of propaganda had been discussed.

Though Hanna constantly reiterated that Georgii's expedition was not a goodwill mission, it nevertheless had that effect. Hanna, once again, failed to recognise the value placed upon her as a symbol of Aryan pride and achievement. In her memoirs she wrote sadly:

> The interest in our activities was enormous. Each day hundreds and thousands of the city's inhabitants trekked out to the airfield to watch us fly. What interested them most were the aerobatics and while my colleagues performed them only rarely, to my regret, I had to fly them almost every day. I would much have preferred to have been taking part in cross-country flights …

Hanna was right where Georgii's backers needed her. While she entertained and impressed the crowds, he could get on with studying thermals, knowing Hanna was flying the flag for Germany. Much of Hanna's subsequent career followed this pattern. She ignored it as best she could. The alternative was to be reminded that she was a mere novelty to her masters, a woman who could fly but who did not deserve the same respect as her male companions.

From Rio, they went to São Paulo and Hanna was involved in a fateful incident that would further thrust her behind her male rivals. It was a fine sunny Sunday morning, the cloud base around 6,500ft. Dittmar and Riedel were to go up first and by the time they were in the sky and silently gliding over the grassland, Hanna was itching to be with them. Her usual impatience did her a disservice. Despite her time with Georgii, Hanna was ignorant of one of the most interesting phenomena to be found in that region – the 'thermal bubble'. The bubble was a rising rush of hot air that could at first appear to be a typical warm thermal, but would pass over an aircraft and could not be used as an up-lift. Instead it left a pilot floundering in down-winds, baffled as to where the thermal had gone. Hanna had not experienced one of these bubbles before, so when she started to feel her glider quiver she believed she was riding a true thermal and cast off prematurely from her tow-plane. Hanna assumed the thermal would quickly take her up to join her friends. Instead she suddenly found herself sinking: the bubble had passed and as Hanna coasted around trying to find her missing thermal her height continued to drop.

São Paulo loomed ahead, a maze of streets and buildings – impossible for a glider to land among them safely. Hanna desperately pulled at her controls and tried to find an up-draught, only to fail again. 'I was in desperation, my mind's eye seeing a terrible slaughter as I crashed into a street, when, in the distance, I saw what looked like an open field.' In fact, it was a football pitch and a game was in progress, but Hanna had few options left and dropping onto the pitch might at least spare others from injury or worse. She came down so low that for a moment she feared she would hit some of the crowd. No one seemed to have noticed her, they were so intent on the match that the silent glider had sneaked up on everyone unnoticed (it was just this sort of stealth that Hitler would utilise during the war). Hanna tore open her window and shouted in Spanish, 'Beware! Beware!' The footballers looked up in astonishment, but no one moved. They all imagined that soon this strange plane would open its engines and fly off, having given them another of the German stunt performances they were fond of. Hanna had no engines to save her.

Screaming at the players, her glider was almost on the ground when she narrowly negotiated a goal mouth. At last realisation dawned on the footballers and at the very last moment they scattered, and Hanna hit the ground, having missed everybody. There was little time for relief as a mob rushed across the pitch and swelled around the glider. Hanna had nightmarish visions of her wings being broken and her glider being trampled to pieces. She climbed on a wing and tried to tell everyone to hold back, but her audience was even more delighted and waved and blew kisses at her, all rushing on, trying to be the first to touch the glider.

Hanna was not naïve in her fears, at least. Early aviators had often had their planes shredded by an enthusiastic crowd keen for souvenirs. Desperately trying to fend off her audience, Hanna spied military uniforms. A small group of soldiers was trying to divert the crowd, but it was not enough. Finally the mounted police arrived. To Hanna's shock they ploughed through the crowd; those who failed to get out of the way in time were trampled and before long ambulances were being summoned. The mounted police formed a circle around Hanna and kept everyone at bay until it was possible to transport her and the glider to safety.

The experience, though largely glossed over in her own account, was eye opening for Hanna. The authorities who were so favourable to Germany had treated their own people with callous disregard. Hanna had spared lives only for her 'protectors' to crush and maim. That the local press spun the event into a German triumph only said more about the casual nature of violence in the country and the way it was routinely covered up. Hanna buried this observation, as she would do many more, beneath layers of blind disbelief.

On the whole, the expedition to South America had been a success. After Brazil came Argentina, long flights across open plains with only pampas grass and herds of wild horses for company and a Silver C Soaring Medal. Dittmar, Hirth and Riedel all contributed world records of their own and by the time they set sail for home the German glider pilots were naturally bursting with pride at their successes. There was one episode of the adventure that Hanna viewed with sorrow rather than joy. She had briefly entertained a fondness for a Spanish pilot, which was reciprocated. On the verge of giving all to this young man, Hanna had got cold feet and fled. A part of her still fought ferociously against the ties of love and romance; she regretted the abrupt parting and sailed home convinced she was suffering a broken heart.

4

FLYING IS
EVERYTHING

Professor Georgii had discovered Hanna and now he would not let her go. In his role at the RRG (renamed the Deutsche Forschungsanstalt für Segelflug (DFS) in 1937) at Darmstadt he regularly needed good glider pilots to help with his research. Dittmar was already signed up, Hanna swiftly followed. Unwittingly she was now firmly established within the Nazi programme of flying research. The RRG, while overtly working on studying gliders, was really helping to redevelop the Luftwaffe with its research. Riedel was equally embroiled as he had taken up work as a commercial pilot for Lufthansa, the German civil aviation company, which was also serving as a front for training airmen and testing potential troop-carrying aircraft. Wolf Hirth went off on his own to form a glider company with Martin Schempp. Schempp-Hirth would go into business in 1935.

Political undercurrents completely passed by Hanna. She was already busy preparing for a trip to Finland, another PR stunt to promote good relations with Germany and encourage gliding. The head of the expedition was a research scientist named Dr Joachim Küttner. In the years to come he would discover to his horror that he had a Jewish grandparent on both sides of his family tree.

Hanna loved Finland and the Finnish, particularly the saunas, to which she attributed the Finns' excellent health and fitness. The trip went down very well with the Reich Air Ministry, which offered Hanna a decoration. Such things meant very little to Hanna at that time and she asked instead for permission to enrol at the Civil Airways Training

School in Stettin. This was by no means a simple request. Civil aviation was treated with very little difference to military aviation; strict discipline was maintained at Stettin, officers keeping the trainee pilots in line. Worse, it was an all-male institution and many of the older officers would find it absurd, if not offensive, to have a woman at the school.

As illogical a desire as it seemed, Hanna had her reasons for wanting to go to Stettin. She still had only limited experience in motor-powered aircraft. At Stettin she would be taught and licensed to use a huge range of bigger and more powerful planes. Hanna had clearly impressed someone enough for the request to go through and she arrived at Stettin to looks of disapproval and amusement. Stettin confirmed Hanna's often unrelenting opinion of male egotism and chauvinism. On one military-style parade she was berated for having a womanly chest, which affected the overall appearance of the line of trainees. At every turn she seemed to be picked on for her femininity. Naturally, she had no experience of military parades, so her early attempts were fraught with errors as she tried to copy those alongside her. She was mocked and ridiculed, forced to do extra drills and generally tormented, with the aim of sending her home in floods of tears. Hanna resisted the abuse and in time it began to ease. As she proved herself in the air, so her colleagues warmed to her and stopped seeing her as an intrusive girl but as another pilot. The commanding officer at Stettin, Colonel Pasewald, found her 'a totally uncomplicated person ... she had no particularly feminine charms and wiles, a very fine instinct for flying, and no sense of danger. When she flew, it was like anyone else going for a walk – she had mastered the medium.'

She may have been unusual in Germany, but elsewhere female aviators were not such an anomaly. In Russia during the war whole units of female pilots were known and accepted. Admittedly, they too had a rough journey into aviation, often mocked and criticised, issued with men's clothing which was far too big (Hanna complained of this at Stettin) and treated as inferior, until they started to prove themselves. But that was still several years away and Hanna had very little concern for what was going on in Russia.

More worrying were political activities in Germany. By the time Hanna was finishing her course in 1935 it was very apparent that the Heinkel, Focke-Wulf and Junkers were not confining themselves to producing civil aircraft. Nor was there any point in prolonging the charade that Lufthansa was only training its pilots for civil flight – anyone noting the military-style training at Lufthansa schools would have questioned that anyway. Germany finally announced the rejuvenation of the Luftwaffe, which it had been building up secretly for years. The world swayed a little and anxiety trickled into everyone except the most ignorant. Hanna could not avoid this; airfields, once deserted, now buzzed with officers and air-craft. Men gave stiff-armed salutes and hung up swastika flags. Peacetime conscription was introduced and Hanna sensed the world was turning in a dangerous direction. Forever the patriot, she blotted out the worst of her fears, concentrating on a planned trip to Lisbon in May to demonstrate German gliding – the PR wagon was off again. Hanna thought of the trip as a means of showing Germany in its best light and downplaying people's fears – everything would turn out all right, after all.

Almost instantly her desire for a peaceful and non-controversial time in Lisbon was shattered when, having made an unplanned stop on a French military airfield, her companion was discovered to be carry-ing a camera. It had been strictly forbidden for such equipment to be brought and it caused natural consternation among the French, who started to ask whether Hanna was a spy. Things rapidly got out of hand. Rumours reached the local inhabitants that two Germans had been detained on suspicion of espionage and a crowd gathered at the airfield. When they spotted Hanna or her companion they spat and jeered at them. The French threatened to dismantle Hanna's plane, but that was the least of their worries if they could not prove themselves innocent. The French were cagey and took hours over their interviews. Hanna asked, unsuccessfully, to make a phone call, and in the end it was only via the intervention of a French soldier that she was granted her request. She managed to contact the German consul, who was far from pleased to hear of her predicament. Through various channels he got an order through to the French commandant that *the* Hanna Reitsch was to be released at once and allowed to fly on to Lisbon. Political pressure asserted, the commandant reluctantly released his suspects.

After the frightening ordeal in France, Lisbon proved a ray of comic relief. The festival was lively and exuberant, the Germans were wel-comed with open arms and the displays went well. But it was with some relief that Hanna returned to Germany and to her old job at Darmstadt. Hanna had impressed enough people to earn herself a promotion and now worked under the supervision of Hans Jacobs, the chief test pilot. A number of experimental gliders came her way, none quite so difficult or as well remembered as the Sea Eagle. The Sea Eagle was a first: a sea-going glider primarily to be used in scientific expeditions (though, of course, with military potential). Hanna's role as test pilot was to work out its kinks and flaws, to check its balance, examine it for possibly dangerous faults and to experiment with its limitations. She was also there to discover if it was actually possible to launch and land a glider at sea. The Sea Eagle was a beautiful glider with tilted wings that did indeed resemble the bird of the same name. She was narrow and could only carry her pilot in a rather cramped cockpit, with little insurance against submerging in the ocean on a heavy landing. Her wingspan was over 56ft, strongly gulled to keep them clear of spray, but she was a lightweight at only 240kg. She needed to reach around 36mph to get airborne.

Hanna's first flight in the Sea Eagle was abortive. The motorboat hired to tow the glider into the air was not powerful enough and could not reach take-off speed. Tests were transferred to a lake at Bodensee and Dornier supplied a Maybach speedboat to act as tow. The Maybach had the speed to launch Hanna into the air, but starting from water proved a new challenge. Originally a 300ft towrope was used, but its weight and the drag caused by it slicing through the water proved an irritation. On her first flight Hanna rose to 30ft, but almost immediately the towrope began to drag her back down and she cast off for fear of hitting the water. Observers from the boat were annoyed; she should have held on.

On the next attempt that is exactly what Hanna did; there was a sudden jar against the plane, the towrope seeming to jerk the glider forward, then a sheet of water flew up into the air and overwhelmed the Sea Eagle. Hanna plunged down, submerging beneath the surface of the lake, no time to think of holding her breath or reacting. She was lucky; the natural stability and buoyancy of the Sea Eagle caused it to resurface a short distance from the spot it had crashed. Both glider and Hanna were unharmed, though she was a little shaken by the experience. Everyone was agreed that this wasn't a practical method for taking off.

The towrope was shortened to 230ft and balsa floats were added to reduce the drag of the rope ploughing through water. This proved a reliable method. Tests were even more successful when the speedboat was switched for a Dornier amphibian flying boat – the Dragon-Fly.

Dragon-Fly could tow the Sea Eagle in most weather conditions and the slipstream caused by its airscrew created another advantage – it left a relatively calm strip of water in its wake in which Hanna could hold the Sea Eagle and thus avoid any heavy waves that the Dragon-Fly might be encountering. The Sea Eagle's biggest test came during a storm. Since her experience in the Grunau Baby, Hanna had been cautious about such weather, but one of the aims of the Sea Eagle's designers was to test her in rough weather. After all, she was designed to land on water in any weather – how would they know if she was seaworthy if she was not tested when a storm was rippling the waters?

Ashore, the anxious Sea Eagle crew and designers stood waiting with every life-saving device they could think of in case the worst happened. Hanna shut that thought out of her mind, if she started to imagine that the Sea Eagle might not survive the landing she would never go up. Hanna had nerves of steel when it came to flying, perhaps even a slight sensation of being charmed, which normally overcame any fear she might feel. As her mother would tell her, placing her life in the hands of God was the only way to get through such dangers. If He chose for her to perish now, there was nothing she could do anyway. With this strange comfort in mind Hanna took off.

Hanna headed into the storm. The winds buffeted her left and right, she struggled to keep the Sea Eagle level and on course for her designated landing spot. Below, the waters of the Bodensee were bubbling and churning. The little boats that had followed Hanna out had to turn around and head for shore. She was alone with the elements. Hanna soared for an hour before coming in to land. She had to reduce her speed to 35mph; fortunately the Sea Eagle had a hull like a boat and landed smoothly on the water. Unfortunately, the storm had churned the Bodensee into a writhing mass of waves that rocked and rolled the Sea Eagle. No boat could reach Hanna in such conditions so she negotiated her craft to a crane that stood at the edge of the waters. Even then it was no simple task to attach the crane's hook as Sea Eagle rocked about. Hanna had to balance herself on one of the wings to maintain an even keel. Finally the Sea Eagle made it to dry land without harm – she and her pilot had proved themselves.

The Sea Eagle was next put to work testing a catapult designed to enable heavily laden transport planes to take off in a small space. Did it occur to Hanna as she climbed into the Sea Eagle's cockpit that she was testing a device that could prove very handy in combat and when launching troop-carrying planes? Apparently not. The catapult consisted of a steel cable which ran over a cone-shaped drum. One end of the cable was attached to the nose of the glider, so that as the cable was taken up by the drum, the Sea Eagle was dragged towards the scaffolding of the catapult set on the shore. Hanna had to judge the moment perfectly to release herself so she could sail clear of the catapult, turn and land. 'Distinctly unpleasant,' she remarked of the task. It required precision and care. Once the Sea Eagle had pioneered the procedure the catapult went on to be tested on powered planes.

The year 1935 turned into 1936. The Berlin Olympics loomed, but Germany was riddled by internal tensions. Jews were being ostracised further and further. Hitler had declared that no Jews would be allowed on the German Olympic team, causing outrage across the globe. The US was threatening to withdraw. If it had, the Olympics would likely have been ruined, for the American team was by far the biggest in the games. Goebbels went into damage limitation; Hitler bit down on his No Jews orders and made token efforts to encourage Jewish athletes. It was all propaganda; anti-Semitic signs were removed for the duration, but no one was entirely fooled and certainly Goebbels' repeated phrase that the games would generate peace between nations was taken by many with a good pinch of salt. Still, the Americans came and for two weeks Berlin buzzed with promise and excitement.

The Olympic spirit was launched with the winter games at Garmisch. Hanna flew in gliding demonstrations with Peter Riedel and Ernst Udet, an ace from the First World War who would soon become a good friend to Hanna. Ernst Udet, Udlinger, as he was nicknamed, had put on weight since he had been a hero of the First World War. His uniform fitted snugly over his expanded form, and his short stature accentuated his dumpy appearance. His square face was jovial, quick to smile or give a sly wink of understanding to the many pilots, designers and engineers he came into contact with. Udet was not a typical Luftwaffe officer: he never wore his cap straight, it was always cocked at a slightly jaunty angle. He dreamed of flight, but the technical side of aeroplanes eluded him and as the war years engulfed him it became more and more apparent that Udet was stuck in a mind-set for a conflict that had been fought and lost two decades ago.

No German with even a passing interest in aviation could fail to recognise the name of Udet. Admittedly Ernst Udet had frozen with fear and was unable to fight in his first encounter with the enemy, but despite this he went on to become one of the First World War's great aces. His final score was sixty-two victories, though still a long way off the greatest ace of all, Baron Richthofen, who achieved eighty kills. In comparison to the scores German pilots would achieve in the Second World War, these figures seem almost paltry, but with the technology and skills of the time they were impressive. Consider that at the beginning of the war the only armament a biplane had was a second man behind the pilot carrying a gun and the figures become more understandable. By the end of the First World War, of course, planes were fitted with machine guns that could fire through the propeller blades, but even so making a kill was remarkably difficult. Udet ended the war as the top-scoring surviving pilot.

Udet's war had been fought from outside the strict German military system. Having learned to fly at his own expense, Udet began the war as a non-commissioned pilot. When he was commissioned it was as a reserve officer, effectively barring him from higher command. Udet was not disheartened; he was not comfortable with leadership, rather he preferred the thrill and excitement of flying. Described by some as a playboy and a talented amateur, Udet was content in his plane, far from the complications of politics and orders. He was very good, however. His rival, Richthofen, was an adequate pilot, compensated by being a superb marksman. In contrast, Udet was an amazing flyer: on one occasion he fought the great French ace Georges Guynemer to a draw. His downside, from a German perspective, was his happy-go-lucky temperament, his failure to be ruthless and his inability to take anything terribly seriously. No wonder he was passed over for command of a squad after the death of Richthofen, in favour of a lesser-known pilot named Göring.

Udet had loved the war for the very simple reason that it had enabled him to fly to his heart's content. Yes, there was always the risk of being shot down, dying in a blazing ball of flames, a fate many pilots dreaded to the point of nightmares, but if you could avoid being morbid there were endless opportunities to fly. After the war Udet crashed back to reality. He drifted from job to job; he had no acumen for business and spent the

1920s and 1930s barnstorming to thrill crowds or acting as a stuntman in Hollywood. He was as uninterested in politics as ever, though on his return to Germany in 1933 his old flying pal Göring persuaded him to join the Nazi Party. In 1935, also under the subtle influence of Göring, Udet joined the Luftwaffe as an oberst and within a year was Inspector of Fighter and Divebomber Forces. It was a new world for Udet, but, at least for the time being, he didn't mind his role, nor the steady income he could now enjoy. Not to mention the people he could meet, such as Hanna Reitsch. It was certainly better than drifting from place to place barnstorming.

Udet experienced his first problems in 1936. The inspector role had suited him perfectly as it involved little more than flying and reporting. Unfortunately, he proved too good at the role and it was decided that he deserved promotion. Udet stumbled into the job of Head of the Technical Office. He was now responsible for supply and procurement for the emerging Luftwaffe; significantly, he was responsible for promoting which aircraft would be produced and the level of manufacture required. This went beyond just knowing that a plane was a good flyer: he had to consider cost of production, level of skill required to build and fly it, available resources and, of course, the timescale of manufacture. Tied up with all the practical considerations was the heckling of politicians, who all had their own thoughts of what aircraft the Luftwaffe should have. Udet was not good at politics and though his technical decisions were good (he promoted the Stuka dive-bomber and Messerschmitt Bf 109), the negotiations and paperwork his new role required, not to mention the diplomacy, were somewhat beyond him. Garmisch was good publicity for gliding and for Udet it was a chance to cast off the shackles of office work. Both he and Hanna had a naïve sense of honour that made them incredulous of the extremes of Nazism. In those wintry days of 1936 Udet had hope and he flew with relish.

In the summer preparations for the big games began in Berlin. The Olympic bell was ceremonially paraded down the grand avenue before the Brandenburg Gate then on to Unter den Linden; months later another parade down the same avenue would mark the opening of the games. Booted soldiers marched between buildings slung with swastika flags and loudspeakers that would proclaim every exciting minute of the games. Visitors were fewer in number than expected and an atmosphere of controversy cast a shadow over the Olympics.

Hanna performed her flying stunts once again and was watched by a British schoolboy named Eric Brown. Brown's father had been invited specifically by Udet because he had served as a fighter pilot in the First World War. Eric was fascinated by the flying aerobatics that were performed over the stadiums, not just by German flyers (though they got all the coverage in the German papers), but by aviators from Bulgaria, Yugoslavia, Hungary, Switzerland and Austria. He was particularly enthralled by Hanna, to whom he was introduced. He fell somewhat in love with this charming aviatrix who would later dash his dreams by staying loyal to Hitler.

If the 1936 Olympics were marred by the reek of racism and anti-Semitism, the taint did not extend to Hanna. Fiercely patriotic she may have been, but she never discriminated against others because of their race or colour. One of her closest friends remained Joachim Küttner, even after he was penalised for the misfortune of having Jewish heritage. Hanna never quite understood anti-Semitism, it didn't fit into her cosy image of how the world should be, but she did understand discrimination for it happened to her all the time. At the 1936 Rhön soaring contest Hanna discovered that women had been banned from competing. Fired up like a furious Valkyrie, Hanna set about reversing the decision, enlisting the help of Udet. Ultimately she was granted permission to compete, but it reminded her that the world of flying was a male realm where women were not welcome.

A growing sense of militarisation was also impeding German women, not to mention fuelling tensions concerning Germany's future plans. At Darmstadt, in between Olympic demonstrations, Hanna was testing out a new safety invention – dive brakes. Ostensibly, they were intended to reduce deaths caused by inexperienced glider pilots diving too harshly and exceeding the limitations of their machines. In reality, these brakes would prove invaluable on the new range of military aircraft being churned out by factories across Germany. Any doubt concerning this must have been dispelled when Udet visited Darmstadt to watch a test, accompanied by his colleague Ritter von Greim.

Von Greim would become an integral part of Hanna's story years later. Born in 1892 in Bavaria, he had served as a leutnant in the early stages of the First World War before transferring to the German Air Service. Von Greim claimed his first aerial victory in 1915, shooting down a Farman while acting as an artillery observer. Two years later von Greim was a pilot flying with Jagdstaffel 34 and scoring his first victory in this capacity on the same day he was awarded the Iron Cross. Von Greim went on to command Jasta 34 and earned his name as a First World War ace in August 1917 with the shooting down of a Sopwith 1½ Strutter (a two-seater biplane with a synchronised machine gun). Von Greim finished the war with twenty-eight confirmed kills; he had served as the commanding officer of Jagdgruppe 10 and 9, had made the first successful aerial assault on armoured tanks and had been awarded the Pour le Mérite and the Bavarian Military Order of Max Joseph. The latter had conferred on him the title Knight – Ritter in German.

Post-war, von Greim found there was no place for him within the remnants of the German army, so he moved on to a career in law, passing the difficult and rigorous German law exams. Flying was his passion, however, and when he was invited to teach in China and to help create a Chinese Air Force he emigrated with his family to Canton. Teaching the Chinese did not rest easily with von Greim. He was already an ardent believer in the superiority of Europeans over Asians and held the view that his Chinese students were incapable of operating aircraft with the finesse required. Von Greim returned to Germany, where National Socialism was on the rise. The Nazi creed and Hitler's oratory appealed to von Greim, who became an ardent supporter and took part in the 1923 putsch when Hitler and other revolutionaries attempted unsuccessfully to seize power in Munich.

A devoted Nazi, von Greim was the ideal choice for Göring when he was trying to rebuild the German Air Force in 1933. Von Greim was appointed to command the first fighter pilot school that was not to operate in secret in 1934, and over the next decade would rise to become a field marshal. When Hanna met him in 1936 he was still training fighter pilots, and little did he know how their lives would intertwine.

For her work on testing the dive brakes, a dangerous task at the best of times as Hanna had to attempt deliberately to stall and crash her glider, she was a awarded her first and only title, Flugkapitän Reitsch. She was one of a few women to be awarded the honorary title and all Hanna could do was beam at Udet and everyone watching. Life in Germany seemed very good at that moment.

5

SNOW AND BROKEN GLASS

It seemed to Hanna that 1937 was a year of promise. In March she returned to Hirschberg for her sister Heidi's wedding. She had not been home much over the years and this too was to be a fleeting visit. Hirschberg seemed slightly more sombre, slightly less welcoming. Anti-Semitism had swept through Silesia and there was a strange atmosphere hovering over everyone. Nazi propaganda was rife, Jewish shops and faces were not. Hanna brushed it off as she always did; politics was politics and she couldn't be troubled with it. Instead she settled in to enjoy the wedding, talking almost non-stop about her new title and mildly annoying her family. Emy looked on, worried that Hanna was being carried away by her successes; she was always anxious for her eldest daughter, fearing her pride and boastfulness would land her in trouble one day.

Hanna moved on to a new challenge: becoming one of the first ever pilots to cross the Alps. The challenge was being held under the auspices of the International Study Commission for Motorless Flight, its chairman none other than Professor Georgii himself. Hans Jacobs had built a tailor-made Sperber Junior for Hanna. The cockpit was so small that no one but Hanna could squeeze in. She was one of five Germans who made the triumphant flight into fame over the Alps. Hanna landed in Italy, over 100 miles from her starting point.

In July she was back at Wasserkuppe. This time she was not the only woman present: an Austrian named Emmy von Roretz was also flying and was worthy of an honourable mention in *The Times*. Hanna, however, made the big news. Both she and Heini Dittmar flew their planes

220 miles to Hamburg, not only enabling them to share the prize for the longest straight glide, but creating a new women's record. In August Hanna found herself in England, a strange thing considering that the tensions between Germany and Great Britain were growing by the day. Under the guidance of the Anglo-German Fellowship, a society trying to promote harmony between the two nations, Wolf Hirth, Hanna and another female pilot, Eva Schmidt, were invited to attend a gliding camp in Dunstable as guests of honour. Gliding in Britain was still fairly new but, as one journalist reported, 'the Germans may find … that although there are few British soaring pilots of outstanding merit, the system has created a big pool of pilots of average ability.' No doubt the Luftwaffe would be taking note, especially as one of their test pilots was attending the camp – Hanna had been flying at the research centre at Rechlin for the benefit of the Luftwaffe for several months. Though technically on loan from Darmstadt, she would spend most of 1937 at Rechlin.

Not everyone was happy to see Germans in Dunstable. Local papers roundly criticised the move, though the national papers were more sympathetic. Gliding enthusiasts seem to have a natural ability to mentally soar above such mundane things as politics, and the glider students and instructors saw no reason to exclude their German friends. Hanna arrived at Croydon on 27 August and was attending the British National Soaring Contest on the 29th. She warranted a small mention in the press as one of the three German glider pilots visiting England.

As Germany ramped itself up for war, Hanna found herself travelling all over the place, completely oblivious to the fact that gliding was being used as a friendly but false goodwill message by the Third Reich. That same summer she went to Zurich for a gliding demonstration. Udet went with the pilots, finding himself placed in an awkward role as unofficial ambassador for German aviation. He was growing increasingly concerned about the actions of the Nazi regime, particularly those of his superior, Göring. While in Zurich he obtained a Swiss pamphlet decrying Nazism and showed it to a number of glider pilots, including Heini Dittmar's brother Edgar:

It described events quite differently from the way they were presented in Germany, where propaganda had been given out which everyone was meant to believe … in the document Udet showed us we saw everything, not as it had been presented to us and as we were meant to believe it, but as it really was. It was dangerous – if one of us glider pilots had said a word in Germany, it would have cost Udet his head.

Udet had told Edgar there would soon be war. 'Of course, I didn't believe in the seriousness of the situation, but the rest of the world saw it differently.'

Hanna was not immune to the changing tides of German fortunes. Udet refrained from exploding her beliefs as he did the others': Hanna was rather too likely to march up to Hitler and confront him on the matter – or at least one of his subordinates – to make this safe. But she knew trouble was brewing. Joachim Küttner was feeling the effects of anti-Semitism. Peter Riedel had gone to America with no intention of returning home (though he would later gather intelligence for Germany), and Hanna and Heini Dittmar were testing more and more military planes – not the sort of thing you expect from a country constantly spouting about peace. Hanna flicked this to the back of her mind, as she had done so often before, to take advantage of a new opportunity. Professor Focke of Bremen had been working on a helicopter, and after years of research had created the first viable model. For years people had explored this incredible idea of a plane that could hover, but no one had as yet succeeded in producing a real one. Focke's design had the potential to be revolutionary, but it needed testing and Focke asked for Karl Franke, chief test pilot at Rechlin, to try out his helicopter.

Franke found Hanna test flying dive brakes on the airfield and asked her if she would care to fly him there in her favourite plane, a Dornier 17. When they arrived at Bremen, where the helicopter was waiting, Professor Focke rushed to meet them. Smiling in astonishment, he declared, 'Oh, it is wonderful that Hanna Reitsch also comes to test the helicopter!' Hanna glanced at Franke, whose eyes were twinkling as he tried to conceal his own smile. 'Thank you, thank you,' Hanna whispered silently to herself. It was as though a dream had come true.

Hanna took time to study the technical drawings and instructions for flying the helicopter. It was quickly apparent she would have to disregard much of what she knew about flying, the helicopter was such a unique and unusual concept. For safety reasons the helicopter was normally anchored to the ground during testing. Hanna was having none of that; she asked that the anchor be removed and the helicopter set in a white painted circle. Perhaps because of her reputation, her requests were agreed to. In any case, Hanna soon found herself in the open cockpit of the helicopter.

There was very little in the way of trimmings with this prototype. In fact, its covering had been kept to a minimum so it was almost skeletal. Hanna could look straight down to the ground and see the machine's three wheels, one at the front, two behind. Taking the control stick gingerly Hanna held it forward slightly and with a little injection of fuel found she could move the helicopter forward; if she pulled back so the machine moved back. With this fundamental knowledge grasped, Hanna revved the engine. Slowly, ever so slowly, the helicopter rose, then it went a little faster. Hanna gained confidence, revved again, she rose 30ft, 60, 150, 250 – 300ft! Ecstatic, Hanna eased off the throttle and hung almost motionless in the air except for the whirling propellers above her. She was flying a miracle; that was the only way she could describe it, hanging mid-air like the larks she had seen hovering over fields. The moment was breathtaking and over so soon.

Hanna continued to the next phase of the test; she moved the helicopter backwards, forwards, left, right, always returning precisely to the centre of the painted circle far below her. Then she lowered the helicopter, dropping almost vertically and landing exactly on the spot she had left. Karl Franke ran towards her and grabbed her hand. 'No more test-flying with you, Hanna – my reputation won't stand it!' Others were curious about the helicopter. American flyer Charles Lindbergh was visiting Germany with his wife Anne and came to witness a demonstration. Hanna remarked that '[His] simplicity of manner won all hearts wherever he went.' Well, maybe not all hearts. Hanna had been won over yet again by a man who would spark controversy with his suggested Nazi leanings.

The Lindberghs' fascination with German aviation had distant origins. Even before her marriage to Charles, Anne had imagined going to Germany to learn to glide. At the time Germany truly was at the forefront of gliding and the rest of the world was only slowly catching on. News of record-breaking German glider flights inspired the British and Americans to try their hand. Charles was swept up in the excitement in 1930 when he went to California to fly in a Bowlus S-18 sailplane. Anne, now Mrs Lindbergh, had missed her earlier chance at gliding and followed her husband to California, determined not to miss out again. Having spent many hours flying a biplane under her husband's instruction, Anne found the transfer to gliding natural enough and was soon ready for a solo flight. In a moment that had parallels with Hanna's earlier glider flights, Anne was launched and soared for six minutes before descending into a bean field, much to the shock and astonishment of the locals. She was the first woman in the US, and only the tenth American, to earn a first-class glider pilot's licence.

The glamour of the spotlight the Lindberghs' were always under came at a price. Hounded by an aggressive media, they had found themselves a rural home far away from the busy urban realm. It was at this retreat that baby Charles disappeared, killed in a bungled kidnapping attempt. The horror of the event, followed not long after by the birth of another son, Jon, forced a change of perspective on Charles and he decided to migrate with his young family to Europe.

England became their home, but Charles was soon making visits to Germany at the behest of the US government, which was desperate for an aviation expert to take a look at the rapidly developing Luftwaffe. Charles Lindbergh had been suggested, partly because he was near to hand, and his arrival was eagerly anticipated by General Hermann Göring, who was enamoured with the idea of showing off his fledgling air force to an American legend. Charles arrived in the summer of 1936, and for ten days he was fawned over by the German aviation community, shown around factories, allowed to pilot military planes and introduced to scientists.

Hanna was as much an admirer as her German colleagues. She had heard of Charles and his achievements and, like many, was swept away by his movie-star good looks. When he first arrived she was performing aerial displays for the Olympics with Ernst Udet. She didn't have many opportunities to meet him as he was ushered from one appointment to another. She was delighted, however, to know that an America had seen her country and been impressed.

Germany was a nation on the rise under Hitler when the Lindberghs had first arrived in Berlin in 1936. The city had then been buzzing with last-minute preparations for the Olympic Games that were due to open in less than two weeks. A new stadium large enough to seat 100,000 people dominated proceedings, adorned with physically perfect Aryan statues and two colossal pillars rising violently into the sky like stone Nazi salutes at the entrance. A recently installed closed-circuit television system and radio network could broadcast the games to forty-one countries. The grandeur of it all was impressive and the Lindberghs could not fail to notice the fantastic stadium and the excitement of the Berliners.

The Lindberghs were enchanted by Berlin. Göring entertained them, asking Anne about her flying and life with Charles. Wearing his excessive, highly ornamented personal uniform and already a man of exceptional girth, he leaned over Anne and wanted to know everything. He was so absorbed he failed to notice that his pet lion was urinating on his gold-braided trousers, though his pretty wife did and giggled as she watched over his conversation, wearing a large diamond and emerald swastika brooch. Anne left Germany impressed by the country's vitality and strength; Charles loved its spirit and clearly superior aircraft technology. On returning to England the Lindberghs were asked to dine with fellow Nazi supporters Edward VIII and his mistress Wallis Simpson, and no doubt much of their conversation was devoted to praising Germany and Hitler.

When Charles returned, once again on a diplomatic mission to observe and report on the growing Luftwaffe, there was no doubt he should see the new helicopter. What better way to spread the word of the German invention than through an American legend? Hanna was ecstatic to be finally face-to-face with a man she had heard so much about. Lindbergh was a celebrity, but, just as importantly, he was an outsider who praised the Germany of the Nazi regime. That made Hanna want to shake his hand even more. Meeting him as he admired the helicopter was a dream come true. He was quiet and reserved, didn't have a lot to say for himself, but his keen eyes could see the potential before him, and he smiled at the female test pilot. Hanna snapped a photograph of her idol.

Knowing the rest of the world would have trouble accepting that the Germans had created a working helicopter, Udet decided to have the machine demonstrated at the International Automobile Exhibition. Hanna was to fly it for one night only, but when the other, male, test pilot made a minor error during a performance, Göring was so alarmed that he insisted only Hanna fly it from then on. The limelight was not entirely to Hanna's taste, surprisingly. She was receiving criticism from her fellow flyers for performing in a 'circus act' – as they deemed her demonstration. Rather unfair, considering many pilots earned their keep 'barnstorming' for the public. Perhaps her friends were already noticing that Hanna was becoming a willing puppet of the Nazi propaganda machine.

Barely a month after Hanna had shown the world what Germany could do, Hitler decided it was his turn. For years Austria had been a thorn in his side; now he moved to annex it into the German Reich. Hanna's uncle, Richard Heuberger, was living in Austria at the time. Having lost his sight in the first war, he had become a history professor and was one of many supporters all for the Anschluss or annexation of Austria. At the time Austria had its own dictators, and Hitler almost seemed a welcome relief. While Heuberger was a little wary of the jumped-up corporal, his youngest son Helmut was an enthusiastic member of the Hitler Youth and ran into the street crying 'Heil Hitler!' when the troops arrived. Overall, the bloodless takeover was almost unanimously approved of by the Austrians (though the statistics were rigged to give the impression that 99 per cent of the population liked the manoeuvre).

Meanwhile, Hanna was headed for America. Udet had been invited to an International Air Race in Cleveland, Ohio, but he could not attend so he sent Hanna and others in his place. Hanna was ecstatic to see the country her hero Lindbergh came from. Her first sight of America filled her with awe: 'There it was before me – the water-front of Manhattan, the Statue of Liberty, the wall of sky-scrapers – that spectacle, so many times described, whose first sight never fails to thrill, amaze and stir the heart.' There was only a week to enjoy the sights and sounds of New York. Hanna picked up a new phrase, 'What a hell goes on here [*sic*]?' and marvelled at the strange, vast city that stretched out around her. 'Sky-scrapers three hundred yards high! That was the height I had flown for my pilot's certificate …' Overall, Hanna loved America. She praised the apparent equality between the sexes, the way women seemed to call the shots, the chivalry of the men and the polite manners of the various workers she encountered. Perhaps this was why she later came to talk so freely to the Americans about Hitler. Hanna had a strong respect for them, not limited to their flying achievements.

One thing did disturb her, however: the use of scantily clad women during the official ceremonies of the air races. They hoisted flags and gave out prizes. Hanna found them entirely inappropriate. The country that had inspired Peter Riedel to vow never to return to Germany left a different impression on Hanna, 'though it thrilled you ... you felt oppressed by it, as if weighed down by some imponderable slab of stone.'

From a distance Udet was pleased at Hanna's reception in America. She was warmly received and interviewed by various papers. Peter Riedel was also delighted. Now appointed assistant air attaché in Washington, he had told Udet that Hanna's presence would give 'American soaring a boost'. Hanna was a pawn once again, but she failed to realise it. So much promise lay ahead; after the races she had been invited to tour America, a prospect that ignited her enthusiasm. It wasn't to be. After Austria, Hitler had set his sights on Czechoslovakia and by the September of 1938 matters were reaching fever pitch. A telegram recalled all flyers to Germany ahead of Hitler's planned coup on the Czechoslovakian government. In October the Sudetenland was relegated to the Nazis. Czechoslovakia was doomed, sacrificed as much as anything by its Allies in Britain.

With all this trouble looming, Hanna put on her rose-tinted goggles once more. 'The Germans did not want war, but justice,' she told herself, assuming quite happily that Hitler wanted peace too. She was not alone in this delusion. On 30 September 1938 British prime minister Neville Chamberlain had told an anxious audience the settling of the Sudetenland crisis meant 'peace for our time'. Hanna could no longer pretend that National Socialism was a flash in the pan, but she looked at it with as much positivity as she could muster. Like many Germans she felt there was much to be admired about the system; even post-war, Germans would state that National Socialism could have worked if only Hitler had not corrupted it. What is often forgotten is that the Nazi Party had reinvigorated Germany, boosting the economy, creating work for all, reducing the crippling poverty and unemployment that had been the country's lot since the First World War. Hanna knew full well she would not have had so many opportunities in her life had it not been for the influence of National Socialism. There was a great deal, pre-1939, that the German people were grateful to the Nazis for.

In 1938 Hanna stated that Hitler had created 'a progressive, dynamic, and prosperous nation, even the critics of Hitler had reluctantly to admit that he had done a creditable job in building up the nation and re-establishing her on the map of Europe'. That people shut their eyes to what was happening to Jews, Communists and political criminals was a matter of self-preservation. People had suffered poverty and depression so greatly that they were prepared to sacrifice a handful of people – who weren't their people, after all – to continue to exist in an apparent idyll. Coupled with her enthusiasm, Hanna maintained a blind loyalty to authority. This was something that had been indoctrinated into her as a child: a leader should be followed to the bitter end as it was the only honourable thing to do. Hanna was not one to question this; in fact, she rarely questioned much unless it affected her immediately. In her mind there was little else to do, so she followed Hitler to the last moments. Anything else would have been betrayal and that would have been more painful to Hanna than any injury or insult she endured during her flying career.

Paris was just beginning to feel the tight clutch of winter in November 1938 as Ernst vom Rath, diplomat and long-standing member of the Nazi Party, was asked to speak to a young man who had entered the German embassy. Vom Rath descended from his office to meet a youth with dark hair and eyes, and a slight look of the American film star Buster Keaton about him. Herschel Grynszpan, the Polish Jew who had asked for a member of the German diplomatic staff, raised a gun without hesitation and shot vom Rath. Grynszpan fled among the screams of the secretaries as vom Rath collapsed bleeding to the floor. A short time later 29-year-old vom Rath died and his death was quickly being referred to in German circles as an assassination.

Why Grynszpan shot vom Rath no one has ever been able to say conclusively (Grynszpan fell into Nazi hands after the occupation of France and died in a concentration camp). Some thought he was upset over news his family were being deported from Germany back to Poland. Others hinted he had had a homosexual affair with vom Rath, but since most witnesses stated that he did not ask for vom Rath by name, it seems unlikely it was a targeted killing. Rather, Grynszpan was making a point – not that many Jews would have thanked him.

The death of vom Rath sparked the worst instance of violence against the Jews of the 1930s. Known as Kristallnacht or the Night of Broken Glass, the retribution was both bloody and mindless. Shop windows were smashed and their goods destroyed; Jewish men, women and children were dragged from their beds; people were brutally beaten in the streets; there were deaths; synagogues were burned. No Jew was safe – there were reprisals in Germany, Austria and Sudetenland, fuelled by exaggeration of Grynszpan's crime by the media. While it has never been proven that the riots were officially condoned, it is clear that little was done to stop them once they began. It was one of the worst cases of civilian disorder in German memory and many were stunned by the chaos and cruelty.

Hanna happened to be attending a DFS outing on the Night of Broken Glass. She first realised that something was wrong when

> I saw two old people being brought out of their house in their nightdresses. They were protesting and struggling and people were jeering at them. This was followed by a number of shop windows being broken. Then I saw some children coming noisily down the street, dragging behind them a Jewish hearse. They took it to the banks of the River Main, chopped it to bits with axes and then pushed it into the river.

Hanna simply didn't understand what was happening. Her first thought was that it was a Communist uprising. Like most good Germans, she had been brought up with a healthy fear and distrust of Bolshevik activities, deeming their politics a dangerous mix of fervent rebellion and idealistic violence – in fact, she should have recognised that that these events were the works of 'good Germans'.

Frightened and outraged, she shouted out to the people around her that they must call for the police. None of her companions moved. Hanna stared at them astonished. 'How can you stand there and allow such things? It is a disgrace that German people should act in such a manner! The Führer would weep if he knew such things were being done in his name!' Her companions looked upon her pityingly. Hanna was aghast that no one was as indignant as she. Worse, Hans Jacobs, who was leading the outing, forced her away and bundled her into a coach before a nasty-looking mob could snatch her for protesting. As the coaches drove away someone told Jacobs, 'The synagogues are burning.' No one seemed particularly concerned by this; some were even revelling quietly in the atmosphere of violence.

More than 100 DFS employees had gone on the outing, yet only a half-dozen showed any sign of distress at the scenes that night. Hanna was the most vocal by far. If nothing else, she hated persecution of any person and was not herself prejudiced against others. If she saw no wrong in Hitler, at least this was offset by the fact that she saw no wrong in a person just because someone said they were the wrong colour, religion or race. She had once been upbraided by Professor Georgii for speaking too openly in support of the Jews. Now she protested to Jacobs and he finally relented a little.

At Darmstadt Jacobs gathered together all the DFS employees. Hanna waited with anticipation to hear what he would say: he had promised her he would publically declare his outrage at the events of the night before. He stared out at his employees, knowing full well that many were Nazis and many had supported Kristallnacht. 'I very much regret that we made our outing on this particular day,' he said. Hanna waited for more, but it never came. For the first time in her life she was ashamed to be German.

Hanna was not alone in her disillusionment. The Lindberghs were back in Germany in 1938. With a whiff of war in the air, America was jittery. As before, Charles was asked to visit Germany and give his expert opinion on its air force. Charles and Anne were blissfully ignorant of any looming catastrophe, they saw nothing wrong or out of place in Berlin. Indeed, Anne began house-hunting as Charles fancied wintering in the city. Göring was equally pleased to have America's flying hero back in his country. At a men-only dinner hosted at the American embassy, he presented Charles with the Service Cross of the German Eagle. Charles wore it happily enough, but when Anne saw it she felt it might cause her husband problems. She was not wrong, but before that storm could hit it was 9 November 1938 – Kristallnacht.

Charles was stunned by the scenes he saw. 'My admiration for the Germans is constantly being dashed against some rock such as this,' he cried. He removed his family to Paris for the winter, but whatever his consternation at the anti-Semitic aspects of National Socialism, his eternal fondness for German culture was to have an impact on his reputation at home. In particular, his rash decision to live in Berlin had been widely reported in America and now his home-grown fans hissed when he appeared onscreen in newsreel footage. Sponsorship was lost and Anne's latest book, though well received by critics, was boycotted by Jewish booksellers. This was to make life difficult for the couple when they returned to America with the outbreak of war.

Charles was incredibly naïve when it came to politics, yet he also held strong, sometimes bigoted opinions. America's golden boy was quickly losing his shine. Two weeks after the outbreak of war Charles delivered a speech opposing the entry of the United States into the conflict. It was a poor job of public speaking and antagonised even those who were on his side. Shortly after, he published an article in *Readers' Digest* with dangerous racist overtones, implying the war was a threat to the white race. Anne also wrote on the subject of keeping the US out of the war, mostly reiterating her husband's views. She would later regret being so blind to the real situation facing the world.

Charles railed on. Göring would have enjoyed the speech presented at Iowa in 1941 when Charles was a key spokesperson for the America First movement, an organisation determined to keep the US neutral. Charles ranted to his audience that it was the British, Roosevelt's administration and Jewish activists who were pushing for America to go to war. Anne, listening at home on the radio, cringed to herself. Though Charles saw nothing racist in his speech, his views were interpreted by others as being at best anti-Semitic and at worst pure Nazi dogma. The Lindberghs were no longer the stars of America; they were finally granted their one wish of privacy, for no one wanted to know them any more. Even Charles' mother found it hard to swallow his views, so against her own were they.

The Lindberghs had been absorbed into the Nazi movement as blindly as so many Germans. As, indeed, Hanna herself was. They failed to see the harm or notice the dark undercurrents rippling through German society. No wonder Hanna was elated to meet Charles and receive his praise. After all, he was Göring's favourite non-German flyer and an American who shared many of the views she did. And, just like Hanna, he suffered after the war for his incredible naïvety and unhealthy opinions.

The retribution meted out to the Jews during Kristallnacht had been horrendous. In Breslau Jewish shops had been systematically destroyed, their windows broken, their wares smashed and trampled. Glass littered the streets and the New Synagogue was ablaze, orange flames flicking up to the sky. The local firemen were standing by and watching, confining their efforts to preventing nearby non-Jewish houses from catching alight. No attempt was made to save the synagogue. When the fury died down, nearly 2,500 Jews had vanished, arrested by the SA, SS or Gestapo. One synagogue was burned to the ground, while two others had been demolished; around 500 Jewish shops and three dozen Jewish-owned businesses had been vandalised to the extent that some would never operate again.

The Nazi paper *Schlesische Tageszeitung* proclaimed 'Breslau gets even with the Jews. Their synagogues are nothing but heaps of rubble.' Unease filtered among the more liberal members of the population as they looked upon the scenes of destruction; some were even moved to angry outbursts – but only in the privacy of their own homes. Ulrich Frodien, a staunch member of the Hitler Youth and loyal follower of Hitler who would, like Hanna, become disillusioned with Germany, later remembered that his father was outraged by the attacks after Kristallnacht, 'But like everyone else, he did nothing, he remained a Party member and only clenched his fist in his pocket.' It was not only Jews who feared the Nazi forces; non-Jews too were afraid to speak out against the violence. It was easier to slip away, pretend it was not happening and hope someone else would do something.

Hanna did stand up, however, along with Jacobs, and they both came very close to disaster for having a conscience. An employee at DFS was nephew to the head of the Nazi administration in the area. He denounced Hanna and Jacobs and they found themselves summoned before a committee of local Nazi officials. Neither would retract their outraged statements over Kristallnacht, nor their support for Jews. Fortunately for them both, they were too invaluable to be removed from Darmstadt and they were released. It is often forgotten by Hanna's detractors, who focus on her days in the bunker, that she stood up for the Jews at a time when it could have landed her in very serious, even fatal, danger.

She had supported Joachim Küttner when he was banned from gliding in 1937 due to his Jewish ancestry and had even helped him to find work abroad as an instructor. Unfortunately, she naïvely believed that Hitler shared her opinions on the Jews and that he must have been horrified by the events of 9 November. She was greatly relieved to learn from an uncle that Hitler had been furious over Kristallnacht and blamed it on Goebbels.

With hindsight, this seems completely implausible, but the German people were drowning in a sea of misinformation and propaganda. They were isolated from the truth, being spoon-fed biased information that shaped their opinions and views. Only in recent years, with the release of such documents as POW interrogation files, has it become clear just how controlled perception was. Many ordinary Germans held a view of Hitler as an almost saintly figure who had saved them, but had then been used and betrayed by such men as Göring, Himmler and Goebbels. Even those who believed in the Nazi Party and hated the Jews found it impossible to contemplate how any government could condone their mass slaughter. Even today our opinions of politicians are largely governed by the media, which are influenced by spin doctors who put a good light on anything bad a politician has done. In Germany this was merely taken to the extreme, helped by the lack of a free press.

In any case, Hanna could not accept that her Führer, the man to whom she had declared undying loyalty, was nothing more than a crook and a bully. It was easier to believe he was misguided than to think she had given her honourable devotion to someone completely unworthy.

6

GIANTS OF WAR

Hitler had designs on gliding for war purposes. At the outbreak of war Hanna found herself testing the DFS 230 glider (originally designed in 1933 for taking meteorological surveys or carrying post) as a potential troop carrier. Shortly afterwards a glider unit was formed and the first potential glider-based operation was imagined.

It has been suggested that Hanna was indirectly responsible for the glider attack on the Belgium fort of Eben Emael, which was the beginning of the 'silent raids'. Eben Emael had been hewn out of solid rock during the construction of the Albert Canal. The canal formed a natural moat on the northern side; the rest of the hexagonal fort was protected by 5ft-thick reinforced concrete walls and roofs, all camouflaged to appear as a grassy field with armed cannon cupolas dotting the landscape. Each of these cupolas had six 120mm cannons and could revolve 360° to attack invaders within a 12-mile radius. A further eighteen 75mm guns were placed in cupolas and casements guarding the approach across the River Meuse and the Albert Canal. Pillboxes, ditches, trenches, barbed wire, machine guns, minefields and anti-tank traps had been placed on the sides not facing the canal to deter attackers on foot. Anti-aircraft batteries, searchlights and sound-ranging equipment scanned the skies to keep bombers at bay. The Belgians had done everything they could think of during the construction of the fort between 1932 and 1935 to make it impregnable and, at first glance, it certainly seemed to be the ultimate obstacle in the path of the Nazi invasion of France.

Late in 1939 Hitler was in Berlin poring over maps of Belgium and constantly being reminded of the impenetrable monstrosity of concrete and cannon that was Eben Emael. A thought had stuck in his mind, something a small female pilot had pointed out to him at a flying competition in 1935. With her eager smile Hanna had motioned to the glider she had flown and commented to Hitler that it was the perfect way to fly noiselessly. An innocent enough remark, until fed into the mind of a dictator. Hitler had summoned the commanding general of Fliegerdivision 7, Kurt Student, to prepare a plan to send in a glider squadron to strike at Eben Emael – a silent invasion that would elude all its defences.

On 10 May 1940, in the early hours of the morning, eleven gliders were loaded with high-powered explosive devices and readied for launch. Lieutenant Rudolf Witzig was in charge of the eighty-five-man team, known as Force Granite, that would storm Eben Emael and disarm its defences ahead of the real invasion force. Inside each glider paratroopers were armed with grenades, submachine guns and the explosive they would have to place and detonate once inside the fort. At 3.25 a.m. they were in the air, but, as Hanna could have told the unfortunate paratroopers, flying in a glider was a very different experience from flying in a powered plane. The gliders were buffeted back and forth, and in the dark confined space the men fought down nausea and fear. There was apprehension among them; few believed they were coming home again.

Problems soon arose. The towrope for Witzig's glider snapped when another plane flew too close. A second tow-plane pilot either mistook the location or lost his nerve and released his glider too early. Out of eleven gliders, only nine were released at the spot that was intended. With no means of communication between tow-plane and glider, the situation was complicated by misunderstandings and errors. To compound the problem, the struggling tow-planes had failed to reach the assigned height of 8,500ft. In desperation, some tow-plane pilots decided to hang on until they were deeper in Belgium territory and ended up under fire.

Despite this, the gliders were on course for their target. Flying silently, completely missed by the anti-aircraft guns, the gliders landed on the roof of Eben Emael without resistance and to the amazement of the Belgium defenders. The paratroopers were shooting as they jumped from the planes, quickly overwhelming the machine-gun posts and defenders who failed to respond fast enough to the strange silent, bat-like creatures that landed before them. Engineers ran to the cupolas and set their explosives and within minutes the cannons and their crews were blasted to smithereens. Huge holes were blown in the 5ft reinforced concrete, not always enough to penetrate the roof of the fort, but adequate to shake the underground foundations, send shrapnel flying and terrify the defenders. The Belgians' feeble attempts to save their fort were without success. The silent and unexpected attack had shaken them too deeply. As a last resort the garrison sealed itself in the underground maze of tunnels that made up Eben Emael. Prisoners in their own fort. By the time the German armies arrived, Eben Emael was truly defeated. The glider team was proudly marching about on the surface, now comfortably in control while the Belgium defenders cowered below ground. With the reinforcement of the Wehrmacht, the garrison had little choice but to surrender. The impregnable fortress had been penetrated by eleven gliders and the power of a surprise attack. The Belgians could thank Hanna Reitsch for giving Hitler the idea.

Hanna was excluded from the plans for glider warfare, much to her chagrin. She had tried to offer her expertise to the new glider unit, but had been rebuffed. When it had initially looked as though the invasion of France would begin in the winter, Hanna had been testing landing skids for the gliders. She was sent to demonstrate the new skids to the glider unit and at last had an opportunity to speak with them. She also learned that the pilots were worried; they had not been allowed practice in the gliders, or to conduct a full-scale rehearsal of the invasion. Most vocal of those concerned was Otto Bräutigam, an expert glider pilot to whom Hanna took a shine: '[He] was the liveliest among us, fizzing with vitality, full of pranks and jokes, yet speaking plainly, almost harshly to the point and, with it all, a most able and courageous flyer.' Bräutigam flew and survived the Eben Emael mission, but Hanna was not destined to enjoy this new friendship for long.

The success of Eben Emael had convinced the German Air Ministry that a similar stealth approach could be used in the planned invasion of Britain. However, in that case it would not just be a matter of transporting men, but vehicles, guns, even tanks. A glider that could carry such a load would need to be very big, so, appropriately it was given the name Gigant. The Gigant was a variant on the Messerschmitt Me 321 military glider with engines to assist take-off and flying. In October 1940 Junkers and Messerschmitt were both given just fourteen days to submit a new glider design. Messerschmitt was the only one to succeed after Junkers found problems obtaining the high-quality timber he needed for his design, along with problems with its stability.

The Gigant also had its problems: it was hard enough to get such a large glider airborne empty; loaded was almost impossible. A Junkers Ju 90 was originally used to tow the Gigant into the air, but it struggled to leave the runway. Messerschmitt knew he would have to alter the designs and ended up giving his Gigant liquid-fuelled rockets to assist take-off. When the lumbering machine finally reached flying height it then had to cast off its undercarriage, another task that was not always successful and could lead to disaster. Eventually a system of three twin-engined Me 110s in a formation known as a Troika-Schlepp were used just to get the Gigant airborne. This added yet another complication: all four pilots had to work in harmony to launch the glider. Once the Gigant had fired its rockets to assist take-off there was no means of shutting them off. This could prove disastrous, if not deadly, if an engine on the planes failed or a rocket didn't fire. The Gigant could end up skewing and sliding across the runway, potentially dragging the tow-planes into a collision. On the first trial of the Troika-Schlepp launch, an accident was only narrowly avoided when the main tow attachment broke.

Hanna was not initially involved in testing the Gigant, but she badly wanted to try out these enormous gliders. Karl Franke eventually agreed to take her up in one. He stood in the empty space where troops and machinery would be stored while Hanna wrestled with the controls. 'It was so primitively built that it was so difficult to fly! You needed so much strength and you see, what is too hard for me in a five minutes flight that is too hard for a strong man in a one hour flight,' Hanna later explained. 'So I tried with this argument to convince Udet to stop it, but he didn't believe me because Messerschmitt said "she is too small, a little girl, not the strong men we have fighting, so don't believe her."'

On only her second test flight in a Gigant, Hanna's fears came true when she had problems while being towed by the Troika-Schlepp:

The left bomber, even while still just above the ground went out [sideways] and he had to release the [tow] cable, and two couldn't do it alone. We had six rockets on the wing which when they once were blowing you could not stop them, so when you lost one towing bomber, also the right bomber was lost. I was hanging on one bomber that was like a little fly compared with my giant! And all six rockets were burning, I knew I couldn't stop it. I could get 150ft high then the rockets were finished after three or four minutes and I knew the single tow bomber had to release me otherwise he would [crash]. So I could just as he released me [glide], before I touched the ground it was [nose pointing down], but I had the good luck as I touched the ground I bounced [and the nose came up]. One [of those in the Gigant] had broken his knees, another had nerve shock, but I was well and only deeply thankful no one was killed [*sic*].

That was enough for Hanna: 'I finished because I was so much against it because it was too big.'

There was another reason for her reticence about the Gigant. Otto Bräutigam had also been testing the giant glider, though he was unwilling to share the experience with Hanna. He took off twice before she could join him in the glider. On the second occasion Hanna was so furious she burst into tears, but within moments she was grateful for being grounded. Bräutigam's Gigant flew into a thunderstorm. It crashed and both Bräutigam and his co-pilot were killed. In Hanna's *The Sky My Kingdom*, her memoirs of her early days of flying, she makes no mention of Otto's painful and untimely death. In fact, the Gigant episode is glossed over, like so much else of her personal history and the experiences of her country, yet the accident had a marked impact on her.

As a glider the Gigant was unfeasible. Realising this, Messerschmitt redesigned it with six set engines and a fixed multi-wheeled undercarriage, making it the largest service transport plane in existence. Hanna was happier with the redesign: 'This was very simple to fly, you see the engine did it all.' Few in the Luftwaffe agreed with her. The Gigant was easy prey for Allied planes and many were shot down before they reached their destination.

The urgency of war was sparking more and more bizarre designs and propositions. Hanna was next called upon to test a flying petrol tanker. The idea was that this could be towed behind the parent plane as a glider and used for refuelling in the air. To work successfully, the tanker needed to be inherently stabe so that it would level itself off after take-off and not hinder its parent plane. The prototype, therefore, would need to be piloted so that notes could be taken on its behaviour in the air and what improvements were needed. Naturally Hanna was suited to this task as she was small and could fit inside the compact tanker with the addition of flying controls. She hated every minute of the flights. In order to ascertain how well the tanker flew she had to lock off her controls during take-off and wait to see what happened. She had to let the tanker get into trouble to identify any problems that needed to be overcome. Very often the tanker flipped over completely and Hanna, helpless inside, fought back waves of violent airsickness and a dreadful sense of fear. Having only just returned from the Gigant experiments, this was hardly surprising. Very soon it became plain that the tanker was impracticable, there was no way to stabilise it and it interfered too much with the flight of the parent plane. Hanna was greatly relieved when the tests were over.

Next she was involved in tests to find a way to land small observation planes on warships, using the smallest deck space possible. Someone had had the idea of stretching several ropes around 100ft in length across the deck at an angle. One end of each rope was attached to the deck, the other to a 20ft-high wooden scaffold, forming a primitive cradle for the plane to land in. Hanna looked at this uneasily; the idea was that the wings would rest on the outer ropes and the fuselage and would slip into the 3ft space between the lower ropes. Each rope was fitted with braking devices to assist the landing in the limited space available. Yet again, precision on the pilot's part was everything. There were many things that could go wrong. The ropes might shear the wings, so the latter were fitted with a steel tube on the underside. The plane might bounce and spring out when it hit the ropes, so a device was made that caused the ropes on either side of the fuselage to spring out into a rigid channel, fixing the plane on a straight course.

Hanna practised on a separate airfield before attempting the real landing. Very soon she realised there was a problem: from the air it was almost impossible to make out the placing or angle of the ropes, so eventually she had several small fir trees placed between the ropes to create depth. Hanna was still worried and decided to make these tests a rare occasion for wearing a crash helmet. In those early days of flight, test pilots often flew without any form of protection – it was seen as a mark of underconfidence or even cowardice to want a crash helmet, though a parachute was normally carried. Like her contemporaries, Hanna never usually bothered with a helmet, but on her very first test of the landing cradle she was glad she had changed her mind. Though her landing was perfect, at the last moment the plane was buffeted by a strong wind. Still going at some speed, the plane twisted and plunged between two of the ropes. Hanna ducked instinctively, but it was the crash helmet that saved her from worse injuries by deflecting the rope. Hannah always insisted in her dramatic way that it had spared her from being decapitated by the rope. In the second test Hanna once more landed perfectly. This time no wind buffeted her, but even with the braking blocks on the rope she seemed to speed towards the 20ft scaffold far too fast. For an awful moment Hanna thought she would crash, but, remarkably, with a few yards to go, the glider stopped. The third test was the worst. A new type of braking system had been introduced after the near failure of the second test, but it might as well not have been. This time, when Hanna landed, she didn't stop at all and the scaffold loomed alarmingly. There was no doubt she would hit it. Hanna ducked her head, closed her eyes and could only thank God that somehow her glider's tail became caught in the scaffolding, preventing a nosedive to the ground. She hung over the edge, the fuselage seemingly poised in mid-flight, as worried onlookers ran to get a fire-ladder so she could climb down. That was the end of landing on ropes.

Next came an experiment in cutting balloon cables. Barrage balloons were a nightmare for the Luftwaffe when making raids over Britain. The cables were often invisible when flying fast, and certainly at night, so planes flew into them, usually resulting in a wing being sheared off, if not worse, and the downing of the plane. Hans Jacobs had come up with the idea of a fender that could be fixed to the front wings of any plane to protect them by diverting the cable and causing it to run into a cutting device at the tip of the wing. The first version looked incredibly unwieldy, like a box section fixed to the front. Naturally, Hanna was sent in to test its capabilities.

Starting with steel cables 2.7mm in diameter, before moving on to cables of 8.9mm, Hanna had the taxing task of flying directly at mock-up barrage balloons and hoping that Jacobs' designs would stand up to the assault. Her aircraft was equipped with sensitive equipment to measure the force of impact as Hanna flew into the cable to help improve the fender. In the initial test there was no knowing if Jacobs' fender would provide adequate protection to the plane's airscrew. If it did not, then there was a real risk that the airscrew would be shattered and broken fragments would be launched backwards into the cockpit – and, of course, into the pilot. Anticipating the worst, Hanna had a second pilot's seat with duplicate controls set into the rear gun-turret of her test plane (a Dornier 17 bomber), near to the escape hatch. Though the plane could not take off or land using the duplicate controls, they could be used to fly in the air, thus lessening the chance of Hanna being injured.

Hanna flew with a fitter who could act as co-pilot when she made the necessary change from front to back pilot seat. The fitter would then ready their parachutes and sit by the escape hatch. In the event of a disaster, Hanna was hopeful both of them would be able to jump out and parachute to the ground. There were some tests she would have to conduct at low altitude, too low to enable anyone to bail out. On those occasions, she informed the relieved fitter, she would fly alone.

With all precautions in place, Hanna took to the air. The designers had fake balloons specially built for Hanna to run the tests, and one now hovered innocently over the Rechlin test fields. Hanna flew high and looked down on it. At a certain angle the cable would flash silver in the sunlight and she caught a glimpse of it. Hanna dived to the level of the cable, but now it vanished from her sight, invisible against the blue sky – this was what made barrage balloons so deadly to Luftwaffe pilots. Hanna circled up again, caught the flash of silver and memorised its position. Then she flew down once more. Using guesswork as much as anything, she aimed at the cable and flew headlong into it. There was a jerk as the cable struck the fender. Hanna and the fitter braced for the shards of plane they were expecting to tear through the cabin. There was nothing. The Dornier flew on as if nothing had happened. 'Next time they need to put something on that cable so I can see it better,' Hanna muttered to herself as they headed in to land. Next time they did: long strings of coloured bunting set at intervals of 100ft. Hanna could fly up and fix on a spot between two strips of bunting, then zoom down, level herself with the same spot and fly forward. Over and over she aimed at the balloon cables and over and over she hit them and returned the data to Jacobs and his team.

Initial results were not conclusive. The fender needed tweaking as each new set of data came in. But for Hanna the constant retests did not feel like a chore, not when she knew that every time she took her Dornier into that cable she was coming closer to saving the lives of other pilots: 'For every test I flew brought us a step nearer to overcoming some of those perils which pilots and aircrews had daily to face in operations against the enemy. Such was my enthusiasm, I was hardly aware that for days I had not been feeling well.'

Hanna brushed aside the headaches that had begun to plague her. She ignored the fever that had her burning one moment and shivering the next. The tests were reaching their conclusion; all that remained was to fly a Dornier fitted with a fender into the thickest cable available and see if it could withstand the impact. Hanna was determined to be a part of that test, but her body had other ideas. One morning she was shivering worse than ever when she noted a faint rash on her skin. As much as she wanted to fly, Hanna could not ignore this new symptom – she had scarlet fever. Scarlet fever, a bacterial infection spread through the air, was a known killer in the early twentieth century. The development of antibiotics would turn it into a minor illness, easily treated, but for Hanna it was going to leave lasting effects. Penicillin had been discovered in 1929, in the 1940s it was slowly coming into use, but that very much depended on the type of doctor one saw. Progressive doctors risked these new antibiotics, old-fashioned ones stuck to their tried and tested methods. Besides, penicillin was virtually unheard of in Germany and impossible to obtain. Hanna Reitsch found herself in the isolation wing of Virchow Hospital, with the windows blacked out, left to lie in bed for hours upon hours and wonder what was to come. The rash had spread to Hanna's eyes; before long she was suffering from common complications of the disease: rheumatic fever and heart problems. Hanna lay on her bed and wondered what was to become of her.

In the background, tests on the fender continued. Hanna's role was taken by a young pilot called Lettmaier who flew the redesigned Dornier on its last few test flights and concluded the experimental stage. Jacobs presented his design to the Luftwaffe. They looked on sceptically. Only one person showed an interest: Ritter von Greim, who recognised the fender's potential to save lives. He and a number of his staff had watched early tests and had seen Hanna's successes. Von Greim asked that all planes fitted with the fender be transferred to his command. It was a small ray of light in Hanna's dark world when letters arrived from pilots who had used the adapted planes and had their lives saved by the fender.

For three months Hanna rested, the hours slipping by endlessly. Her mother wrote daily and provided news on the Reitsch family. Kurt was now married and in the German navy. He had survived the sinking of his ship during the Nazi invasion of Narvik, Norway, in early 1940. Heidi had recently had twins, a boy and a girl, to complement her elder son, who was now 3. There was much to be grateful for, Emy wrote in letters that varied from prose to verse, reminding her elder daughter to keep strong and hold tight to her patriotism. The senior Reitschs had aged dramatically in the last few years. Emy had gone grey and wore her hair tied back in a bun. Her face was lined with years of worry. Herr Reitsch looked even worse: a frail figure worn thin by the passing of time. His heavy brow shadowed his eyes, he hunched slightly as he moved, there seemed a heavy burden upon him. Emy ignored her husband's decay; she must buoy him up as she buoyed Hanna up. Somehow she kept the despondent threads of the family together, clutching her children as close as she could and dreading each day the news that either Hanna or Kurt (or perhaps both) had perished.

Through those long dark months Hanna thought of God. Her faith, childlike as it was, remained strong and rigid. She thought of Hitler and knew she must remain loyal and continue her work for the sake of Germany. She thought of the many pilots whose lives would be saved by the innovations of men like Jacobs, and longed to get well again. Finally the day came when she was removed from isolation. Her body was weak from so long lying down, her heart had been permanently damaged, but she was too eager to get back in the air to worry. Hanna returned to Rechlin and picked up where she had left off.

Operational flights with Jacobs' fender had shown that while it offered good protection, it was rather heavy, and if a plane lost an engine the weight of the fender would become too much. The boxy construction, serving somewhat as a sturdy, protective fence ahead of the plane, needed to be modified. Jacobs tried another idea – a razor-sharp strip of steel attached to the leading edge of the wings and designed to cut through a cable. Unlike the fender, which had mainly acted to protect the airscrew and guide the cable clear of the plane, the new design would leave the airscrew exposed, but would cut the balloon cable; thus taking the balloon out of action. There were pros and cons to the new design, not least because testing the cutting power of the steel razors meant constantly losing balloons. As soon as a cable was cut the balloon floated away and could only be retrieved with extreme difficulty. Testing was therefore both costly and time consuming as balloons had to be regularly deployed. To make life somewhat simpler, the tests were moved to the balloon-testing station at Saarow.

An unforeseen difficulty arose, however. When the balloons were cut loose during the tests they were naturally taken by the wind, dragging their heavy cables. On blustery days this sometimes meant they towed their cables into overhead electric wires, causing endless damage. 'We must have cost the State a fortune,' Hanna mused as she watched another balloon wander into a power line. In desperation, fighters were deployed to shoot down the balloon once it had been released, or sometimes the pressure release valves were closed so that the balloon would explode when it reached a certain height. Neither method was entirely successful and both meant more lost balloons. Still, the tests continued and word spread to the Luftwaffe of the new design.

One breezy day Ernst Udet touched down at Saarow. He was on his way to a conference with Hitler and wanted to see the balloon cutters in action. He had arrived just as Hanna was about to fly another test; he was even more delighted when he learned exactly who was flying the plane. He joined the balloon crew to watch. It could not have been a worse day to visit. Hanna was about to test her plane on a particularly difficult cable. The cable and balloon were genuine British made. The balloon had drifted across the ocean from England and been captured as an ideal means of testing Jacobs' cutter. On inspection, it was realised that the cable was not quite the same as the ones the Germans had been using for tests. Though only 5.6mm in diameter, the cable was made of five or six strands of steel thread, each much thicker and tougher than the ones Hanna normally used. To make matters worse, the balloon had been captured with only a short length of cable. It could not be flown at the usual height, instead Hanna would have to come at it quite low, far too low to enable her to bail out. To compound the difficulties, a stiff wind was blowing and the balloon had been anchored in a wood to try and stop it being blown about. Hanna had to skim over treetops and aim for a balloon that was turning in the wind.

Had Udet not been there, the test would have surely been cancelled, but he was present and he was eager. Hanna climbed into her plane with a last look at the balloon. Her heart sank as she saw that it had not turned into the wind as expected (with its nose pointing in the direction the wind was blowing from), but was sitting side-on, so that the full force of the weather was hitting it broadside. The drag on the cable must have been enormous and there was a real risk that it might break loose. If only Udet had not come! Hanna took to the sky and quickly saw that the balloon was dragging its cable at an angle, the steel rope was slanting over the tops of the trees. It was not a good position to try and cut it, in fact it was fraught with difficulties. But the test-crew had given the all-clear, so perhaps, reasoned Hanna, such conditions were commonly encountered on active duty and must be tested for.

Hanna flew close to the cable. There was a strange sound, metal under tension. With a loud whipping noise, the balloon cable snapped. Fragments of steel thread flicked into the air and caught Hanna's airscrew. Metal splinters shot through the cabin as Hanna frantically ducked and covered her head. The cable had taken off the lower edge of two propeller blades on the starboard side and now the engine was racing uncontrollably. Hanna reacted instinctively, switched off the damaged engine and engaged the electric motor in a desperate attempt to halt the propeller in a neutral position where it could no longer turn by auto-rotation. She had to hurry; the starboard engine was in real danger of breaking loose from its mountings. If it did so, Hanna would crash. Too low to bail out, she would die in the impact.

From the ground the test-crew looked on in horror as the cable sheared and snapped, and debris flew through the air. The sound of an engine racing filled the sky. As Hanna vanished from sight Udet waited for the seemingly inevitable crash and plume of smoke. For several moments everyone waited for the explosion. When nothing happened, Udet turned and raced from the balloon crew: 'Ready my plane!' He flew over the treetops and followed Hanna's usual route back to her take-off site, his eyes primed all the while to see the twisted, burning carcass of a plane on the ground. There was no sign of anything until he reached the nearby airfield. There was the Dornier, sitting on the ground looking as if nothing had happened and a pale Hanna Reitsch climbing out. Udet landed and almost ran to her. 'You look as shaken as I feel,' he said. Hanna gave him a wan smile.

Udet flew on to see Hitler when his nerves had recovered, very relieved not to have to tell the Führer his favourite test pilot had died in a crash. In fact, he had a very different story to tell, one that would delight Hitler as it demonstrated the courage and resourcefulness of the German people. Hanna Reitsch had defied the odds yet again and for this she would receive the Iron Cross, Second Class – the first woman ever to do so.

Hanna had long-ago realised her leaders were not the great men she had dreamed of, but her staunch honour and patriotism would not allow her to admit it in public. She had briefly met Hitler when she was made a Flugkapitän and he had left a dismal impression upon her. She confessed to a friend that he was so huge a disappointment that she locked herself in her room and cried for three days – was this the man she was fighting for? Hitler had appeared in a crumpled suit, looking dishevelled and small. He sounded uncultured when he spoke and, to Hanna's unparalleled horror, picked his nose. She was torn between her disapproval and the knowledge that to forsake her patriotism was to be a traitor to her country; worse, to be a traitor to her parents.

For three days these emotions warred within her, until finally her iron-willed loyalty to Germany won out. Hitler was not the man she had believed in, not the man she had turned into a hero in her mind, so she would have to ignore that impossible fact. She would not disgrace her honour by diminishing the Führer to others, she would not disgrace her family. Nor would she admit that she, or her beloved mother, had been wrong about the Führer. Hanna stuffed the notion away and to all intents and purposes appeared to her friends to be overly loyal and unquestioning of the Führer. In many regards it was the only way to retain her sense of patriotism; if she let her mind wander to that figure who had stood before her in a crumpled suit, then awful questions loomed in her mind as to why she was flying for her country.

If Hanna was reluctantly revising her image of Hitler, she was far less concerned about who knew of her distaste for Göring. On 27 March 1941 Hanna stepped into Göring's lavishly decorated Berlin home to receive a special version of the Gold Medal for Military Flying with Brilliance. Göring liked to imagine himself a connoisseur of art and antiquities. All his homes were stuffed full of paintings, sculptures and ceramics, many notoriously 'stolen', others bought with his ill-gotten gains. As early as 1941 he was using his position as head of the Luftwaffe to pursue his cultural interests rather than pay attention to Germany's Air Force. Hanna was a simple girl at heart and the brash interiors of Göring's home were not about to impress her. Nor was the man himself.

Overweight, decorated with glittering baubles and surrounded by his generals, when Hanna entered his room he completely ignored her and looked over her head. Udet let the embarrassing moment drift on too long, then smiled apologetically and murmured that *this* was Hanna Reitsch. Göring looked at her with undisguised amazement: 'What!' He moved towards Hanna, hands on his hips as he stood enormous before her. 'Is this supposed to be our famous "Flugkapitän"? Where's the rest of her? How can this little person manage to fly at all?' Hanna bristled, she was sensitive about her height, something her fellow pilots had picked on from her earliest days of gliding. She glared at Göring. 'Do you have to look like that to fly?' She swept a hand at Göring's huge girth, her hot temper overcoming restraint. As she said it, she knew it was a mistake. So often her words, spoken too quickly, had dropped Hanna into trouble. But this surely had to be the worst time of all for her restraint to fail her. Hanna inwardly cringed, but fortunately Göring took the remark as a joke. He and his generals laughed. After all, who would take the words of this little girl seriously?

Swaddled in a grey uniform, overly ornate with medals and gold braid, insignia blazing on every spare patch of cloth, the obese and gormless-looking Hermann Göring was far too easily parodied as the incompetent leader of the Luftwaffe. His history and road to success had been marked by luck, though he would rather think of it as fate. Born in 1893, as an awkward and rather inane young man he had flown across the battlefields of the First World War, indulging his love for hunting, be his prey animal or man. His minor successes belied the grandiose claims later made by the medals on his uniform. He finished the war with a score of twenty-two kills, far behind his comrade and rival Ernst Udet.

Göring's skill as a fighter pilot was questionable, but a lucky chance landed him in the position of leader of Jagdgeschwader 1, originally led by the flying ace Baron Manfred von Richthofen. Richthofen's death had passed the leadership to Wilhelm Reinhard. Shortly afterwards, Reinhard and Göring went to test a new fighter plane. Göring flew the craft successfully, but when Reinhard tried the same, the aircraft broke up and he was killed. Five days later Göring was promoted to the leader of JG 1. Unfortunately, it was now 1918, and within months of his promotion Göring was having to retreat with his squadron, finally deliberately destroying their aeroplanes so they would not fall into enemy hands. Göring came away from the war with the strong impression that it had not been the skill of the Allies that had defeated Germany, but betrayal within the German Empire, particularly by Jews, Marxists and republicans.

Göring had had a brief taste of power, which he had savoured for all it was worth. Arrogant and dogmatic, he had not found favour with his men, but what did that matter? He had been in command, they had had to do as he said, and any glory they attained eventually came to him as their commander. Göring had found his place, only to lose it. Now his one goal was to seek out that sort of power again. Falling in with Hitler was natural enough. The Nazi movement offered the glory, authority and fame Göring craved (not to mention satisfying the blood lust). He became leader of the SA, but again it was a short-lived dose of power; he was badly wounded during the Munich putsch and fled the country to recover. Ending up reliant on painkillers, he was considered by many as a trumped-up drug addict with an over-inflated ego who had somehow become one of Hitler's closest associates.

Göring returned to Germany in 1927 and set about reinstating himself as a prominent Nazi. Whatever his failings (and there were many), his family background and reputation as an ace of the First World War (albeit one of the lower-ranking aces) made him indispensable to the struggling Adolf Hitler, who needed influential people to fuel and empower his cause. Göring was a ticket to meeting the best people, he opened doors that would otherwise have stayed closed to an upstart army corporal, and before long Hitler was winning over high-ranking officers and industrialists. After Hitler came to power in 1933, Göring was the golden boy of the regime, controlling the slowly expanding Luftwaffe, which he claimed would be the key to success in future conflicts. The 1930s were a heady time, when Göring made big promises without having to deliver on them. He showed off his planes and his pilots and basked in the friendship Hitler bestowed on him and the wealth, power and luxuries such friendship brought. By 1938 Göring had been promoted six times and now held the rank of generalfeldmarschall; he was President of Prussia and the Ministries of Aviation, Economics, Forestry and Hunting, and Minister of the Interior for Prussia, through which position he gained control of the Prussian political police and was able to found the Gestapo.

Göring was powerful, but imprudent. He could whip a crowd into a fever of patriotic Nazism, but it was all words and so little substance. He had so many responsibilities it was impossible to uphold them all, and though he devoted time to the Luftwaffe in the early years, it slowly drifted from his grasp, until even he was unaware of the failings of his own force. Göring wanted power; he did not want responsibility. He wanted to wine and dine pretty mistresses, show off his fanciful and ludicrous uniforms and collect expensive *objets d'art* (though by the inexpensive means of stealing them). However, as much of a dreamer as he was, Göring was also a realist. At the back of his mind was the nagging doubt that things might not last, and in the final weeks of 1945 Göring was working on his exit strategy at the expense of his former friend. It had been good while it lasted, but Göring was not an idealist and once Nazism turned a fatal corner, he was quick to make his escape.

'Göring had a kind of charm,' said V2 designer Wernher von Braun:

> In his way, he could even be said to have been likeable. With his perfume and his gaudy uniforms, I thought of him as a Renaissance prince who had been born into the wrong time. He was a re-incarnated Borgia, lover of food and drink, patron of the arts – with a little poison in somebody's wine at midnight, just for the fun of it.

If the public loved him for the pompous and absurd speeches that buoyed them with confidence, those who knew him found him distasteful, boastful and egotistical. Goebbels in particular despised him, but he was not alone. Hanna Reitsch found Göring impossible and completely out of his depth. She could never forgive his failings towards the Luftwaffe.

The day after meeting Göring, Hanna met Hitler, only her second encounter with him since 1937. She was received in the Chancellery, that grand building of old paintings, glittering ornaments and sturdy, Teutonic furniture. Hitler was to present Hanna with her Iron Cross. He wanted to know about her work on dive brakes and balloon cables, and gave the impression of being knowledgeable on the subject. Hanna liked to talk about her flying, so the conversation was easy enough. Later Hanna spotted one of her friends and couldn't resist calling out, 'Guess where I've been! Hitler invited me! Come with me and I'll tell you all about it.' Then, continuing in a confidential whisper, 'I find that Hitler a dreadful fellow.'

7

A CHILD OF SILESIA

Hanna was a national heroine, but there was a special piece of her heart reserved for Hirschberg, and her hometown had taken its long-lost little Hanna into its bosom. When news of her award circulated, Hirschberg was determined to celebrate its home-grown celebrity and Hanna was invited to a great reception. Strangely for someone who didn't mind talking about herself, the thought of the big party and greeting of her hometown worried Hanna and she turned down the invitation. Not to be deterred, the mayor of Hirschberg drove to Berlin and fetched her in person.

Hanna soon realised the clamour she had caused in her old town. All along the roads leading to Hirschberg flags hung from windows to welcome her, flowers were thrown upon the car and more than once the mayor had to stop to allow local schoolchildren to sing to Hanna, shake her hand and give her homemade gifts. Hanna was speechless at the impact she had made. She posed with her parents on the town hall steps while flash bulbs popped on all sides. The Grunau Gliding School welcomed her with enthusiasm, current pupils forming a 'guard of honour' for her alongside the local Luftwaffe detachment. It was a far cry from those days when she was teased for being a girl and told to go back to the kitchen. As a brass band played and the streets were filled with people eager for a glimpse of the Führer's beloved test pilot, Hanna was given a scroll of honorary citizenship, a distinction she shared only with Gerhart Hauptmann, poet and playwright. It was a rather ironic honour to share, as Hauptmann had been a pacifist during the First World War.

Hanna carried on to her old school, where she spotted the faces of old friends among the current students. It was a bittersweet moment. Hanna was not quite 30, but a lot of time seemed to have passed and she found herself looking at these girls with their whole future ahead of them and thinking, 'I seemed to catch a reflection of my own youth.' She had to smile, though, at the careful spin her teachers had placed on her academic career. When her award was announced Hanna was held up to the girls as a model student: 'Do well in your studies and you too could be like Hanna Reitsch. She was industrious, attentive and well-behaved!' That was far from the truth as the girls had discovered, unfortunately for the teachers, when they had leafed through an old class book. Page after page illustrated Hanna's failures as a pupil, with many black marks against her name. They were usually given for talking too much, or for being in high spirits during class. The girls were elated; the teachers were not. The offending pages were removed and specially bound as a memento for Hanna (and to ensure future attempts at school propaganda could not be so easily found out!).

The gliding school had one last surprise for Hanna: she was presented with her own Grunau Baby. Since she now flew Dornier 17s, Messerschmitts and Junkers, the Baby looked rather old-hat, but Hanna warmly accepted the gift. In a rare moment of sentiment she christened it 'Otto Bräutigam' after the young man she would never see again.

Excitement was soon tainted by tragedy. The first blow was delivered by her old companion and supporter Ernst Udet. For some time he had been struggling and it had exacted a heavy toll. His friends wondered how Udet survived sitting behind a desk day-in and day-out, the idea of this daredevil being constrained to one place was so ludicrous as to seem impossible. Udet was not the sort to sit still; he craved adventure and freedom, and he didn't like being told what to do. While his friends wondered how he survived, in truth Udet was floundering fast. Udet had virtually stumbled into his new role – for Göring he was a poster-boy, one of the surviving air aces of the First World War, the Udlinger who was well known to the general public as the face of stunt flying and barnstorming. From Göring's perspective, Udet was great publicity, and if his one-time comrade treated him with a mix of disdain and mild amusement, what did it really matter? Even better, Udet had no intention of getting mixed up in Nazi politics; he was effectively non-political with very little clue as to the way his future would shape up. His only concern was with the world of flying; everything else could take care of itself.

Udet failed to grasp the power games politicians played. He initially worked well with another commander, Erhard Milch, whom he had in fact taught to fly. Göring resented Milch's power and, in a strategy he and other high-up Nazis would use time and time again, he decided to play off Milch and Udet to undermine the former. Göring reorganised the Luftwaffe so that Udet now reported directly to his commander-in-chief, cutting Milch out of the process. The two men, though once friends, became suspicious of each another and were soon antagonistic. Determined to undermine Milch further, Göring fast-tracked Udet through a series of promotions until by 1939 he was generaloberst.

The new responsibilities and stress of working against others gnawed away at Udet. He was failing fast; his biggest triumph was also his biggest downfall. While in South America he spotted a new type of plane in development – the dive-bomber. Convinced this would be a key weapon in any future Luftwaffe arsenal, he returned to Germany full of news of the amazing craft. The plane could swoop down in a near-vertical dive, pulling up at the last moment to deliver a lethal payload of bombs. At first his enthusiasm was dampened by his colleagues, but he caught the attention of Göring and persuaded him to put funding into the development of the Stuka dive-bomber. When Hitler went on his campaign of invasion it at first appeared that Udet had been completely right about the aircraft. Using the Stukas to bombard cities and populations in a stunning and unearthly raid that levelled the ground, crumbled buildings and set people screaming in terror, the early campaigns were easily won and Udet was flavour of the month.

All too soon the glory came to an end. The Allies studied the Stuka and realised it was vulnerable during its dive; it exposed itself as a highly visible target as it plunged. Before long, Stukas were being shot down before their lethal dive could be completed. Suddenly the wonder weapon was useless. Udet took the full blow of the disaster – he had pushed for Stukas, so clearly he was the one to blame for the Allies outsmarting them.

Udet began to crumble like the buildings his Stukas had once demolished. On a miserable October evening he stood in his villa on the outskirts of Berlin and poured himself a brandy. The Battle of Britain had been another disaster; his Stukas were being annihilated at every turn. All criticism fell on his shoulders and Udet could not take the burden. Walking into his gun room, he selected a revolver from a rack on the wall. He raised his arm, stared down the barrel and pulled the trigger. The quiet room erupted with the roar of the bullet as it spiralled through the air and thudded into a far wall. More bullets followed – bang, bang, bang – until the gun was empty and Udet lowered his arm.

Slumping into a chair, Udet looked at the wall, the bullet holes conjuring ideas in his disillusioned and disconnected mind. He had taken to drinking heavily to cope with the strain of his responsibilities and this spoiled not only his temper, but his aim. Udet was spiralling out of control. 'I'm doing the best I can in this job, but don't expect too much from me,' he had once said. His plea had fallen on deaf ears. Faced with endless challenges thrust at him by Hitler, fighting a war on too many fronts and with not enough forces, Udet was facing defeat after defeat after defeat. But he was not giving up yet. Outside his villa he beamed jolly smiles, visited the airfields and test centres and praised the work being done. He would not spread his depression, not while those under him needed his calm, though fraudulent, comfort.

A year later, the upkeep of the pretence had become too much. Udet's plans for reinvigorating the Luftwaffe had failed, Göring's constant mishaps and incompetency were tying his hands. When Göring failed, so too did Udet, and the pressure was becoming unbearable. The higher echelons of the Luftwaffe were now managed by politicians rather than airmen. As a neutral, Udet was rapidly sidelined, and no matter how sensible his project or suggestion, it was ignored as not being part of the political scheme. Göring was no help at all. When Udet went to him with his troubles, he simply smiled and told him to get some rest. Rest? Rest from a perpetual nightmare? Trapped in a hornet's nest, judged on all sides, pursued by the Gestapo, who distrusted his foreign connections, and promoted far beyond his ability, Udet's health rapidly deteriorated. On 14 November, just over a year after his target practice in the gun room, an almost identical scene began to play out. Udet rose and dressed in his red dressing gown. He went to the gun room and selected a revolver. Loaded it. He poured out a brandy and went back to bed. Lying very still, he remembered the words he had only recently spoken to a friend: 'I have no one to fear now. No longer.' He placed the revolver against his head; none of them could get him now. He pulled the trigger.

Three days later Goebbels had worked the tragic suicide of Udet into a heroic sacrifice. Udet had died, not in bed, not with a revolver to his head, but testing a new weapon. It was a terrible accident that had robbed Germany of one of the greatest pilots of all time. At Udet's funeral Göring was there in all his glory, puffed up with vanity. 'Now we must take leave of you,' he told 'dear' Udet in a public speech. Neither Goebbels nor Göring blanched at the hypocrisy, by now they were well used to it.

The shock of Udet's death tore at Hanna. She had idolised and worshipped him, he had replaced Wolf Hirth as her father figure, the man she could always turn to when she needed advice or help. More than once Udet had personally removed obstacles to enable her to fly. Now he was gone. She blamed Göring. She would blame him even more when she learned the true nature of Udet's death. Tragedy now seemed to haunt Hanna. As each blow was weathered so another was added to bring her down. Her brother-in-law was killed a month after the death of Udet, leaving Heidi widowed, heavily pregnant and with three small children to look after. Emy rallied round, but even so the shock affected Heidi's unborn baby. It was born sickly and died within eight months. To add to the growing losses, Kurt's latest ship was sunk and there was no news to tell them if he had survived or not. All this weighed heavily on the shoulders of Herr Reitsch, who bowed further under the load and sank into a deep depression.

At the same time Hanna found herself at odds with an old flying colleague, Heini Dittmar. It seemed years since they had stood on a ship heading for South America and Hanna had complained to Peter Riedel about Dittmar's attentions. Riedel was now married to an American and Dittmar was testing early rocket planes. He had grown resentful of the influence Hanna had with the upper levels of the Luftwaffe. 'Hanna pays more attention to prettying up new gliders with parsley to impress the generals than to pioneering test-flying,' he complained bitterly. It was an unfair comment. Hanna had risked her life more than once. It was not her fault that as the only female test pilot in the Luftwaffe she was regularly singled out for special praise and used as propaganda – not that she was an unwilling victim, far from it. But Dittmar was jealous of her influence and the way she so readily smoothed over obstacles in her path by speaking to one of the superiors she was friendly with; she would do it for others too, though – it was partly her influence that had enabled Riedel to marry a foreigner in wartime.

There was another reason Dittmar agitated against Hanna; it came in the form of a rocket plane, the Me 163b. When Dr Alexander Lippisch designed the first Me 163, it was following the principles he had been promoting for years that a plane need not have a tail. The Me 163b or Komet had no horizontal tail surfaces, instead it was controlled by elevons, which acted as either ailerons or elevators. The plane almost looked like a cartoon drawn by a child, with its shortened body, stubby nose and rounded girth. In fact, the few surviving pictures of the Komet fail to do it justice; it was not the tiny plane it might appear at first glance. Its wingspan was only a little less than that of the Bf 109, while the actual surface area of the wing was 20 per cent greater. It was its length, or rather its lack of it, that made it look squat. Unlike its elegant cousin the Bf 109, the Komet was more of an egg-shaped flying bubble. It was comical in appearance, but this belied its deadly potential.

Dittmar had been testing early versions of the Me 163 and had had considerable successes, first reaching 400mph, then 571mph, then 623mph. The world speed record was just under 470mph. Before his death, Udet had seen some of the early flights and been both mystified and impressed by the stubby plane that flew so fast. After his suicide, development of the 163 looked to be in peril as it now had to compete with other projects, including the V1 and V2 rockets. Lack of funding delayed both, and the rival development teams each furtively guarded their pet projects and believed they were the answer to the war. One of those rocket men working on the V1 and V2 was none other than Hanna's old gliding pal, Wernher von Braun.

Lippisch was determined to push through his project and wanted to recruit Hanna to take part in the latest tests. There may have been a degree of subterfuge to this request. Hanna was well liked by the higher echelons of the Third Reich, a poster-girl for German flying, with good contacts among the Luftwaffe generals. If she was on a project there was a good chance it would attract the notice of Ritter von Greim, Göring or even Hitler. This was how Lippisch intended to secure funding for the Me 163. Heini Dittmar was appalled at the idea of working with Hanna.

'There are women who cannot bear it if a man comes into town whom they haven't already been to bed with. For Hanna, aeroplanes are like men for other women. As soon as a new plane appears anywhere, her sole aim is to fly it,' he told his colleagues bitterly.

Hanna, who was under the impression that she and Dittmar had reached a truce, would have been disappointed to learn of his unpleasant comments. Lippisch was unconcerned with Dittmar's griping. He asked Hanna to come for a special one-off flight in the Komet in May 1942. Hanna was ecstatic: 'To fly the rocket plane … was to live through a fantasy of Münchhausen. One took off with a roar and a sheet of flame, then shot steeply upwards to find oneself the next moment in the heart of the empyrean.' Dittmar was relieved when Hanna left the airfield, thinking that now she would be satisfied and leave him alone to test fly the rocket. He was unimpressed when a colleague who had watched the flight remarked what an asset Hanna would be to the test team. Unfortunately for Dittmar, his relief was short-lived; he stalled a 163 during a test and injured his spine, effectively removing himself from the programme. Lippisch took this opportunity and replaced him permanently with Hanna.

The Messerschmitt 163b or Komet was designed as an interceptor with a liquid-fuelled rocket motor. The advantages of the rocket engine were that it gave incredible speed and a fast rate of climb, but the Komet drank fuel like there was no tomorrow and a pilot was lucky to get eight minutes of powered flight, despite the fuel load weighing more than the empty aircraft. To try to improve performance the Komet had no retractable landing gear, instead it was launched on a wheeled trolley that was ditched in the air and landed using a retractable skid. This was hardly ideal and as the Komet had a landing approach speed of 137mph, miscalculation was painful, often resulting in back injuries to the pilot (as Dittmar had discovered).

From an operational point of view, the Komet was an excellent fast interceptor. It had to be held in reserve until the very last moment due to the short lifespan of its fuel supplies, but when it was released it would soar up into the air at amazing speeds, reaching enemy bombers within two or three minutes. Though the smoke plume from its rocket jets hardly made the Komet capable of stealth, its speed prevented enemy fighters from assaulting it as it launched among the slow bombers.

Komet pilots would try to inflict as much damage as possible before their fuel ran out and the Komet turned from a rocket ship into a glider. Even without fuel it was a wily opponent for the Allied fighters; it could dive safely at over 500mph and while its speed remained over 250mph it was nimble in the air. The only problem was landing, which had to be done in one attempt as there was no means of powering the Komet away once it was heading down.

Initially the Komet put the fear of God into Allied flying crews. Zooming out of nowhere, its speed was devastating and though its attacks were short, the confusion and panic it caused put a severe dent in Allied morale. American pilots began to think their operational flights into Germany were at an end. The Komet was a complete unknown; unique in design and performance, it genuinely seemed that the Nazis had superior technology and would soon be winning the war. The Komet could have been the Nazi superweapon. So why wasn't it? The main problem with all the rocket-powered jet aircraft in the Luftwaffe stable was the volatile nature of the fuels used. Hellmuth Walter had developed the 109-509 rocket motor for use in such aircraft. A previous engine using a 'cold system' had been tried in the Me 163a by Heini Dittmar and had broken the 1,000km/h barrier, but Walter was unsatisfied with the low thrust. So he created the 'hot system' for the 109, a mixture of C-Stoff (C substance) for use with the T-Stoff fuel found in the V1 flying bombs. When C-Stoff (a mixture of methanol, hydrazine hydrate and water) mixed with T-Stoff, it ignited and caused the latter to decompose into hot steam and oxygen. Though the mix was effective, it was highly toxic and prone to spontaneously exploding. The various tanks and fuel systems were also prone to leaks. Dripping T-Stoff was corrosive and anyone working around it had to wear a rubberised suit (as it could eat through organic materials, including human flesh). Pilots also had to wear special protective suits in case of a crash or leak that would send the corrosive fuel rushing over them. Just fuelling the plane was hazardous. C-Stoff was usually added first, the tanker carrying it hastening off the airstrip before a second tanker full of T-Stoff rolled up. Despite precautions, Komets did explode without ever taking off. In fact, it is believed that more Komet pilots were killed in accidental explosions caused by leaks than by the enemy.

On 23 June 1943 test pilot Rudolf Opitz attempted the first powered flight of the Komet using Walter's 'hot system'. It was close to a disaster.

The Komet's take-off trolley detached itself before he had fully left the ground and Opitz barely clambered into the sky. Then a pipe cracked, leaking burning T-Stoff into the cockpit. Opitz managed to land safely and escape the plane, but it was a clear sign of how dangerous the Komet could be to its own pilot.

New volunteers were roped in to learn to fly the Komet. Introduced to the radical design by flying in an unpowered version (the 163a), they were soon moved on to testing the real thing. The dangers inherent to flying the Komet were kept quiet, but the pilots were soon to witness the horrors an accident in the prototype could cause. On 30 November Alois Worndl misjudged his landing in a Komet and the aircraft flipped and exploded. He was lucky as he was killed quickly. Far less lucky was 'Joschi' Pohs, who released his take-off trolley too close to the ground (a danger Hanna remembered vividly). The trolley bounced back up and hit the underside of Pohs' Komet. The engine failed abruptly. Pohs was too low to bail out, but landing was going to be dangerous too. Pohs desperately tried to get his craft down; the Komet was full of fuel, making it heavier than was usual for a landing. The plane proved difficult to control, Pohs clipped a flak tower and dropped heavily to the ground. Observers held their breath for an explosion. Remarkably there was none, but the screams of a man in agony suddenly rose from the downed Komet. Rushing to his aid, the rescuers made a gruesome discovery: Pohs had been eaten alive by the fuel of his plane. It had leaked through the seams of the overalls supposed to protect him and he had been cocooned in a terrible, flameless fire as the fuel burned through anything it touched. What remained of Pohs was discreetly removed from the Komet.

Accidents seemed to be becoming more and more frequent. Explosions were all too common. Despite this, the Komet was desperately needed to try and stem the flow of Allied attacks and it was rushed into production. This caused an added danger as forced labour was used to produce the aircraft. A Komet in the collection of the National Museum of the United States Air Force appears to have been sabotaged while under construction. A small stone was wedged between the fuselage fuel tank and a supporting strap. Eventually this would have caused a dangerous leak. Contaminated glue was also found in one of the wings, which would have caused the wing to fail in flight. Inside the Komet's skin the saboteur had left a message in French: *Manufacture Fermée* ('Factory Closed') and *Mon coeur est en chomage* ('My heart is unemployed'), referring to the occupation of France. How many Komets exploded due to such sabotage, or simply the inadequate sealing methods of the time, we can never know. They were certainly not the wonder weapon Hitler had envisioned. Two hundred and seventy-nine Komets had been delivered by the end of the war and one operational group, JG 400, had been formed. End-of-war scores were nine kills by JG 400, with a loss of fourteen aircraft.

When Hanna climbed into the cockpit of her first Komet it was to be an experience she would never forget. There was nothing comparable, at the time, to rocket-powered flight. Test pilot Erich Warsitz, who flew in the He 176 and the Me 262, described his first taste of rocket power vividly:

> … this thunder, this gigantic noise, and always the air pressure which sur-
> rounded one and which one felt forward in the cockpit region … When
> it started, the full power of the rocket thrust tugged at the machine's
> anchorage so that I had to grip the flange and play the strong man, oth-
> erwise the pressure would have ripped me off. I was extraordinarily
> impressed – enchanted.

Warsitz was describing a dummy plane, a carcass for testing the rocket engine which was strapped securely to the ground. Being escorted around it by Hanna's old gliding friend Wernher von Braun, he felt its power, but he was also aware of the inherent dangers involved in rocket-powered craft. Near to the test ground a twisted lump of metal components was all that remained of a previous experiment – in fact, most tests had resulted in an explosion. A mechanic merrily pointed out the warped remains to Warsitz: 'They exploded. And if you are unlucky, Herr Warsitz, and do not take great care, you will finish up on top of them.' Von Braun was cagey on the matter, attempting to brush off the obvious signs of failure. He was keen to get a pilot into his rocket, even if it had not as yet proved stable. For him progress was more important than the life of one man. Still, the rocket plane held an enchantment all of its own which attracted willing pilots to test their luck. Hanna remembered:

> To sit in the machine when it was anchored to the ground and surrounded
> suddenly with that hellish, flame-spewing din, was an experience unreal
> enough. Through the window of the cabin, I could see the ground crew

start back with wide-open mouths and hands over their ears, while, for my part, it was all I could do to hold on as the machine rocked under a ceaseless succession of explosions. I felt as if I were in the grip of some savage power ascended from the Nether Pit. It seemed incredible that Man could control it.

There were unkind eyes watching Hanna as she flew. Fellow glider and test pilot Wolfgang Späte shared Dittmar's anger over having Hanna on the team. Späte had crossed paths with Hanna several times over the years, usually at gliding competitions. The gliding world was not so big, at least at its higher levels where the best pilots flew. Dark-haired, dark-eyed Späte had proved himself a skilled pilot over the years, if not a very pleasant one. Nicknamed 'Count Späte' because of his arrogance, he had earned a number of awards, but not many friends, during his career. The problem for Hanna was that he was in charge of the secret unit of test pilots for the Me 163b. He was determined she would never fly a powered version of the rocket plane. Hanna had to content herself with flying an unpowered Me 163a that was towed into the air for her and then released to act as a glider. Hanna had done this enough times to have become quite contented with the 163 – it was just an awkward-shaped glider after all. But, as Dittmar had discovered, it was just when things seemed to be going well that they were likely to go wrong.

On her fifth flight things went horribly wrong. Hanna took off on a typical flight, towed by a twin-engine Me 110. Just under 30ft she was supposed to drop her removable undercarriage. She had done this four times before and reflexively reached for the release lever and pulled it. At once the plane juddered violently, shaking Hanna. From the ground red verey lights were launched and glowed in the sky. Something bad had happened: the red lights were a warning. Uncertain what had gone wrong, Hanna tried to contact the pilot of the Me 110, only to discover her communication system was out of order. What was she to do now? Hanna glanced at the tow-plane and realised someone was trying to attract her attention from the rear gun-turret. It was the observer who flew in the lead plane. He was waving a white handkerchief up and down, and the Me 110 was raising and lowering its undercarriage. It only took a moment for Hanna to realise what was wrong: her undercarriage had not released.

Not sure what to do and thinking Hanna might try to land from a lower height, the pilot of the Messerschmitt was towing her in circles around and around the airfield. Hanna didn't fancy her chances from such a height, rather she wanted to go higher, try to cast off and hope her plane might respond to the controls. With no way of speaking with the pilot in the tow-plane, she resolved not to cast off until he guessed that she wanted to go higher. They soared up to 10,500ft before Hanna was happy to release her towrope. She pulled out tightly, trying to dislodge her recalcitrant undercarriage. Nothing moved below, but the plane shuddered violently, its natural line dramatically altered by the bulky weight and mass of the undercarriage. Hanna tried to think calmly: here, after all, was an opportunity of testing the capabilities of the 163 when hampered by a stuck undercarriage. There wasn't exactly much else to do until she dropped low enough to land. Hanna turned the plane this way and that, testing all its angles. It did respond well, considering a huge mass of metal was hanging off its fuselage.

Hanna had lost most of her height; she now needed to make a decision. Would she abandon the plane to its fate or attempt to land it? It went against her pride and professionalism to abandon now, when there was a slight chance of landing the plane. Of course there were great risks too, there was no knowing if the undercarriage would be ripped off as she came in to land, nor could she know if it was still completely fastened to the fuselage. It might be hanging off. In any case the 163 was designed to land on its belly, not on wheels. Hanna refused to bail out. She approached the airfield high, planning on side-slipping in the last 100 yards to land on the grass beside the runway, perhaps lessening the impact of the landing. In normal circumstances the manoeuvre might have worked, but the turbulence caused by the undercarriage was creating all kinds of drag and difficulties. As she attempted to side-slip, the plane stalled. In a split second the emergency landing turned into a crash. The ground raced up before Hanna's eyes. There was no time to think, just to hunch down and brace for the shock as the plane plunged nose-first into solid earth. There was the crunch and whine of metal being torn and bent. The Me 163 flipped over, perhaps once, maybe twice, Hanna never knew. When the motion stopped and the plane creaked and groaned into a stationary position, Hanna cautiously opened her eyes and realised she was sitting upright. The plane had righted itself and was now sitting on its belly.

Hanna was shaken, but her first thought was to open the cockpit canopy. Fresh air rushed into the plane, rousing her slightly. Next she examined her arms and legs with a great deal of trepidation. Through the shock she was numb to pain, so it was impossible to know at first if anything was missing. A miracle seemed to have occurred. Hanna had all her limbs, fingers and toes, there were no gaping wounds or broken bones. She relaxed a little, she had survived her first major crash.

It was then she noticed the thin trickle of blood running down her neck. With cautious fingers she followed the stream; there was still no pain as she came to her nose – or, at least, where her nose had been. There was nothing now but an empty hole, a sharp cleft in her face. When she breathed, bubbles of air and blood formed along its edge. It seemed she had not survived intact. Worried, she moved her head to the side and almost blacked out. Now she was really anxious; had her spine been damaged too? Was it a head injury? Hanna tried to calm herself by reaching out for a notepad and pencil in the cockpit, all the time keeping her head motionless, and writing down with a quick sketch exactly what had happened to her. Perhaps it would spare someone else. At least it would prove the accident was not her fault and that she had not been responsible for the wreck of the plane. Even now Hanna was worried about her reputation in the eyes of her fellow test pilots. Lastly, Hanna pulled out a clean white handkerchief and tied it around her face like the cowboys did in movies, masking her ruined nose and sparing the rescue party the sight of her mutilated face. It was her last act before the darkness of unconsciousness took over.

As news reached Wolfgang Späte of Hanna's last actions before she was taken to hospital he was overcome with a new sense of respect for the tiny pilot. 'What a woman!' he remarked, seeing the notes she had made before passing out. Hanna awoke in the Hospital of the Sisters of Mercy in Regensburg. She had been x-rayed and the results showed the worst possible results; her skull was fractured in four places in the basal area and two places in the facial area, resulting in compression of the brain, displacement of the upper jaw bones and separation of the bones of the nose. She had also broken several vertebrae. The loss of her nose now seemed the least of her worries, though, as in many cases of trauma, it was this minor detail that occupied her thoughts. 'Will I have to live my life without a nose?' she wondered morosely. It was easier to worry about that than to dwell on the serious brain and skull injuries she was suffering.

Fortunately, Hanna was in the hands of a first-class surgeon and he managed to piece her back together in the operating theatre. When Hanna at last regained full consciousness her head was wrapped up like a mummy, only her lips and bruised eyes peeking out. Her mother was standing before her with an adoptive aunt. Reaching out for Emy Reitsch, Hanna felt a mixture of relief and homesickness. Emy kept a straight face as she comforted her daughter. Life had thrown a number of ordeals at her in the last few months and the sight of Hanna suffering so was hard to bear. The doctors were cagey about her likely chances of survival. Hanna was not afraid to die, but if she was likely to do so, she at least wanted to know so she might prepare herself. No one in the hospital would give her answers, so in the end she asked her mother to send for Edelgard von Berg. Von Berg was a female surgeon and a close friend from Hanna's days as a medical student. She worked at the Robert Koch Hospital in Berlin and Hanna believed that if anyone would be honest with her it was Edelgard. Emy dutifully summoned Edelgard, who promised to come at once and even rang from Leipzig to promise she would soon be there.

Then nothing. Hour after hour there was no sign of Edelgard. Hanna became distressed: had her friend changed her mind? Was she delayed somehow? Ill herself? Emy, much to the disapproval of the doctors, told her the truth: Edelgard was dead. Perhaps she had driven too fast to reach her seriously injured friend; perhaps her car was not in the best repair after three years of war. In any case, she had skidded on wet leaves and crashed. Edelgard was dead and Hanna fainted from the shock.

Back at the airfield, Wolfgang Späte had overcome his initial admiration for Hanna. Day after day his team analysed the crash and the notes Hanna had left behind, trying to work out what went wrong. There was an unpleasant atmosphere in the workshops and offices; someone, or at least something, had to be blamed for the terrible crash that looked likely to cost Germany its only female test pilot. As so many months before, when Udet had watched Hanna appear to crash after the failed balloon cable-cutting incident, no one wanted to have to tell the Führer his Hanna was gravely injured. There was even a suggestion that Späte should be deemed responsible for the accident. 'How could anyone suggest such a thing!' he ranted angrily. 'At the time of the ill-fated forced landing I was after all 800km away in Peenemünde.' He believed the crash had been caused by a series of mishaps, all minor on their own but combining to make a deadly situation. Besides, Späte was convinced that Hanna should have been able to land the plane without crashing. He threw everything back at her, forgetting his earlier admiration: 'Through the impact of the landing Flugkapt. Hanna Reitsch hit her head on the visor. This was made possible because she used a thick cushion behind her back and therefore sat forward and had probably not strapped herself in very firmly.' He did not mention that Hanna needed the cushion because the seat, designed for men, swallowed her up if she did not have support, nor that she might have trouble reaching the controls if she was forced to sit too far back. It was incredibly ironic that she was so maligned, considering Dittmar had landed himself in hospital for a year after stalling his Me 163 and received nothing but sympathy. Fortunately, cocooned in her sickbed, Hanna was mostly unaware of the criticisms being levelled at her behind the scenes.

Others were less inclined to blame Hanna, instead the accident and her triumphant survival (though it was still uncertain whether she would live) were treated as yet another example of German heroism. Göring, along with other Luftwaffe leaders, decided that Hanna should be awarded the Iron Cross, First Class. Hearing the news, Emy Reitsch was concerned. She felt no good would come from the award and was worried about the impression it might make on Hanna. Emy's exact concerns are unclear; did she simply think it would increase her daughter's pride? Or was she worried it might tie her even more inextricably to the Nazi Party? She should perhaps have been more concerned about a small parcel of chocolate and fruit juice Hanna received while recuperating, which bore a message of well wishes and speedy recovery from Himmler. 'Himmler reminded me of Robespierre – a half-educated fanatic who actually believed that the extermination of the Jews was the way of truth. I'm sure he died without scruples about his crimes,' commented Wernher von Braun.

Himmler was also a controversial name within the Reitsch family. He was prominently atheistic, to the point of persecuting the traditional Church. As a Protestant former Catholic, Emy had always disliked Himmler from what little she knew of his political views. The present from him was therefore unwelcome and Hanna and Emy uncomfort-ably ignored it. Further presents arrived from Himmler, each with a short, friendly note to Hanna. Such was the simplicity and kindness of the missives that Emy began to doubt herself. Hanna, who liked to see the good in everyone, preferred to think that they had been led astray by the official news they had heard of this man. Forgetting that all news was carefully controlled and manipulated to say exactly what the party desired, Emy and Hanna convinced themselves Himmler had been misrepresented and must be a good deal kinder than they had thought. 'When you are well you must visit him and thank him for his kindness,' Emy told her daughter, as if she was just discussing a kind neighbour.

Hanna's recovery would be a long one, however, and the matter of visiting Himmler would have to wait. Hanna was offered a place in a sanatorium to recuperate, but she had other plans. Family friends owned a small cottage halfway up a mountain surrounded by a park-like garden and picturesque views. Hanna asked if she could go there. Perhaps an odd place for an invalid to go, but Hanna was desperate for solitude and time to think. A depression had risen over her, drawing her down into melancholy and a desire to shut out the world. Would she ever fly again? She asked the question over and over. As much as she hid her condition from her family, she knew the odds were not good. Hanna still suffered from giddiness and sickness when travelling, even on short journeys. Her head ached constantly and her balance was impaired – hardly auspicious for a return to flying.

Hanna went to the cottage and there began a savage programme of exercise and mental exertion to retrain her body and mind. She walked every day, at first growing despondent that she could only manage short distances before feeling exhausted, but improving with time. Even more important was her desire to restore her equilibrium; Hanna attempted this by feats of daring that would have had her doctors screaming at her.

The cottage had a steep-gabled roof, with a chimney on one side. Hanna climbed up and carefully placed herself on the ridge, sitting astride it and holding tight to the chimney. She kept her eyes shut as she did so in case she glimpsed the ground and was overcome by vertigo. From this vantage point Hanna opened her eyes and focused slowly on each tile on the roof, from the apex down to the gutter, first one side and then the other. The first time she attempted this feat she took herself to the brink of complete exhaustion. But the next day it was a little easier, and the next day after that, and so on until after endless practice of this exercise Hanna could stare all about her without dizziness, could let go of the chimney and balance perfectly, could even scoot herself to the middle of the roof ridge and look out at the dazzling countryside.

Sometimes, for a bit of variety, Hanna would climb a pine tree instead of the roof, creeping from one branch to another to see how high she could go. Once again, her first efforts were pitiful and Hanna despaired, but each day she was a little stronger and the top of the tree came a little closer. Her will to succeed had overcome Hanna's physical difficulties. In collusion with a friend she went gliding at Breslau-Schöngarten, at first just testing her basic flying skills before attempting powered flight. Then she was in the air performing dives from greater and greater heights to see if her brain could cope with the pressure and indulging in all manner of aerobatics. When she finally returned to her doctor he remarked on her fitness and gave her a clean bill of health. Hanna was fit to fly again. But just as important, she had a new nose, one so skilfully created that it was impossible to know there had been any damage. Hanna had survived the worst and was looking forward to flying again.

8

LIVING WITH DISILLUSIONMENT

Himmler's headquarters in East Prussia were neatly arranged as Hanna paid her long-postponed visit in July 1943. It was early evening and Hanna was worried about the meeting, not least because she had several burning questions to put to Himmler. He greeted her warmly, invited her to dinner and introduced her to his officers. Over their meal Hanna was intrigued to see the easy camaraderie between Himmler and his subordinates. After dinner, Himmler showed her to his study. Hanna's unease returned. Never one to soften her words just because she was facing one of the most dangerous men in Germany, she began her explanation for her visit with an apology. 'This is rather difficult for me, Herr Himmler. I have come to thank you for your kind gifts during my convalescence, but I confess your name has only ever been mentioned in my family with trepidation.' Himmler observed her calmly. 'Do you always form your judgements so hastily, Frau Hanna?' he asked as he directed them to a pair of armchairs. 'What exactly do you find in my name to alarm you?' 'I hardly know where to start,' Hanna said. 'For one thing, how can you bring yourself to try and root out of men's hearts their most sacred beliefs when you have nothing remotely comparable in worth to replace them?' Himmler was amused, but his response was quick. He delivered a speech on the implausibility of the Bible and thus of Christianity, illustrating his argument with examples from the Bible and others Hanna had not heard of. Hanna could not hope to match this rant, so simply said, 'We are concerned with a religious belief. I cannot compel you to share this belief, but in your position you should respect and not interfere with the religious feelings of others.'

Asking Himmler to show some respect to other religions! Now, better than ever before, Hanna demonstrated her complete naïvety and her misconception that everyone could be a better person, should they only listen to reason. Himmler was naturally unmoved. When Hanna spoke on to a subject she felt passionately about – Himmler's opinion that women were only useful for reproduction – it was plain she was getting heated and Himmler attempted to calm her. He had been misunderstood, he stated plainly, he too was concerned. Hanna had heard rumours about the SS that could potentially undermine German morality. She may have meant the proviso that had been issued enabling illegitimate children of SS men to be recognised legally, and the general policy that SS soldiers breed as profusely as possible so as to populate Germany with the right sort of person. Himmler shook his head; all wrong, all wrong, he said. Naturally he was lying, but he wove a web around Hanna, leaving her believing his words had been misused and the rumours she had heard were malicious.

Hanna was easily swayed all her life. A kind explanation would be to deem her very forgiving and determined to like everybody. A less kind one would be that playing the Nazi game enabled Hanna to continue flying, and thus it was best to ignore the worst excesses of the party. A plain example of this came in 1944. Peter Riedel, briefly back in Germany, found Hanna at a flying club and threw a booklet down on the table before her. 'If you want to know what is going on in Germany, look at this! This is what we find on our desks in the Embassy.' The booklet told of the gas chambers in use in concentration camps, now notorious, but for much of the war not known to most Germans, or, if known, not believed. 'And you believe this?' Hanna asked angrily. 'In the First World War, enemy propaganda smeared the German soldier with every imaginable barbarity – and now it has come to gas-chambers!'

Hanna genuinely believed the stories were no more than Allied propaganda. Such awful cruelty was unthinkable to her, thus, she reasoned, so it must be abhorrent to everyone, especially her gracious and kindly Führer. Riedel was somewhat relieved at her vehemence; he too had been struggling to believe the stories and was desperately hoping someone would tell him he was wrong. 'I'll believe that from you,' he said.

'But perhaps you'd best inform Himmler.' Hanna agreed. She arranged a meeting with Himmler and presented him with the booklet. 'What do you say to this, Reichsführer?' Himmler flicked through the pages. It was all very familiar to him, but he glanced up casually and with a quiet smile said, 'And you believe this, Frau Hanna?' 'No, of course not,' Hanna responded loyally. 'But you must do something to counter it. You can't let them shoulder this onto Germany.' Himmler laid down the booklet and looked Hanna directly in the eye. 'You are right,' he said, and the meeting was at an end.

An almost fully recovered Hanna went to Peenemünde, the German rocket test centre, in time for its first air raid. Peenemünde had so far avoided being bombed, but its luck would not last. However, for three years there had been so many false warnings that the scientists, mechanics and various staff on the site had become complacent when the air-raid sirens went off. Everyone worked long hours and on the night of 17 August 1943 few were in bed before midnight. Wernher von Braun was heading for his quarters under a brightly moonlit sky when the early warning siren sounded. He barely heard it. For too long that siren had gone off to announce that Allied aircraft had been spotted flying towards Germany without there ever being any subsequent attack. The planes would fly across Germany, aiming for Berlin. Peenemünde would shield itself in a cloak of darkness; lights were turned out and the anti-aircraft batteries manned, though there was a standing order never to fire unless the test site was directly attacked. For all anyone knew, Peenemünde had yet to be identified as a worthwhile target for the British.

Von Braun had not been long in bed when the next siren sounded. This one summoned the weary scientists and workers to the concrete shelters. Machinists only had moments to shut down their workstations, close valves to prevent fire and hurry down dark streets to the nearest shelter. After fifteen minutes an officer would close the steel door, and those left outside had to take their chances with the Allied bombs. No one was that concerned, however, as they ran in the darkness. If someone was missing it was not deemed greatly urgent, they would probably just get a reprimand in the morning. That Hanna Reitsch failed to respond to the siren went unnoticed.

At the shelter von Braun reached there was no rush to close the steel door. Instead he stood with fellow scientists watching a low fog rolling in across the test site. A scattered blackout squad was rushing around checking for forgotten lights and in general enjoying a little action after the usual tedium of the day. Von Braun was just beginning to think of his bed and the heavy tiredness that was weighing him down when the first sign came that this was not to be an ordinary night. Somewhere high up a plane dropped a flare. Von Braun and his companions watched as the bright lights descended, fluttering outwards to give the impression of a vivid, Christmas tree shape hanging in the sky. There was no doubt now that false warnings were in the past; the Allies had decided to take out Peenemünde.

Complacency dissolved instantly. As the anti-aircraft batteries started to bark at the swarming planes, at last being allowed a taste of action, von Braun and his companions jumped into their shelter and pulled the heavy door shut. The loud explosions began almost at once. A rain of bombs crashed onto the site and violent, thunderous crashes echoed within the shelters. The walls shuddered and people clapped their hands over their ears as the world erupted in fury. As hard as the anti-aircraft crews worked, the planes slipped among them and delivered their horrendous payload. The raid lasted only minutes; it was over almost as soon as it had begun. Their bombs dropped, the Allied planes turned for home. The guns continued to squeal into the night, but soon there was nothing to aim at.

When Wernher von Braun stepped out of his shelter he looked upon the destruction. The light fog was now replaced by thick smoke. Fires lit up buildings, flames licking at walls and windows. Acrid smoke hit the back of the throat, making people cough and eyes stream. The inferno before von Braun was a scene he could never forget. As he headed out with a team of volunteers to recover what he could from the debris – important files, papers and test parts – more bombers were heard approaching. Between search operations and attempts to damp down fires, the men had to flee into the nearby woods as more bombs hit the site now lit-up like a beacon. It was plain the Allies were determined to leave nothing standing.

The local fire brigade tried to come to the assistance of the beleaguered base and surrounding town. In between air raids they attempted to bring their engines down roads now completely destroyed or blocked with burning debris. Loose electric wires sparked dangerously all over the place, combining with water to make a horrific barrier to helpers.

Those who avoided electrocution choked on the black, stinking smoke, collapsing where they stood. Somehow people kept moving. A first aid station was created and canteen staff valiantly worked in the heat and destruction to bring out fresh soup and coffee to the men.

Slowly the night drew to a close. A sole surviving plane enabled von Braun to make an aerial survey of the site and to realise despondently that the British had achieved the close to complete destruction of Peenemünde. Using maps and aerial photographs the RAF attack had been meticulously planned, the main targets established and accurately bombed. Six hundred bombers had dropped around 3 million pounds of high explosive and killed close to 800 people, including many important scientists. V2 production could no longer continue at the site: aside from a lack of men, machines and supplies following the raid, the British now knew where to look and would keep an eye on Peenemünde and thwart any attempts to rebuild. Wernher von Braun was relocated. Peenemünde would continue as a research and test facility only.

'I'm terribly ashamed to say I slept through the whole night,' Hanna later confessed:

> They forgot I slept in the house where the ... officers slept and when there was the siren I didn't hear it, I slept so deeply and everybody thought the others had fetched Hanna. So I was quite alone in this house sleeping deeply, I didn't hear anything and the next morning I was so ashamed. I thought, oh it's misty, but it was the smoke from things burning and you see the main attack was East and I was in the West. It was not so near.

February 1943 saw the disaster of Stalingrad. Five months of close-quarters fighting and a bombing campaign reduced the Russian city to rubble, and still the Germans found themselves ultimately overrun and defeated. As Germany was awaiting the spring, part of its army was trapped in the ruined city, surrounded on all sides by the Russians, low on supplies, almost out of ammunition and utterly exhausted. There was no hope left for them as Hitler shrieked from safe quarters that they must continue to fight to the last man, to the last bullet. A pointless waste, but Hitler had lost all perspective and he would rather lose his army entirely in the fight than see it come home defeated. In the end those troops that remained surrendered, having lost all faith in their Führer.

What few at the time realised was that the Russians' triumph was partly down to bands of valiant and courageous women acting as soldiers and as pilots. In other circumstances Hanna would have been impressed to know that some of the best fighter pilots coming out of Russia were female and they were making their mark on German aircraft. In this Russia was unique. Women in Germany, France, Britain and America could not expect to fly as part of squadrons, no matter how desperately they wanted to. In the UK and US there was the alternative of Auxiliary Transport squads, though even these took time to recognise the valuable contribution women could offer. In Germany women in the air force were few and far between. As far as Hanna knew (and she seems right), she was the only one to be specifically working with the Luftwaffe. As a test pilot she had already broken through a male barrier which her female contemporaries in Britain could not attain, yet even though she had achieved this level of respect, no amount of begging, persuading or tantrum pulling would get her closer to action than a test runway at Rechlin.

Things were different in Russia, where German men were dying by the thousand. Hanna's Soviet equivalent was Lilya Litvyak, affectionately known as the White Rose of Stalingrad. In another world the two women could have been friends, or at least comrades in the pursuit of female flying. As it was, they were natural enemies. Lilya was younger than Hanna, born in 1921, but she had a similar passion for the pursuit of freedom in the open sky. She didn't survive the war to give us a full understanding of her personality, but she was spirited and strong willed. When she entered the Russian air force she was expected to have her hair cut in the same fashion as a male pilot; Lilya refused for as long as was possible. On another occasion she cut the fur tops off her pilot's boots to make a collar for her coat, and an irate superior made her put them back. Hanna would not have entirely understood this longing for identity and femininity in a male world; she conformed as much as was possible, though she retained her own foibles, including dyeing her hair blonde.

Russian women had found their way into flying clubs with a little more ease than German women, though they still faced the stigma of being the 'wrong gender'. When war was announced with Germany, the Russian female flyers wanted to fight to protect their country. There was reluctance among the authorities – was it even ethical for a woman, the mother and peacemaker, to take to the skies or battlefields and kill? Germany was having similar doubts; in fact, most of the fighting countries could not quite bring themselves to have women in the air.

Stalin's hand was forced over female pilots in two ways. First, it was becoming more and more apparent that women were running off to fight with the army. Some were dressing as men, others were simply finding a gun and helping out frontline troops where they could. They stated that they were protecting their family and should be allowed to do so. At the same time, there had been a concerted effort by female aviators to steal planes in order to participate in the air battle that the Germans were currently winning. Second, Stalin was coming to realise that he was facing a war of attrition and losing men faster than he was replacing them. Was it unreasonable to tap into a ready army that just happened to be female?

News on female flyers was slow to reach Germany. Few Luftwaffe pilots knew that at times they were being attacked by, or shooting at, women. Lucky crash survivors learned on the ground that they had been shot down by a woman, much to their chagrin. There was no sense of respect or admiration for these flying women. Lilya made her first kill over Stalingrad, on her third mission to provide air cover for troops fighting below. This made her the world's first female fighter pilot to shoot down an enemy plane. She later became the first woman to earn the title 'fighter ace'. Her time covering the air at Stalingrad earned Lilya her nickname. Hanna, like her male colleagues, preferred not to know that a woman was beating Germans at their own game.

The Battle of Stalingrad was clearly over, but Hitler would not let his troops admit defeat. They would fight on until none was left, while those at home were told lies of triumphs and successes. Even so, the defeat could not be entirely ignored by the media. Propaganda tried to put a gloss over the worst, but people still knew something awful had happened. 'After Stalingrad, the shadows began visibly to descend over Germany and in spite of official propaganda, which was still turned to victory, month by month the feeling grew that the end was inexorably approaching,' Hanna recorded. She was not to know the extent of her Führer's madness, but a trickle of doubt was creeping into her mind. As blindly as she followed him for patriotism's sake, now she wondered if Hitler would not be the end of Germany.

Hanna's restoration to health was followed by a visit to Göring, who invited her to his over-furnished house in Obersalzberg. Externally Göring was still projecting the image of a man confident of victory; privately he was working on worst-case scenario plans to evacuate his collection of art and antiquities. At lunch Hanna discovered to her horror that Göring believed that the Me 163, so recently the cause of her life-threatening injuries, was already in mass production. Whether he had been told this or had just made the assumption was not clear; what was apparent was that he had consoled himself with the notion of the new secret weapon about to save Germany. In some regards Göring and Hanna shared a common condition of being able to fool themselves into believing everything would be all right. Hanna was distressed to think Göring was so misled and tried to explain that the Komet was nowhere near the production level he thought. Her words fell on deaf ears. In fact, Göring was furious with her for bursting his bubble. He stormed out of the room, only returning at his wife's insistence. Afterwards he refused to talk to Hanna on the subject of the Komet and he never invited her again.

Hanna's brush with death had left a lasting impression upon her; not least because she now realised it held no fear for her. Strangely the experience had almost immunised her to the normal human horror of annihilation. She was walking through life almost numb. It was at this point that her thoughts turned to one of the most desperate schemes of the war – suicide flights, or, in other words, the deliberate ramming of enemy aircraft.

'I wouldn't have rammed anyone. It's sheer idiocy. Life mayn't be much, but one does cling to it after all,' commented one Luftwaffe pilot while a prisoner of war, completely unaware the British were recording his every word. It was June 1942, and even at this early stage in the war suicide missions were being discussed among pilots. If you couldn't shoot down a plane, then ramming it might be the only option for taking out an enemy combatant. Unfortunately, chances of pilot survival during such actions were minimal.

By 1943 the increasing success of the Allies was threatening both morale and Germany's hopes for victory. Thoughts were turned to alternative means of eradicating the British danger; if a decisive strategic hit could be dealt, perhaps that would cripple the attacking power of the RAF? If nothing else it might buy the Germans a breathing space. In August 1943 Hanna sat in a canteen with Luftwaffe doctor Theo

Benzinger and glider pilot Heinrich Lange discussing the changing tides of the war. The idea came up that if manned V1 flying bombs were launched they could be aimed at highly specific targets and strike a decisive blow against the Allies' ability to continue fighting. Hanna revelled in the idea, which was formalised in a memo by Benzinger and Lange:

> The military situation justifies and demands that naval targets be fought with extreme means like manned missiles whose pilot voluntarily sacrifices his life. [This would represent] a form of warfare that is fully new in Europe.

Benzinger and Lange reasoned that as German pilots were losing their lives in huge numbers anyway, they might as well take out a large number of the enemy in the process. The memo was passed to Field Marshal Erhard Milch in September 1943. At this point the Japanese kamikaze pilot was unknown and with the air situation looking bad and Göring constantly criticising the Luftwaffe for cowardice and lack of results, suicide missions held a certain appeal. Milch conferred with his subordinates and plans were drawn up to load planes with explosives and crash them into enemy warships and bomber formations. Milch, however, baulked at the idea of a true suicide mission; wouldn't it be better, he argued, if pilots dived at enemy targets but then ejected and parachuted to safety before the actual impact? Even so the Luftwaffe commanders were unconvinced by the idea. Wasting good pilots on one-off missions did not appeal and there was still optimism that with new planes and advances in technology Germany would regain control of the air.

Hanna was disappointed. It is hard to fathom why a young woman would so eagerly push for her own and other pilots' deaths, but Hanna's very recent brain injury may well have played a part. Hanna later rationalised her behaviour by imposing a humanitarian angle on her actions. If manned missiles could strike at important, non-civilian targets and cripple the British, then it would spare a lot of lives, she argued. It would also enable Germany to negotiate peace on its terms, if it so wished. Hanna justified herself by saying that the sacrifice of a single German pilot would spare hundreds of civilian lives. A manned missile would hit a target precisely, not accidentally take out neighbouring houses or miss completely and massacre the local population, as was so often the case with bombing.

There was another draw towards the ultimate sacrifice: Glory. Hanna had sought success and accolades since she first jumped into a glider. She was always fighting to be the best, to prove herself, often in the face of derision. Unlike in Russia, there were no German female fighter pilots. If Hanna wanted to make her mark in this war, if she wanted to be remembered and glorified forever, she had to be more than just a test pilot. Manned missiles presented a golden opportunity; Hanna could die a hero, she would never be forgotten. Fuelled by a heady mix of patriotism, Nazi fervour and dreams of idolisation, Hanna was completely prepared to fly and die for the Reich.

Then something changed her mind; perhaps her return to health and the freedom to fly had rekindled her love for life. In any case Hanna backed out from personally participating in suicide missions. In some regards this is not entirely surprising – Hanna had no experience of combat flying, though nor did many of the volunteer suicide pilots. Exactly what changed her mind remains personal to Hanna. She made the excuse that she was of more use alive as a conduit between the team and Hitler and Himmler, than flying to her death. In this Hanna dramatically over-inflated her own importance. She was neither that influential nor that close to either the Führer or his Reichsführer. Hanna honestly believed her opinion mattered to these men, a delusion that was both egotistical and frustrating to her colleagues and friends. The irony was that Hanna would later criticise the head of the project for refusing to fly on a suicide mission, when she herself had done just the same.

There was still one stumbling block: Hitler himself. Hanna visited the Führer at the Berghof. During a conversation which Hanna recalled years later, she mentioned the suicide squads she was helping to organise. Hitler was appalled. What was the point, he wondered in horror, of German heroes crashing to their deaths and being unable to savour the glory they had achieved? Hitler was forever keen on the image of warrior celebrity, but for that you needed a living, breathing person who could be paraded before crowds, adorned with medals and could give interviews to inspire others. Dead pilots couldn't do that. What if, pondered Hitler, the missiles were manned by lunatics or criminals? Then they would be disposing of undesirables who could regain some honour for themselves and their families by making a last sacrifice. But no, that wouldn't work: they might be incapable of flying, or might try to escape their fate. Hitler rejected the idea, but that did not prevent his subordinates trying to circumvent his orders. In July 1944 he had to intervene personally to stop a plan to load thirty-nine Fw 190 fighter-bombers with explosives and crash them into an Allied armada in the Baie de la Seine.

Hanna left Hitler, despairing. It was not the first time she had perceived her leader struggling with the reins of power. He ranted at her in lengthy monologues on the psychology of the suicide idea and how it was not the right moment to convince the public to let its young men deliberately fly to their deaths (not that they had been doing much different recently). Hanna listened but realised that much of Hitler's raving was irrelevant to the subject at hand. He was enjoying hearing his own voice, his ramblings were just that – rambling. When she tried to point out the need for desperate measures Hitler told her not to worry for the new jet fighters would tip the war in Germany's favour. Hanna's heart sank as it had done when she sat in Göring's dining room. For the first time she realised how distant from reality Hitler truly was: '[he] was living in some remote and nebulous world of his own and the appalling implications of this discovery suddenly burst upon me.' Hanna could hold her tongue no longer. If others would not tell Hitler the truth, she would. 'Mein Führer, you are speaking of the grandchild of an embryo.' Hitler stared at her in astonishment. His adjutant's face fixed in an expression of horror. Hanna refused to recognise the danger and carried on, speaking fast, as she explained how far off jet-engine aircraft really were. Hitler seemed to stare at her a long time. When he spoke, it was with clipped sentences and stony glances. She had spoiled his good humour, but Hanna resolutely pressed on. 'At least let us make experiments with the type of aircraft we would use in the suicide missions. Then, when you think the moment is right, you can announce them and they will be ready to fly.' Hitler slowly agreed, mainly to be rid of Hanna. He cut the interview short and left her to tell her friends the good news.

The notion of suicide flights had not been born out of thin air; there was a very recent precedent – which Hitler was still sore over: the Russians. Russian pilots, often flying antiquated planes, had a habit of ramming an enemy plane in desperation to take it out of the air.

Stories about these air tactics and the scare value they had on German pilots had filtered through the Luftwaffe and made an impression. There were even a number of female Russian pilots prepared, as Hanna had been initially, to sacrifice themselves for the good of their country. On 12 September 1941 Ukrainian pilot Ekaterina Ivanova flew her Su-2 into a Messerschmitt Bf 109, ripping it in half. Out of ammo and fighting seven German planes, it was an act of desperation that cost her her life, but it was remembered by both the Germans and the Russians. The Soviets had a nasty tendency to ram planes with seeming disregard for their lives. They even had a name for this flying tactic – the *taran*.

Lilya Litvyak used a variation of the *taran* on a Messerschmitt Bf 109 when she found herself surrounded and with a shrapnel wound in her leg. Lilya was flying the woeful Yak-1, made from plywood because aluminium was difficult to get in quantity. Against Messerschmitts firing 30mm cannons, it was like a gnat attacking a lion. Desperate to escape the onslaught, Lilya tried one of the most daring moves in the Russian flyers' arsenal. She slipped to the side of the enemy planes, standing the Yak-1 on its tail to pull it as high as she could as fast as she could. The Yak-1's engine struggled valiantly to lift her into the sky, her plane's body was ripped by cannon fire and she was fighting the blood loss and pain from her leg. Just as the engine seemed about to stall, she rolled over and dived straight at the marauding Messerschmitts. Height turned into acceleration, the Yak-1 roared straight down at two Luftwaffe pilots, Franz Müller and Karl-Otto Harloff. Terror seized them as the mad Russian pilot plunged towards them in a deadly dive. Naturally they had heard tales of the *taran* and equally naturally they ducked their planes. Lilya had never intended to ram another plane; she had, however, intended to frighten them. As the Messerschmitts ducked, Lilya pulled out of her dive and opened fire with her 20mm cannon. Müller and Harloff were both caught and went down, their mighty Messerschmitts defeated by a flimsy, torn flying plywood box. Lilya made her escape while the other pilots were recovering from the shock; she lived to fight another day. Lilya had performed the *sokolin udar*, the Falcon Blow, a manoeuvre similar to the *taran*, but not suicidal. The Falcon Blow relied on the Luftwaffe's fear of the Soviet proclivity for fatal ramming attacks.

The impact these Russian tactics had on Luftwaffe morale was worsened by the terrible fighting situation in the east that faced the Germans.

Hanna would have been aware of the psychological effects of such actions, the anxieties they caused pilots and the feeling that it was difficult, if not impossible, to defeat an enemy who was prepared to sacrifice himself to kill you, particularly as it seemed as though the Russians had an endless supply of men (if of nothing else!). Adding all these factors together, the idea of a German suicide squad became more and more feasible, and even vital, as the war dragged on. Hitler handed development of the suicide squads to the Reich Air Ministry. One of the men involved was Heinz Kensche who, as luck would have it, had already volunteered for Hanna's idea (and would subsequently reject the notion of personally flying, much to Hanna's dismay). While the necessary administrative work began and designs were formulated, Hanna received a request that she visit the Eastern Front from none other than Ritter von Greim, now colonel general. Von Greim was fighting a losing battle commanding an air fleet in the middle sector and trying to supply air support for the troops with insufficient aircraft. Times were desperate and his men were constantly wavering between hope and defeatism. Von Greim hoped that a visit from a woman who had received military decorations might give morale a good boost; all his men knew the name Hanna Reitsch. Hanna agreed at once. She had great respect for von Greim: 'Both officers and men ... looked upon him as a father,' she remarked, and it wouldn't be far from the truth to say she shared their view.

Hanna made her way east in November 1943. She found von Greim in his headquarters in the woods near Orscha, where the thunder of guns echoed continuously, day and night. It was like a scene from the First World War, where men ate, slept and manned their positions under the constant noise of shelling. The endless barrage wreaked havoc on the men's nerves and mental stamina. At dawn von Greim flew Hanna in a Fieseler Storch to his advanced Ack-Ack positions. The Russian winter was beginning to take hold and the cockpit was freezing. They hedge-hopped to avoid detection, finally abandoning the plane for an armoured car which took them close to the front. For the last few metres there was no option but to leave the vehicle and run crouching across fields and open ground, hoping to avoid being spotted by the enemy. What had induced von Greim to bring a civilian into such a situation? Hanna could have been injured or killed at any moment – only extreme desperation could have brought him to such a decision.

No sooner had they reached the Ack-Ack guns than the Russians opened fire with a heavy bombardment. Everyone dived for cover, Hanna crept into a hole in the ground and hugged herself tightly into a ball as overhead shells screamed and crashed to the ground with mighty explosions. The German guns returned fire and the roar became deafening. A squadron of Russian planes flew over and dropped more bombs. Hanna tried to bury herself deeper in the ground, her terror worse than anything she had experienced in a plane. She was convinced none of them would survive the onslaught and threw all her energy into just trying to stop her knees from knocking, and shutting out the shouts and yells of the wounded and dying. It was rather ironic that while Hanna had been willing enough to fly to her death in a suicide plane, the thought of dying in a shell blast filled her with unimaginable dread.

The onslaught slowly concluded. In the aftermath Hanna crawled from her hole and helped to tend the wounded, gagging at the sight of mutilated and broken men. Von Greim suggested he take her back from the front, but Hanna controlled her fear long enough to refuse. She had seen the delight and enthusiasm her surprise appearance had produced in the men on the guns, and felt she could not neglect the other positions when she could strengthen morale. As ever, Hanna was thinking of her patriotism first and it could overcome almost all anxieties. She travelled from position to position, talked to countless Luftwaffe units and all the while was aware of her own inadequacies at the front. What could she offer these poor souls? When they asked about the war situation she tried not to raise false hopes; when the shelling began again she tried not to display her panic, all the time wondering at the pointlessness of the exercise. She came home more aware than ever that Germany was lost.

Meanwhile, the idea of suicide missions was being developed further. It should not be supposed that Hanna, Benzinger and Lange were alone in contemplating German kamikaze flights, even if Hanna would have liked later historians to believe her notion unique. Luftwaffe fighter officer Hans-Günther von Kornatzki was also contemplating the air conflict situation in autumn 1943 and proposed the 'Storm Attack'. In a Storm Attack, as envisioned by Kornatzki, a group of fighter pilots would fly directly into enemy planes, the result being a massive collision that would bring both aircraft down. As tactics went, it would be virtually unstoppable once the German plane was on course and close enough. Even killing the pilot would not prevent ramming if the distance was narrow enough. In fact, this had happened all too often in the course of normal operations, sometimes by accident, sometimes purposefully, out of sheer desperation. Even Kornatzki, however, could not quite reconcile himself to the loss of good pilots. His missions would be almost suicidal, but with the insurance of parachutes, the pilots could eject at the last moment and have a fair chance of survival. The only problem was finding large enough formations of Allied planes near enough to send the swarm at quickly, before they had a chance to bomb anything. There was also the cost in planes to consider. As was often the case among the higher ranks, this issue of material costs was overlooked, in the assumption that German production could keep pace with demands.

Generalmajor Adolf Galland accepted Kornatzki's plan, even if he was dubious about pilots purposely flying into the enemy – it was not a spectacle the German people would like to witness. Despite his reluctance, in May 1944 the first 'Storm Fighters' were initiated, swearing that they would attack the enemy at close quarters and, if they failed to shoot them down, they would ram them. Three units were formed comprising around fifty specially modified Fw 190s. Galland need not have worried about massive sky battles where planes crashed into each other; for the most part, the Storm Fighters were able to shoot the enemy down at such close range. When they did occasionally fail they rammed the aircraft. Kornatzki's 'fair chance of survival' proved to be about 50 per cent for those who took this decisive action.

Ramming missions continued with renewed enthusiasm from certain quarters. Colonel Hajo Hermann decided the war situation in autumn 1944 required a radical reassessment of air combat and suggested that one or two thousand new pilots be recruited from the ranks of the Wehrmacht to fly their planes directly into the enemy. Experienced pilots would be held back for 'traditional' flying missions. Galland was appalled with the idea, but that did not stop him discussing the matter with Hitler in January 1945. Hitler announced to his troops that he would have the highest respect for any man volunteering for these ramming squads, and that no soldier would be forced to participate.

As before, the missions were defined as 'almost' suicidal: the pilots would have the option of parachuting out.

An alleged 2,000 men volunteered, of whom 300 were selected. Unfortunately, when informed of their mission – to fly into American bombers – the volunteers' zeal dried up. They had expected to give their lives taking out aircraft carriers or battleships. To die for the sake of one B-17 Flying Fortress was harder to swallow. By the time they were called for their mission, on 7 April 1945, there were 183 volunteers ready to make the sacrifice. These inexperienced pilots aimed for an American bomber unit over Magdeburg; 133 of them were shot down, seventy-seven were killed. Only twenty-three of the American bombers were lost, though German propaganda reported the number as sixty. Goebbels wrote in his diary:

> The first use of our suicide fighters has not produced the success hoped for. The reason given is that the enemy bomber formations did not fly concentrated so that they had to be attacked individually. In addition our suicide fighters encountered such heavy defensive fire from enemy fighters that only in a few cases were they able to ram. But we must not lose courage as a result. This is only an initial trial which is to be repeated in the next few days, hopefully with better results.

One last suicide mission was tried by the Luftwaffe ten days later on 17 April. The Russian Red Army was on the banks of the River Oder east of Berlin and the Wehrmacht had failed to destroy the bridgeheads. A Luftwaffe attack had also failed, so the 7 April volunteers were recalled and told to dive at the bridge and ram it, again with the proviso that they *could* parachute out. In reality the odds were slim. The first pilots crashed into the bridges over the Oder as Russia launched its major assault on Berlin. If ramming B-17s had seemed pointless, taking out the bridges was even more so as they were easily repaired or replaced with pontoon bridges.

Heinz Kensche had agreed with Hanna to try using a Me 328 as a suicide plane. Designed as a long-range fighter or light bomber (Hitler and Göring being obsessed to the point of idiocy with fighter-bombers!), the Me 328 looked like an ideal candidate for the task. But after only two tests it became plain that it was not feasible to use the powered version of the 328. Instead the engine was removed and the 328 was tested for its potential as a human glider-bomb. It could not take off alone and was carried to a suitable height piggyback-style on a Dornier 217. The pilot could release himself from the Dornier without having to leave his seat and the plane would then become a glider capable of flying at 470mph. The Me 328 fulfilled all the requirements of the experiment and, satisfied with its potential, a contract for mass production was given to a factory in Thuringia in April 1944. The Me 328 never went into production, dropped for another plane, a Fieseler. Hanna was disappointed, but, with resources stretched tight and many designs being put into production, it was often the case that a particular model was never built.

Hanna bitterly regretted the decision to focus solely on the Me 328 at the expense of tests on a manned version of the V1. It worried her that Hitler might suddenly expect a suicide squad to be ready and they had nothing but a few tests flights to show. The day was saved unexpectedly by a phone call from Otto Skorzeny. Skorzeny has gone down in German history for his daring rescue of Mussolini. The Italians had become disillusioned with the war by 1943 and Mussolini had been overthrown and imprisoned by his own government. Hitler, running rather low on allies at this point, felt the Italian dictator still had potential and put Skorzeny in charge of the operation to effect his release. The operation proved trying as the Italians rapidly moved Mussolini from one secure location to another. A first botched attempt saw him briefly freed before being recaptured. At last Mussolini was held in a mountain-top hotel accessible only by cable car. Skorzeny led a well-organised airborne raid on the hotel, managing not only to maintain the element of surprise, but to rescue Mussolini without a shot being fired. The stunned Italian guards were completely overwhelmed and Mussolini was flown out to enjoy a brief return to his former glory in northern Italy.

After his success Skorzeny was promoted within the SS to SturmbannFührer and given the Knight's Cross of the Iron Cross. By 1944 he was working on the development of special weapons and was in direct contact with Himmler, who had told him about the tests for a perfect suicide plane. Independently Skorzeny had been wondering about the possibility of developing manned V1 flying bombs and now he contacted Hanna to discuss the matter urgently. She could only tell him of the unforeseen stalling of the project. Skorzeny brushed that aside:

'Hitler has vested me with full powers and has expressly called for a daily progress-report.'

There were to be no further delays or obstacles. Skorzeny set to work organising a team of engineers and constructors and with his constant support they had soon succeeded in converting a normal V1 to accommodate a pilot. Hanna later estimated that he achieved this remarkable feat in four or five days. The modified V1 was given the codename 'Reichenberg', few knew about it, even those who were working on the normal V1 at Peenemünde. It was Hanna's work with the V1 that created one of the biggest myths circulating about her.

Initially the test version of the piloted V1 was equipped with cushioned skids and a pilot's seat behind the wing, along with a power unit and landing flaps, since pilots were expected to land the rocket, not crash it. A second version had two seats, one in front and the other behind the wing. It had dual controls and was intended for training volunteers. The power unit was removed as it was only intended to glide. This could lead to some frightening landings. The V1 was not easy to handle and its unorthodox shape (for a plane) meant that bringing it to earth safely was extremely difficult. It was too much for most pilots (though they might be skilled in ordinary flight) and fatalities were not infrequent. This presented another problem as constant losses among the instructors would have made training impossible. Only the best of the volunteers were picked to take over the role of teaching others, and even from that select group only those who had proven themselves in a V1 would become instructors.

The power unit of the operational model was restored but its landing flaps and skids removed, since it was not intended for this model to land. As Hanna put it, 'Its first flight would also, inevitably, be the last.' Hanna wanted to test the Reichenberg, but was turned down. She was told bluntly that it was a man's job. Hanna kicked her heels and resigned herself to watching the tests from the ground. Since the Allies' capture of the original V1 launching sites in France, methods for launching the rocket had had to be changed. Initially they were sent up by catapult, but this was no longer possible if they had to be launched from Germany, so a Heinkel III bomber was adapted to carry the V1 under one wing and release it when sufficiently close to the target. In any case, launch by catapult would have been impossible for a manned V1 as the g-force caused by the high acceleration would have been too great for a human to stand.

The first test of the Reichenberg was conducted on a warm summer morning. The Heinkel took off with its strange cargo, climbed into the sky and released the rocket. The Reichenberg began to glide at once, building speed 'like some small, swift bird'. The rocket glided in tight turns, finally levelling onto a dead straight course. Then it dipped steeply, and a moment later it was losing height rapidly. As Hanna and the team watched on anxiously the Reichenberg disappeared over the horizon. There was a loud explosion and a plume of black smoke rose into the sky. It was every pilot's worst nightmare: a crash landing. While men raced off to find the rocket, Hanna and Skorzeny paced the airfield, awaiting dreaded news of a dead pilot.

Half an hour passed before men came rushing back. The pilot was alive, they cried feverishly, but very badly injured. A survey of the rocket revealed the cause of the crash. The pilot had accidentally pressed the catch for the sliding hood of the cockpit. The shock of the air whipping in at such speeds had momentarily stunned him, causing him to lose control of the plane. It was not an auspicious start. Nor did things improve when a second test pilot launched the next day and crashed his Reichenberg, though he too was lucky enough to survive.

Two disasters had stripped Rechlin of its badly needed test pilots and it became necessary for Heinz Kensche and Hanna to take their places. Hanna could not have been more delighted. Her first flight in a Reichenberg was not only successful but an exhilarating experience; it now seemed a long time ago that she was lying in a hospital bed wondering if she would ever fly again. Over the course of eight or ten flights (she lost count!) Hanna learned the quirks of the V1 and avoided several disasters. On one occasion the Heinkel launching Hanna accidentally grazed the back of the rocket as it was released. Hanna heard awful rending noises and half expected to find her tail completely torn off. She landed the rocket with difficulty only to discover her tail had been crumpled and twisted 30 degrees to the right. It was remarkable she had landed at all.

Another test almost ended in disaster because of a decision Hanna had made before take-off. Being so small, she was inevitably also light, which could present difficulties flying a craft designed for men. To test it accurately Hanna insisted on having a bag of sand added to the cockpit to mimic the greater weight of a male pilot. On a test in a two-seater Reichenberg the sandbag was wedged into the front seat and came loose during the launch. Flying at speeds of 530mph, Hanna discovered she could not move her elevator. Too low to bail out, she had to do her best to land. As the ground rose up before her, she pushed down the nose sharply, then quickly pulled up again with all the response she could get from the elevator. The abrupt manoeuvre was just enough to check the speed of the rocket and Hanna skidded into a heavy landing, splintering her landing skids and the hull, but herself emerging unscathed.

To test the Reichenberg to its operational limits a water tank was installed to mimic the weight of a fully loaded V1. This was too heavy to land with (the true Reichenberg not being required to land safely), so a plug operated by a lever in the cockpit was installed to drain the water in the air and enable the test pilot to land safely. As with her disastrous flight in the Me 163, Hanna was soon to discover the limitations of release mechanisms. She tested one of these modified V1s at 18,000ft as she had been instructed, hardly thinking that the cold at such heights would freeze the water tank plug into its hole. Coming down to 4,500ft, Hanna went to drain the water and found the lever would not move. She was rapidly losing height and, as this variant had no engine, time was of the essence if she wished to avoid crashing. She clawed at the lever desperately, pulling on it with all her strength, wrenching the skin off her hands and making her fingers bleed, the ground looming closer and closer. Then, just as all seemed lost, the lever released and the water drained away in sufficient time for Hanna to land almost perfectly.

Testing came to an end just as Britain was finalising the plans for the D-Day landings. By the time Hanna and Kensche had handed over to trained instructors the suicide programme was already too late. The Allied invasion had begun and long-distance rockets were not going to help against troops streaming from both east and west into Germany. Many of the volunteers had also developed cold feet; the glory of giving one's life for the Reich had seemed a powerful motivation before the actual reality of the operation had sunk in. Hanna might have spoken of hundreds of volunteers, but in actuality she had seventy who had signed an oath to fly to their death. Some of these had perished in test flights; others, witnessing the fatal crashes, had become reluctant to risk the same. After all, what was the point? Germany looked pretty doomed with the Allies pushing towards Berlin. Hitler was ranting about the impossible and the other high-ranking members of the Reich were either arguing with each other or casting men into pointless deadly situations. No wonder even Hanna felt disillusioned. She was angry with Himmler for not appreciating the skill required to fly a V1 and hated Goebbels for turning their mission into another propaganda ploy. By the time the suicide unit was ready to fly it was no longer of any use.

Hanna's vision of a noble suicide in the name of the Reich was never going to happen. Hitler was never really convinced by it. He was later won over on the Storm Fighters and missions of April 1945 because they were high risk, but not deliberately suicidal. For Hanna's men there would have been no second chance; this was the reason her plan never took off. Hitler refused to see good pilots wasted unnecessarily. Paradoxically, he often ordered the Wehrmacht into suicidal situations and told them to fight to the last bullet and the last man, praising their inevitable self-sacrifice. But cannon-fodder soldiers were far easier to come by than experienced pilots, not to mention planes. In short, Hanna's experiments with the V1 were never going to bring her the fame and glory she craved. Instead, they brought her a strange memorial. The film *Operation Crossbow* blended truth and fiction to give the impression that Hanna flew V1s to test their suitability as rockets. This confusion of the true nature of her tests has become an oft-repeated 'fact'. That she was testing them as suicide craft was never suspected – one of those cases of truth being stranger than fiction.

9

THE END OF THE WORLD

Hanna's world had crumbled a long time ago, only she had failed to notice – or rather she chose to ignore the signs. Her association with Himmler, going to the extent of defending him as being misunderstood, had earned her the anger of some of her colleagues, who could not believe that she was so blind. But Hanna was desperate: desperate to believe there was some good left in Germany and its leaders, desperate to know that she had not devoted her career to aiding madmen and murderers. Such desperation is a powerful motivator when it is mixed with pride and patriotism. 'She was too good for what they made of her,' her friend Otto Fuchs recalled.

Hanna did not see the subtle shifts and ulterior motives around her. She was honest to the point of stupidity; she was rarely devious, she could not lie (except to herself) and she bounced around the Nazi world taking at face value everything that was said to her. If Himmler said there were no gas chambers, well, that must be the case. Hanna could not conceive that her leaders and superiors would lie to her face. Such subtleties were lost on her. Not all her family were so blind. In desperation over Göring's misunderstanding of the strength of the Luftwaffe, Hanna told her cousin Helmut Heuberger about her meeting with the chief of the air force and his conviction that the Me 163 was already in production. If he believed this then surely he had convinced Hitler of the same? The horror of knowing her superiors were so ill informed was hardly imaginable.

Helmut seemed a good person to voice these concerns to. An enthusiastic member of the Hitler Youth, he had joined the army empowered by propaganda and Nazi righteousness. A severe injury had prevented him participating in the disastrous Stalingrad campaign, but had earned him the Iron Cross, Second Class. Now invalided out of the army, he was watching the war from the side lines. Hanna's news fed into worries that had already been troubling him. Doubts had entered Helmut's mind and he started to wonder what he had fought and been injured for. He came to the conclusion he could no longer support Hitler. He had to stand for Germany, to save his country from further destruction. Doing that meant opposing the Führer. Helmut went on to become one of the leaders of the Austrian resistance, completely unbeknown to Hanna.

Hanna's ignorance of the worst excesses of the Nazi creed was far from unusual. Many Germans, especially women who were not involved in the fighting, were ignorant of the crimes of Hitler and his cronies. Even those who hated the Jews found the concept of mass murder impossible to swallow and even harder to imagine on the scale the Allies claimed. Nearly seventy years on, the facts are undeniable, but it should be remembered that in the blinkered, controlled world of Nazi Germany truth was a scarce commodity. Papers reported what they were told to. Those who lived in the areas of concentration camps must have had some idea of the conditions, but mostly they were kept at a distance. Ignorance was widespread. Besides, it is very hard to believe that your leader, the man you have placed your trust and hopes in, could be so evil and bloodthirsty. Unlike some, Hanna could not claim complete ignorance. She had been shown evidence of Nazi crimes; she just refused to believe it. In that she was far from alone in Germany.

In October 1944 Hanna was hurt running to an air-raid shelter during a bombing raid on Berlin. Her injuries were relatively minor: a concussion and damage to her elbow, but she was taken to hospital and there fell in with Colonel Hans-Ulrich Rudel, a veteran of the Eastern Front who had recently had his leg amputated. Hanna put to Rudel a question that had been troubling her – how would the wounded be evacuated from Berlin once the city was in ruins and navigation by air almost impossible? Planes sent to airlift civilians would find it impossible to land now that the city was being blown to smithereens and all landmarks were lying in rubble.

Rudel considered the problem and agreed with Hanna that the situation would call for advanced planning. Hanna thought a helicopter might be the answer: it could land much more easily than an aeroplane. Once sufficiently recovered, Hanna began searching for evacuation routes through Berlin. She used an Ack-Ack tower as her target, the space on the top of the tower being just big enough for a helicopter to land. Then Hanna plotted routes from all sides of Berlin, all angles, all compass points. She memorised each course so that she could find the tower even in a night air raid with smoke obscuring her view. The project certainly kept her busy, but what was the point? Hanna alone in a helicopter could rescue a handful of people only; a mass evacuation of Berlin was simply unfeasible. Still, the experience had kept her distracted from other concerns, such as the fast encroaching advance of the Russians, who even now were making inroads into Silesia. Rumours of Russian atrocities had reached Berlin and frightened everyone. Hanna became afraid for her friends still living there and phoned Otto Fuchs and begged him and his wife to leave the city as soon as they could. Fuchs was touched by the phone call; he had not spoken to Hanna for some time – since they had fallen out over her dogmatic defence of Himmler and Hitler.

Hanna was equally concerned about her own family. She had made a trip to Breslau as pilot to State Secretary Naumann. The city had been under siege for some time and the depression and distress all around filtered even into Hanna's rose-tinted worldview. Naumann had gone to try and raise hopes and brandish Nazi propaganda, but the dying city was past being saved by words. The inhabitants had already conceded defeat mentally and Hanna left with a deepening impression of the despair Germany was destined to suffer. Her parents were still in Hirschberg, but the pressure of the Russian advance, and the persistent pleading of the Hirschberg mayor, finally persuaded them to leave their home and travel to Salzburg, where they found accommodation in the attic of a once-grand mansion. Herr Reitsch's depression was worsening. Having been called upon to treat the wounded because of his medical knowledge (even if he was only an eye doctor), he had seen first-hand the brutality of the Russians: women and children raped repeatedly, old men and wounded soldiers tortured and beaten. He had seen cruelty he had never imagined and it haunted him. It seemed the Bolshevik threat Hitler had scared them with over the years and which had gained him power, had proved too much for the Führer to hold back. In contrast to her husband, Emy Reitsch settled well in Salzburg and began to make plans for the future. Heidi's children were growing up and Emy wrote an Easter play for them in verse and made them all costumes. As usual, she was the glue holding the family together.

Hanna made a final trip to Hirschberg in the April of 1945. Only a few years before she had walked through the streets of her hometown a heroine, greeted by flags and smiling faces. Now the roads and houses were empty. Everything was quiet as those few who remained awaited the arrival of the Russians. Hanna walked the old routes, looked upon the tramways she had once used, peeked in at the empty school and stood outside her house. She took it all in one final time. She would never see Hirschberg again. She travelled on to Salzburg and paid an unexpected visit to her family. Emy was ecstatic and hugged her daughter tight. Hanna was able to stay the whole day, a treat she had not experienced since Christmas. She played with her nieces and nephews, enjoyed a family meal and overlooked the quietness and reserve of her father. It was a happy occasion despite the dark clouds looming over Germany.

On 25 April Hanna received a call from Ritter von Greim. He had been summoned by Hitler to the Führerbunker, in the heart of besieged Berlin. The mission was no doubt suicidal, but von Greim's honour as a soldier would not allow him to ignore the command. Getting to Berlin was tricky enough, so he decided to ask Hanna to fly him in via helicopter, having heard of her experiments in 1944. Later authors have suggested Hanna was an unwanted guest on the mission to Berlin, that she wheedled her way into flying with von Greim to pay a final farewell to the Führer. This makes a better case for a sycophantic Hanna Reitsch, suggesting she was desperate for one last minute in Hitler's reflected glow, but it is in fact untrue. Von Greim knew Hanna was probably his best chance to get in safely because of her knowledge of all the routes through Berlin. The fact he sought permission from her parents to allow her to accompany him also shows he wanted her and not that she was an unwelcome tag-along. The knowledge that Hanna was requested by a superior to fly him to Berlin and did *not* insist on going for the sake of some egotistical hero-worshipping foible, casts a whole new light on Hanna's time in the bunker.

Hanna said a final farewell to her family in Salzburg. Despite her eternal optimism, Hanna had to admit that there was little hope of her returning and her parents knew this as they kissed and hugged her goodbye. There was still no news of Kurt, who had vanished after his ship had sunk and now Emy's eldest daughter was flying into a war-ravaged city and probably to her own death. Hanna flew with von Greim to Rechlin. There the news was bad: for two days no plane had been able to get past the Russian defences. There was no knowing the condition of runways nearer Berlin; a pilot would probably have to improvise. The airport at Gatow was still in German hands, but it was completely encircled and under almost constant enemy artillery fire. Just to finish off the catalogue of disasters, the helicopter Hanna had intended to fly had been destroyed in a recent air raid on Rechlin.

Von Greim was still determined to reach Hitler. A Focke-Wulf 190 was put at his disposal, along with a pilot who had made several successful trips into Berlin and back, and knew the safest routes. He would land the colonel general at Gatow then take off immediately, since the Russians were expected to take the airport at any time. Hanna queried how von Greim expected to get from Gatow to the Führerbunker, a considerable distance through a ruined and bombarded city. Von Greim would have to pilot himself, but naturally it would be difficult for him to navigate, especially as he had spent many of the last months on the Eastern Front and Berlin was a very changed city. Hanna decided that she still could be of some use, showing von Greim the route through the city she had memorised during her flights in 1944. Von Greim agreed. Hanna was one of the few people who knew how to navigate through the wreckage of Berlin.

Hanna made her way to the pilot who would fly von Greim into Berlin and asked if it would cause him a great deal of difficulty to include her on the flight. The pilot laughed: 'Frau Hanna, your weight will not matter, but where should I put you?' The Focke-Wulf was a single-seater, though the 190 von Greim would travel in had been equipped with a second seat for a passenger. Aside from that there was no room for anyone else. Hanna took a look at the 190 and decided she would have to squeeze into the rear of the fuselage, crammed between oxygen cylinders and the metal struts of the plane. There was no dignified way of entering and Hanna was literally threaded into the aircraft feet first. Once wedged in, the metal struts digging painfully into her flesh, Hanna was completely immobile. She could not pull herself out of the tight crawl space. Should the worst happen – the plane crash and catch fire

– Hanna would be trapped in her own coffin waiting to cook to death. A sudden panic engulfed her at the thought; but she was doing this for von Greim, because he had been a loyal supporter and friend since the loss of Ernst Udet – a loss that still pained her. She was very alone in the world of the Luftwaffe and von Greim had made the constant obstacles and criticisms bearable. For this reason she wanted to see him safely into Berlin, but the confinement of the 190 almost proved too much. She had to bite down firmly on her fears and ignore the vivid nightmares her imagination drew just to remain calm.

On the airfield thirty or forty fighter planes were running their engines, preparing to escort the valiant general and his stowaway. The noise was deafening, but it gave Hanna hope. It was the largest contingent of Luftwaffe aeroplanes she had seen in a long time. Von Greim climbed into his passenger seat, unaware of Hanna's presence until a little voice called out to him. 'Kapitän, where are you?' he said. Hanna just had time to tell him before the engines roared and the aircraft rumbled down the runway, each bump forcing a metal strut painfully into Hanna's back or side. The flight would take an estimated thirty minutes. Hanna could just see the luminous dial of her watch and counted off each minute, knowing that at any second a Russian fighter might spot them and attack. The air over Berlin was swarming with Russian planes. It was remarkable, in some regards, that they were spotted only when they were just short of Berlin. Hanna knew nothing of what was happening outside, but when the Fw 190 pitched forward and dived, screaming, into a headlong plunge, she feared the worst – they had to have been hit and she was about to endure a fiery death. The sheer force of the dive was agonising: still pinned in her coffin, Hanna was plunging head-first at colossal speed, squeezing her eyes shut, awaiting the explosion that would either kill her quickly or leave her to suffer an agonising death. Pain sparked through her head, if she was lucky she might fall unconscious …

Without warning the Fw 190 started to level off. The blood stopped pounding in Hanna's head. The crash had been averted. She only later learned the terrifying dive had been a deliberate move to avoid a Russian fighter. Gatow emerged through the smoke and fog of dying Berlin. There were no more attacks. No fiery deaths. Hanna's plane landed and she was tugged out of her hiding place with a great deal of relief. General von Greim made a dash for the nearest air-raid shelter and asked for a telephone at once. It was somewhat remarkable that almost until the last moment Hitler's bunker retained a working telephone line. Even so, placing a call wasn't easy. With shells bursting overhead von Greim finally reached Colonel von Below, Hitler's Luftwaffe adjutant. Hanna listened uneasily as von Greim tried to get information from the colonel. Was he still wanted at the bunker? Yes, come at once! But what was all this about, why did Hitler have him flying a suicide mission? Below could not say, he just repeated that von Greim must come at all costs.

There was nothing for it but to make the last dash for the Reich Chancellery. Below explained that most of Berlin was under Russian control; in fact, the bunker was almost surrounded and places to land were few and far between. However, it was still possible to land near the Brandenburg Gate. Hitler's pilot Hans Baur had been there recently to survey the possibility of transforming the avenue beyond the gate into a runway. Perhaps von Greim could land there? While he was still wanted, von Greim could not conceive of disobeying his orders. He and Hanna prepared to fly again, only to learn that the plane they had intended to take had just been destroyed by artillery fire. There was one last Fieseler Storch remaining. At 6 p.m. von Greim took position in the pilot's seat and Hanna sat behind him. They had agreed that he would fly and she navigate, as Hanna had never flown under fire before. Just in case, Hanna checked that it was possible for her to reach around von Greim and take the controls in an emergency. It would not be necessary, she told herself, but at least she knew she could if the worst happened.

The take-off was smooth. Von Greim kept low and hoped the rapidly dimming light would mask their approach. Russian planes, after all, could not be everywhere at once. They made it to the treetops of Grünewald without incident and then, like wasps swarming near a picnic, fighter planes emerged on all sides. Bang! Something swooped up from the trees. Hanna looked down at tanks and men with machine guns, all aiming at the Storch. All Hell broke loose: bullets and shells flew at them from the ground and the sky. It seemed for an instant as though the whole might of the Russian army was focused on this one tiny plane. Gun muzzles flared, tanks thundered, fighters zipped overhead. A yellow explosion flashed over the engine. 'I'm hit!' Von Greim slumped backwards. An armour-piercing bullet had smashed through the fuselage and mangled his foot. In moments he was unconscious.

Hanna reached around him and grabbed the control stick. Somehow she weaved and dodged as best she could despite more and more bullets hitting the Storch. She noticed in horror that both wing engines were leaking petrol, dark fuel running down them and dripping away. The plane should have been doomed but somehow it struggled on. Hanna kept tight hold of the controls and her own panic. Von Greim opened his eyes once or twice, reached convulsively for the control stick, then sank back into oblivion. Had she not been there he would have crashed and never learned of the fate Hitler had in store for him. Ahead was a radio tower, just visible through thick swirls of acrid smoke. The ground fire dwindled as they came back into German-held territory. Those weeks of running routes through Berlin now served a purpose. There were no landmarks to navigate by, and it would be far too dangerous to search around for one, but Hanna knew the exact position of that Ack-Ack tower that had guided her so well, and using her current position she knew exactly how to find it and turn off for the Brandenburg Gate. Von Greim could not have reached the Führerbunker without Hanna; that was why she went to Berlin. Not to court Hitler one last time. Not to beg to die with him. She went as a simple act of friendship towards von Greim.

Hans Baur was supervising the conversion of the avenue at Brandenburger Tor into a landing strip when he heard the wailing of an engine. Glancing up he spotted a Fieseler Storch just above the buildings. The plane was looking for somewhere to land under heavy bombardment from the Russians. Finally it appeared to land some distance from the airstrip Baur was hastily trying to construct. He climbed into his car and headed for the spot he thought the plane had landed, but when he arrived its occupants had vanished. Two soldiers informed him a general and a woman had left the plane and driven off at once in a car. The general had been wounded. Baur had witnessed the arrival in Berlin of Hanna Reitsch, but he was more interested in von Greim, whom he remembered from the First World War and found in the bunker being pieced back together by Dr Stumpfegger. The general had arrived to learn his fate. Hanna's decision to join him would prove one of the most significant of her life.

The Führerbunker has developed a mythical aura all of its own since the details of the last days of Hitler were first revealed to the public in the 1950s. It has baffled people why Hitler chose to stay in Berlin when it was clearly lost and he was in very real danger of falling into Russian hands at any moment. From a practical perspective it was illogical. It would have been better to continue commanding his forces from somewhere else, such as Prague, where there was still a strong SS force. However, abandoning Berlin to the Allies would, in itself, be the end for Hitler. To run away seemed cowardice and only a delay of the inevitable.

By 1945 Hitler had become morose and depressive for much of the time. While he had occasional mad moments of inspiration and optimism, far more often he was contemplating death, both his and the figurative death of Germany. He was also angry and paranoid, convinced the German population had betrayed him and that if he must fall then he would do so with as much destruction of the country he ruled as possible. In the end Hitler was an insane despot, far removed from reality and without the energy or strength to leave Berlin. Hanna recognised this, even if it was only after the war that she admitted as much to herself and her interrogators.

From an ideological perspective, staying in Berlin made even clearer sense. Like a captain going down with his ship, Hitler would stand staunchly in his capital until the very end. In those last heady, confused days Nazi fever raged through the occupants of the bunker, making a future without Hitler seem impossible. Cut off from the world, detached from reality, they drifted into dreamy contemplation of a heroic, sacrificial death as in the ancient legends upon which Hitler sometimes modelled his regime. Propaganda demanded that Hitler remain to the end if there was to be any hope of a revival of National Socialism postwar. Goebbels realised this. As perhaps the only intellectual left in the bunker, he saw an irony in a last stand at Berlin, as well as comparisons with the ancient history he relished. Hitler would be like a Roman emperor throwing in his lot with his people. What he would not be like was the Kaiser, who ran away in shame at the end of the First World War. Goebbels, above all, was influential in persuading Hitler to stay in Berlin.

If there was to be a last stand, however, there had to be a suitable location for it. As early as 1935 construction had begun on a reinforced cellar beneath the Diplomat's Hall of the Old Reich Chancellery to act as an air-raid shelter. This would ultimately develop into the Vorbunker or Front Bunker, where essential staff had their quarters and where Hitler's personal kitchen was situated. The Vorbunker covered 6,000 square feet, but the useable area within the interior was significantly smaller, much of the space being taken up by the thick 18in walls which divided the bunker into cramped, narrow rooms along a central corridor that was used as a dining room. By the time Hanna arrived, Frau Goebbels and her children had taken over a suite of rooms in the Vorbunker, opposite those reserved for Hitler's personal police.

After the bombing raids on Berlin of 1943–44 Hitler grew increasingly paranoid about the strength of the Vorbunker and ordered the design and construction of another deeper, stronger, thicker bunker. This would ultimately come to be known as the Führerbunker. Construction began in April 1944. According to Albert Speer, Hitler's architect, the specifications were a 'ceiling 3.5 meters thick and sides 3.5–4 meters thick' situated in a pit '10 meters deep'. In total, the new bunker covered 3,350 square feet, its interior being marginally larger than the Vorbunker's, though the overall building was much smaller. Workmen created a connecting staircase between the Vorbunker and the Führerbunker. All the steel doors were gas proof and a ventilation tower stuck up from the ground to provide inhabitants with relatively fresh air. The rooms were around 30ft beneath ground, their ceilings supported by angled steel girders and covered with steel mesh and then granite slabs to explode bombs before they could penetrate the bunker. Again there was a central passage divided by a wall into a conference room and a general sitting area. To one side were Hitler and Eva Braun's rooms and a map room sometimes also used for conferences, though its size made it inconvenient for large groups. On the opposite side were rooms for Martin Bormann, Goebbels and Dr Stumpfegger, along with the telephone exchange. At the back of the bunker was a common latrine and the heavy-duty diesel generator.

When Hitler moved into the bunker in March 1945 work was barely completed: the plaster on the walls was still wet and teething problems with the ventilation and pumping systems made life underground uncomfortable. The marshy soil near the Reich Chancellery made the bunkers damp, the Vorbunker occasionally flooded and water constantly leaked into the generator room, which had to be mopped three times a day. With so many people in close, stuffy quarters tempers became frayed, there was a constant smell of human body odour as hot and bothered staff and soldiers bustled about the confined environment. There were limited facilities for washing and when the common latrine blocked up the smell became even worse, nauseating at times. Residents would risk a break outside during a bombing raid just to get some fresh air. The diesel generators were a constant nuisance: noisy and reeking of diesel fumes, they drove residents insane. Hitler would demand them switched off during conferences, but this only resulted in making the acrid air of the bunker grow staler and stuffier until his guests complained of headaches. One SS captain described the bunker as like being in 'a cement submarine, or buried alive in a charnel house … Towards the end when the drainage packed in, it was as pleasant as working in a public urinal.'

The bunkers did not exist in isolation. Beneath the Reich Chancellery was a vast network of underground cellars linked in places to form a long bunker. So big were some of the passageways that lorries were able to drive down into them from the surface. In better days those lorries had carried coke to fuel the many furnaces in the Chancellery; now, as the Russians pounded the city, they carried in the wounded and the homeless. A hospital was set up in one area, and other cellars swarmed with refugees, largely women and children. So in March and April 1945 a regular underground hive of people formed beneath Berlin. The last necessity of the bunker was its phone line, one of the few ways Hitler could keep in touch with the outside world and continue to command. It was also a link to reality, sorely missing in most aspects of Hitler's life. Down in his bunker, cocooned from the worst, Hitler could believe all would come right, that this was just a blip in his great plan. As news of betrayals and further defeats trickled in to him, it now became apparent his war was lost.

On 25 April Hitler received a telegram from Göring informing him that the latter had opened negotiations with the Americans. Hitler's anger polluted the atmosphere of the bunker and he raved over Göring's betrayal – how could he? It was treason! Hitler furiously sent a message back informing Göring that he could be executed for his cowardly turncoat behaviour. Hitler ordered him to give up all his offices and appointments within the next twenty-four hours. Cowed, Göring quickly relinquished his authority and left Hitler facing the tough task of appointing his successor. His tormented mind settled on a man he felt worthy of fulfilling Göring's role, a man who would not betray him in this final battle. General Colonel Ritter von Greim had remained on the

Eastern Front to the last, had been a loyal servant to the Führer. Now he would become the overall commander of the Luftwaffe. So great was the honour that Hitler insisted on presenting it in person – thus von Greim was set on the path for a disastrous flight across Berlin, which in the end would prove utterly pointless.

For the moment, however, no one knew the fate in store for them (except for Hitler). As von Greim was helped into the bunker, Traudl Junge, one of Hitler's secretaries, came to catch a glimpse of the famous man and saw Hanna. She made a brief entry in her diary:

> Hanna Reitsch lands in a Fiesler Storch on the East-West axis just outside the Brandenburg Gate, bringing General Greim, an excellent Luftwaffe officer. Today is the first time I've seen either of them. Hanna Reitsch is a small, delicate, very feminine person, you'd never have thought she had such masculine courage. She wears the Iron Cross on her smooth black rollneck sweater. Greim limps into the bunker on one leg, leaning on her shoulder. He was wounded on their adventurous flight here, shot in the leg by Russian fighter pilots. Now he has come to succeed Göring and take over command of the Luftwaffe. But first he disappears into the operating theatre to be treated by Dr Stumpfegger, the silent, pale, reserved doctor. Hanna Reitsch hurries to see the Führer. She must have been one of those women who adored Hitler unconditionally, without reservations. Today that seems to me amazing, because she was the only woman who knew Hitler not just privately, as a man, but as a soldier and a military commander too. She sparkled with her fanatical, obsessive readiness to die for the Führer and his ideals ...
>
> In the evening she put the Goebbels children to bed. Eva Braun kept her company. Their mother hardly had the strength to face her children with composure now. Every meeting with them made her feel so terrible that she burst into tears afterwards. She and her husband were nothing but shadows, already doomed to die.
>
> [First written down as memoirs in 1947–48]

As we shall see, Hanna's memories of her arrival in the bunker were slightly different.

Hanna was not prepared in any way for the madness of the bunker. As she walked down the steps to the Führerbunker Magda Goebbels appeared in the entranceway, stared at Hanna, then burst into hysterical tears and clasped her in her arms. What was Hanna to make of such a spectacle? Her astonishment had barely passed when Hitler appeared. Hanna trembled to seem him, a shadow of the man she had once spoken to about flying: 'His head drooped heavily on his shoulders and a continual twitching affected both his arms. The eyes were glassy and remote. He greeted us in an expressionless voice.'

What Hanna could not know was that Hitler was being fuelled by a heady and dangerous concoction of drugs mixed by his personal doctor. One compound was heavily laced with strychnine, but Hitler would hear no word said against his doctor. Stress, lack of sleep and a deadly mix of various poisons and drugs had all taken their toll on the Führer and had utterly addled his thinking. Always behind Hitler was the pretty Eva Braun, his mistress. What was Hanna to make of Eva Braun? She was not a woman Hanna could come to like deeply, a complete opposite to the woman Hanna herself was. Some found Eva simple and charming. Hans Baur remarked that he both liked and respected her. Hanna found it harder to come to the same conclusion. Eva was naïve, or perhaps just stupid, she had no interest in Third Reich politics despite her association with its leader. Instead she attached herself like a devoted dog to Hitler and followed him unswervingly. Hanna found her rather silly, an opinion shared by von Greim. It says a good deal about Hanna's views on the Führer's lover that when she was entrusted with Eva's last letter from the bunker she opened and read it. Considering it unsuitable and pathetic, she destroyed it. For a woman normally dominated by her own sense of honour, this was a remarkable thing to do.

Von Greim limped from the operating theatre to greet the Führer and give his report on his flight to Berlin. When he relayed the part Hanna had played, Hitler turned to her and flashed a smile, 'Brave woman! So there is still some loyalty and courage left in the world!' Hitler went on to explain the betrayal of Göring and his reason for summoning von Greim: 'Nothing is spared me, nothing! Every disillusion, every betrayal, dishonour, treason has been heaped upon me. I have had Göring put under immediate arrest, stripped him of all his offices, expelled him from all Party Organisations.' He ranted to the room, shouting and pacing, waving his arms and working himself into a fury, before he paused and stood before von Greim again. 'From now on you shall be Chief of the

Luftwaffe in place of Göring, with immediate promotion to the rank of Field Marshal.' The award was bittersweet, as Hanna well knew:

> Commander-in-chief of an Air Force that no longer existed! In the circumstances and for [von Greim], whose conception of honour was entirely immutable and selfless, it could have only one meaning – to stay here, in the Bunker, with Hitler, to the end. And if Greim stayed, then I would stay with him.

Why did Hanna choose to stay? Well, partly there was very little choice. There seemed little chance of getting another plane into Berlin. The Fieseler Storch they had flown in was damaged beyond repair and without fuel. A pilot might risk flying in to rescue von Greim or one of the other officers, but Hanna Reitsch? She was not worth the risk, not when her propaganda value was nil now that the war was drawing its last breath in favour of the Allies. If she couldn't fly out, her options were limited. Cars were few and far between and the roads had been badly damaged. Besides, a vehicle would be spotted by the Russians. An escape on foot was possible, but it was a slim chance and would involve running roadblocks and large parties of Russian soldiers. If captured, Hanna would face an unhappy fate: as a woman she was likely to be violated. In recent times it has been common to play down the atrocities the Russians inflicted on the inhabitants of Berlin, but they were very real and very widespread. Russian soldiers raped and killed as they raced through Berlin: figures for these crimes are shockingly high. If Hanna was captured she would have been treated brutally; if she was lucky she might be recognised, in which case she would find herself in Russia facing interrogators every bit as unpleasant and cruel as the Gestapo. If she survived she would be sent to a concentration camp to starve to death or die from disease. Faced with such grim choices, was it any wonder Hanna considered the best option staying with von Greim and the other officers, enjoying at least some limited protection from the SS men who stood on guard?

Hanna can hardly be blamed for thinking it safer to stay. Talk of honour aside, Hanna had witnessed entry into Berlin and was afraid to try to escape alone. Even if she could get hold of a plane, she had just seen what had happened to von Greim. There is no need to talk of Hanna's patriotism, loyalty or even Nazi beliefs (which were few) to explain the decision – it was simply the most obvious and most sensible one to make! Hanna never voiced this logic, preferring to suggest her decision was based on her sense of duty. If she had, she might have been spared some of the criticism she later endured.

Hanna became familiar with the interior of the dank, smelly bunker, its corridors smelling of stale food and human sweat. Frau Goebbels befriended her as the only woman in the bunker (aside from Eva Braun) who was on a similar social standing to her. There were other women in the bunker, but they were secretaries and it was not appropriate for Magda to associate with them. Besides, they were young girls who knew so little. Hanna was closer to her in age and had seen the world. Frau Goebbels took Hanna up to her small suite of rooms for a much-needed wash. As Hanna entered the rooms six small faces peered over the top of double-decker beds. These were the Goebbels children, soon to be some of the last innocent victims of Hitler's tyranny. Trapped in the bunker themselves, when not frightened by the shelling, they were bored, so a new face was a good surprise. They quickly rose and, as Hanna washed, asked her question after question about her flying.

Though Hanna had no children of her own she was fond of young people and had been a good aunt to her various nieces and nephews. She liked the Goebbels children and in a world gone mad there was something refreshing about their openness, good-humour and playfulness. From then on she was invited to spend every mealtime with the children and to regale them with tales of her adventures:

> Each of them was a delight with its [*sic*] open-hearted naturalness and bright intelligence. Their concern for each other was touching. One little girl was isolated for a time in the next room with tonsillitis and when telling a story to the others, I had to pause every so often, so that one of them could tell the patient next door 'what happened next'. I taught them part-songs and how to yodel in real Tyrolean style. The crash and thunder of the shells bursting above failed to disturb them. It was their 'Uncle Führer', as they had been told, busy conquering his enemies, and when the youngest got frightened and began to cry, he was quickly pacified with this explanation.

Hanna was fearful for the children's future. She wanted to fly them all away, but it was simply impossible. She consoled herself by thinking that separating the family at such a time would be a greater cruelty. Perhaps her mind was straying back to her own family; her mother and father worn into premature old age, Heidi a young widow with three small children, Kurt lost somewhere …

Then there was her own fate to consider. On the night of her arrival the Russians finally found the correct range for the Reich Chancellery and began a steady programme of intense artillery fire. Even in the Führerbunker, the deepest portion of the underground labyrinth, every explosion produced a rain of plaster from the ceiling and walls. Cocooned in this strange isolated world, the bunker inhabitants became divorced from reality. Hanna noted how they clung to the most fanciful of hopes, not least the Führer himself, who was constantly talking about rescue from one source or another. There were thousands of troops waiting for just the right moment to strike, just when the Allies thought they had won, he would say – or he would talk of new wonder weapons and masses of planes awaiting delivery to the Luftwaffe. For Hanna, who knew all this to be lies and misinformation sold to Hitler by his cronies, his talk of a sudden victory for Germany was pitiful. Unlike the grovelling creature portrayed in *Downfall*, Hanna knew all too well how pathetic were Hitler's plans. '… their self-deception was particularly noticeable,' Hanna later wrote, referring to the bunker inhabitants. Hanna was in the bunker on the 27 and 28 April, living in a strange atmosphere of suspense and false hope. Rumours of triumphs or disasters spread through the bunker like wildfire and kept the inmates alive with dreams of rescue for a little longer. Caught in this world, Hanna felt her beliefs in the German Reich shaken. News of the murder of SS Group Leader Fegelein was whispered. The rumour made Hanna 'feel that the very ground beneath my feet was beginning to give way'.

Fegelein had disappeared without permission from the bunker. No one seemed to know where he had gone, not even his sister-in-law Eva Braun. He was finally discovered in his own flat, but he refused to appear before Hitler, claiming he was too drunk. Hitler, by now paranoid about betrayal, sent a group of SS men to fetch Fegelein. The SS group leader still refused to come, promising he would arrive at the bunker when he was sober. He did not. Another party was sent for him, this time Wehrmacht, and once again he promised he would come when he was ready. Around midnight he appeared at the bunker, by which point Hitler had decided his fate. Tired of Fegelein, Hitler ordered him investigated for desertion. If Fegelein expected any sympathy for being brother-in-law to the Führer's mistress he was gravely mistaken. Despite Eva Braun's pleas on behalf of her sister (who was heavily pregnant) and her brother-in-law, Fegelein was found guilty, stripped of his rank and executed in the deserted, ruined streets of Berlin. The execution brought a new thought to Hanna's mind: what would be her fate if the Führer decided she was a traitor? If she was to request to leave now, without von Greim, would she be viewed as another turncoat? Perhaps shot? Fegelein had only gone to his flat for some temporary respite from the misery of the bunker, but he had been shot for betrayal.

Around 27 April a Ju 52 managed to make the dangerous flight into Berlin to collect von Greim. Hanna later claimed that it had come to take her as well. Bearing in mind she was a last-minute addition to the original flight in, this was optimistic thinking. The Luftwaffe had come for its new chief, but von Greim refused to go and the plane was sent back. Hanna was stuck. Though she might have made the dangerous run to the aircraft which would have, necessarily, landed some distance away, she would have had to ask special permission and overridden von Greim's orders to do so.

Hanna's belief in her own self-importance does her a disservice in this part of her story. She writes in her autobiography as if the plane was sent for her as much as for von Greim, making it seem that she chose to ignore it due to a misguided sense of loyalty to Hitler. In reality the plane were not for her at all, and she had very little say in the matter. She was stuck with von Greim and had to abide by his decisions, since he was probably her only means of escape. At the return of the Ju 52, Hanna was summoned to Hitler's study:

> His face was now even paler, and had become flaccid and putty-coloured, like that of a dotard. He gave me two phials of poison so that, as he said, Greim and I should have at all times 'freedom of choice.' Then he said that if the hope of the relief of Berlin by General Wenk was not realized, he and Eva Braun had freely decided that they would depart out of this life.

Hanna had come to the conclusion that even if Hitler's vain hopes of victory, which he pinned solely on General Wenk, were realised, 'his vital energies were by now too depleted to sustain him alive.' Hitler had turned down options for escape. 'He believed his presence·in Berlin would make a decisive difference to the defenders' morale: indeed, this thought alone was keeping him alive.'

Hanna retreated from the depressing atmosphere of the bunker to von Greim's sick room, where he rested uncomfortably. His foot was painful and he needed proper attention in a hospital, but von Greim had thrown in his lot with Hitler and was not expecting to be alive for very much longer anyway. The Russians would storm the bunker eventually; he was not blind to that fact as the others were. He would commit suicide before then. The relationship between Hanna and von Greim has been subject to much debate. Eric Brown, one-time devotee of Hanna turned arch-critic, suggested their relationship was intimate. This is unlikely; von Greim was married, not exactly a disqualifier for being Hanna's lover, but he was a man of staunch honour. More importantly, Hanna's principles concerning sexual relations were decidedly puritanical. The closest she had come to losing her virginity was many years ago with a Spanish pilot, but she had baulked at the last moment – she could not relinquish her strong religious fears, or her sense of propriety. Hanna retained that strong sense of honour throughout her life, and committing adultery was simply not feasible for her. Contemporaries who witnessed her relationship with von Greim record that it was a close friendship; she looked up to him, as she had done so often to older men in her life. Her loyalty to him was born out of the care and respect he had shown her. Throughout her life Hanna had latched on to father figures, and von Greim was the last in a long line of men who had fulfilled a role in her life as protector and supporter.

On 29 April, a few minutes past midnight, Hitler appeared in von Greim's room. His face was 'ashen-white, like a dead man's', and he was clutching at a piece of paper containing the transcription of a wireless message and a map. 'Now Himmler has betrayed me,' he said, swaying slightly in the musty air. 'You two must leave the bunker as quickly as you can. I have had news that the Russians are going to storm the Reich Chancellery tomorrow morning.' He showed them the map: 'If the enemy concentrations in the streets leading to the Reich Chancellery can be destroyed by air attack, we can gain at least twenty-four hours and enable General Wenk to reach us in time. Already at Potsdam they can hear his artillery fire.'

There was an Arado 96 waiting for them, Hitler explained. They had to escape and von Greim must organise the air attack. Both protested; from von Greim's perspective the attack was hopeless. He was also very ill and in a great deal of pain. At that point he wasn't sure what the future held for a German general, let alone a Nazi, and he had resolved himself to death. Hanna protested because she was afraid, because she wanted to remain with von Greim, because even in this dark hour she felt some shred of loyalty to Germany's leader. Unlike later myths concerning her, these protests were neither demonstrative nor dramatic. She did not weep and cling to the Führer. In one autobiography she makes no mention at all that she refused to go.

The problem was that Hanna was not so stupid as to believe Hitler's fantastic plans for the relief of Berlin. She had seen the situation outside – the wrecked roads, the ruined houses, the masses of Russian troops, guns and tanks. She had seen the large number of planes in the sky and in contrast the depletion of the Luftwaffe. Both she and von Greim realised the attempt would be futile. However, Hanna did want to leave the bunker. When the Ju 52 had managed to land in Berlin she had grasped at the hope of escape with both hands. She did not want to remain underground awaiting the Russians, but nor did she want to throw her life away on futile gestures of resistance.

In any case, after almost four days in the bunker, Hanna was leaving. A tearful Magda Goebbels clung to her as she prepared to go and sobbed that Hanna must do absolutely everything in her power to save those left behind in the bunker. She pressed a letter into Hanna's hand and asked that it be delivered to her son from her first marriage. Goebbels also gave her a letter to this same stepson and she took one from Eva Braun to her sister. They were last goodbyes to loved ones outside and Magda was in a terrible state as she handed over hers. A tentative friendship had formed between Hanna and Magda; Hanna does not appear to have been aware of Magda's intention to murder her children. Frau Goebbels struck Hanna as a sorry creature, the bunker was no place to end your days and certainly not for small children. But Frau Goebbels had thrown in her lot with her husband and refused to leave. She was ready when the time came to murder her children before taking her own life. 'You know ... life hasn't really given me very much,' she explained to Hans Baur:

> I bore children to my husband; I went to all the big meetings because he wanted me to; and I did my best to devote my life to him and my children. It wasn't always easy. My friends, who envied me, made me see a good deal. They would tell me about this or that woman I ought to keep my eye on. I knew quite well, of course, that my husband ... didn't take his obligation of marital fidelity very seriously ... He often hurt me, but I have forgiven him. I know we shall never get out of this bunker alive ... Every evening I put [*sic*] the injections for the children ready, and when the time comes the doctor will make them for me. The Russians are not more than a couple of hundred yards away now, and every night when I tuck my children in and say goodnight to them I never know whether it's for the last time.

Hanna understood self-sacrifice, but the deaths of the children upset her, she couldn't resolve herself entirely to the murder of such innocents, especially when she knew she had offered Frau Goebbels a chance to leave the bunker. Magda refused to leave, time and time again, condemning herself and her children. Hanna, who looked at the Goebbels offspring and thought of her own sister's children, could hardly know that soon they too would fall under the self-destructive whim of their father. Goebbels himself was one of the few who had not abandoned Hitler and so earned some respect from Hanna. He was a small, plain man, who lit up a room with his conversation, which was always lively and amusing. For that reason alone Hitler liked his company. 'You could tell Goebbels what was on your mind,' Hitler's valet Heinz Linge recalled years later. Wernher von Braun was less complimentary: 'Goebbels had a diabolic intelligence and an appreciation of his own power. I remember his boasting once that "it is three days' work for me to change this nation's mind".'

Goebbels was also the main rival of Göring, whom he viewed as ample target for his sarcastic slings and arrows. Göring's betrayal only galvanised Hitler's faith in Goebbels – had his propaganda chief not told him time after time that Göring was not fit for his command? Hitler's fondness for Goebbels offset his acute dissatisfaction with his philandering ways. Goebbels had an eye for the ladies, and though far from handsome, his position, charm and sense of humour drew many attractive women, including film stars. One such blatant affair had almost ruined his marriage to Magda, but both she and Hitler had hung on to Goebbels, and the Führer had restored at least a semblance of harmony.

Hanna said goodbye to the dysfunctional Goebbels family and left the bunker with Hitler's last words to her ringing in her ears. 'God protect you!' he had said to her briefly, his attention already wandering to more maps and more grandiose imaginary schemes. Von Greim, in a great deal of pain, hobbled out of the bunker assisted by Hanna and von Below. Berlin appeared to have devolved into Hell since their descent. The sky was thick with sulphurous clouds and smoke that stung the back of the throat. The horizon was stained a yellow-red by the flames of many huge fires and the din of shelling was unceasing. The psychological pounding on the senses was overwhelming; if Hitler had been forced to emerge from his burrow and seen this, could he still have believed in rescue?

The trio found an armoured car and made the journey through the ruins of Berlin, hoping to God they did not stumble upon any Russians. They were lucky: they pulled up at the plane unscathed and Hanna discovered that their escort was the same pilot who had flown them in only a few days before. He had braved the hellfire of Berlin once more for them. Who this pilot was we do not know; all that remains of him is Hanna's impression of his great courage in the face of absurd odds. They flew out of Berlin for the final time and landed at Rechlin around 3 a.m. The air base was almost deserted, but there were enough left of the operations staff to aid von Greim in his thankless task of raising a fictional air assault on the Russians. While Hanna stomped on the runway, trying to work up some warmth in her body, deep underground her Führer was marrying Eva Braun.

Hanna became von Greim's personal escort, first taking him to Plön to meet with Grand-Admiral Dönitz, soon to be the last leader of the Third Reich, then to Dobbin to Field Marshal Keitel. Hedge-hopping in a small plane to avoid attack or sometimes travelling by car, von Greim relied on Hanna to get him safely from one place to another. It was while they were at Lübeck that they heard the news that Hitler was dead. He killed himself on 30 April and was soon followed by his most loyal followers. Among those who chose to live and try to evade the

Russians were Hans Baur and Hitler's valet Heinz Linge. Baur made a desperate dash across Berlin, but was shot in the leg and ended up in the hands of the Russians and would vanish for the next decade.

Dönitz was now head of the German government. Von Greim was determined to get to his command in Bohemia, but his foot wound was causing complications and he landed instead in hospital for four days. Lying in his hospital bed he learned on 7 May that the German capitulation, arranged by Dönitz, would be signed two days later. The war was over. The Nazi regime was finished. Uncertain what to do, von Greim insisted on Hanna flying him to meet with General Field Marshal Kesselring. Kesselring was said to be at Zell-am-See, so Hanna flew von Greim over the Alps, trying to locate the elusive field marshal. The peaceful mountains were a stark contrast to the calamity happening around Berlin and for a brief moment Hanna could breathe. Then they landed and von Greim learned that Germany had surrendered unconditionally.

Von Greim was a desperately ill man. Running around on a badly damaged foot, with the stress and pressures of trying to fulfil the last orders of the Führer while avoiding capture, had inevitably taken a toll on him both physically and mentally. Von Greim was feverish and sometimes delusional. He ended up once more in hospital. There Hanna remained at his side and they talked for a long time of the last few years and of what the future held. Von Greim was a long-standing member of the Nazi Party and this now weighed heavily on his conscience. The Americans were close and they would take him prisoner and probably wish him to testify against Göring. Von Greim detested the idea, it went against all his ideas of loyalty and honour. Over and over again he talked to Hanna about suicide. They still had the vials Hitler had given them. Just supposing they took them? Von Greim might have been ready for death but Hanna was not. Her resilience and her natural optimism had once again resolved her to live a little while longer. Her reasoning was that if they both committed suicide it would arouse suspicions of them being lovers. If von Greim felt he must end everything he must do it alone so that no such rumours would besmirch his honour after death. Hanna might have briefly considered suicide, but her will to live was stronger. Dark days were soon to overtake her, but in all that time she never turned to her suicide capsule.

There was one last unexpected visitor. Eric Brown had spent the war testing British planes and the odd German craft recovered intact. He was in Germany during the capitulation and was given a list of important people the British wanted to speak with. Aside from names such as Wernher von Braun, on the list was Hanna Reitsch. Eric had heard rumours that she was in a nearby hospital when he stopped in Kitzbühl. This was the last place she had been with von Greim. Hanna was suffering from acute exhaustion after the tempestuous last few days. Eric tracked her down and found a defeated woman. He toyed with the idea of saving his one-time heroine for the British (she was in American-occupied territory), which would have involved kidnapping her. In the end he decided, reluctantly, to leave her where she was and inform the Americans of her presence. Hanna was destined to become a prisoner of war.

10

WHEN ALL HOPE IS LOST

There had been little to sustain the Germans in those last days of war. Hanna could not look towards a glorious future for her country or even an agreeable surrender. In that darkness what was there to keep her going? Hanna pegged her hopes on her family. They had fled to Salzburg and there, at least, she felt confident they would be safe. Her last meeting with them had been sad, she had been about to fly into Berlin, possibly to her death. Hanna knew she must get a message to her parents and sister as soon as possible so they would know she was alive and well. Hanna penned a letter on 10 May and gave it to a doctor who was paying a visit to Salzburg that day. A flicker of joy burned inside as she anticipated the reply from her mother. Emy Reitsch always knew what to say to cheer Hanna and she would get her daughter through these hard times. There would probably be no more flying, of course, not with the Allies on the doorstep. But she could return to her family, help Heidi with the children and work out what she was going to do with herself.

For a brief time there was new hope, and then the doctor returned. He visited von Greim before seeing Hanna. 'It is bad news for Frau Hanna,' he said. 'Her family are all dead. Will you tell her this, Herr General?' The doctor revealed the sad saga of the Reitsch tragedy. After Hanna left for the Führerbunker rumours began to spread among the civilian population that once the Allies took hold of the country all German refugees would be returned to their district of origin. The German people had given up on their Führer before he had even concocted his great 'General Wenk' plan. When Herr Reitsch heard the rumours of what the Allies would do with refugees he grew fearful. Silesia was in the hands of the Russians. If his family were returned there they would fall straight into Soviet hands. The Third Reich had been building a terror of the Russians for years, using it as propaganda to keep people fighting and sacrificing their husbands and sons. The image of the average Russian was a hairy, ferocious, cruel monster. The truth was not so different. The Germans suffered greatly in Russian hands, just as Russians had suffered greatly in German hands. The hostility between the two nations was great, the hatred even worse. Within the Russian zone of occupied Germany secret police operated day and night, stealing people from their homes to send to concentration or prison camps for the most mundane of reasons. Persecution was rife; food was restricted; starvation common.

Herr Reitsch was terrified of the thought of his family returning to Hirschberg. He imagined his daughter and grandchildren being violated, his wife being tortured and killed, and him not being able to prevent it. Slowly, slowly these thoughts festered in his already tormented mind. When Hanna left Berlin, General Koller claimed to have informed the Reitsch family. He can't have done, for when the Führer died and reports spread over the radio of his death, the Reitsch family had no knowledge of where Hanna was. It was natural for them to assume she was still in the bunker, either dead or in the hands of the Russians. Herr Reitsch favoured the former answer; he couldn't bear the idea of his daughter being a prisoner of the Soviets. With no news of Kurt either, the elder Reitschs resolved themselves to the fact their two oldest children must be dead.

On 4 May a family friend called on the Reitsch household. She knew of Herr Reitsch's fears and had even found the family a refuge on a farm where they might hide in secrecy. But Herr Reitsch would not leave the attic rooms of Salzburg – if Hanna lived they would be the first place she would go to find them. On that May morning, as Germany wondered what Dönitz had planned for his people and whether a navy man knew what he was doing, Herr Reitsch told his visitor that the family were suffering from upset stomachs. 'They drank some bad fruit juice,' he said. 'They should be better tomorrow.'

The friend left, wishing them a speedy recovery and promising to return the next day. On 5 May when she approached the house there was an old cart drawn up outside. Its cargo was covered with old blankets, but it was obvious it contained bodies. Herr Reitsch had shot his wife, daughter, grandchildren and maid, before shooting himself. The day before, he had tried to poison them with cyanide, causing the upset stomachs but not proving fatal. He had left a note for Hanna, just in case she had survived. He told her she must be comforted and even made happy by the knowledge her loved ones were safe in the arms of God. No torture or torment could befall them. Herr Reitsch had done his duty by his family.

Von Greim broke the news to Hanna. She was bereft. She had no idea how she would continue with her life without the mother who had been her rock throughout the years. How terrible to have survived so many brushes with death only to have the people she loved most in the world snatched away. Hanna hardly knew how to cope. She turned to von Greim, who was supportive and allowed her to place some pictures of her family in his room with candles. There they sat together in silence contemplating the dead of the Reitsch household, while Hanna knew von Greim was planning his own death. Then she would have no one.

On 22 May von Greim was officially arrested by the British. He would be transferred to England and would then have to testify at the Nuremburg trials. On 24 May von Greim bit down on the suicide capsule he had been given by Hitler and died. Hanna was at last truly alone. She toyed with the idea of suicide. This was the closest she would ever come to such a decision. Without family, without friends, without even a true Germany to sustain her, what was left for Hanna Reitsch? The only thing that stayed her hand was her promise to von Greim that she would delay her own suicide so it was not associated with his. Even so, she was close to giving in.

During that first week of total loneliness Hanna had a visit from three American officers. They wanted to know if she would come to America. She would be able to fly to her heart's content and would probably become more famous than she already was. If she didn't agree, well, they would have to leave her in the hands of the American CIC (Counter Intelligence Corps). Hanna wasn't interested; she flew for Germany and Germany alone. Selling out to America struck her as a betrayal to her country. She was hardly to know that her old gliding pal Wernher von Braun was happily contemplating his own transfer to the US. She turned them down, but accepted their offer to take her to see von Greim's grave in Salzburg – perhaps they thought it might shake her loyalty enough to reconsider their invitation.

On the journey they presented her with photographs taken at Dachau concentration camp, from which they had just returned. They reminded Hanna of the pamphlet Peter Riedel had once thrust at her, the one Himmler had so adamantly denied. Hanna was stunned into speechlessness. She was genuinely a kind, giving person who would not inflict cruelty on others. The images broke her. So this was the Germany she had fought for? She tried to deny the images to herself, but it was impossible faced with the sad, emaciated faces staring at her from the black and white photographs. If this was true, then the Germany she had devoted herself to had not deserved her loyalty. Her efforts suddenly seemed so worthless.

Hanna turned this over and over in her mind. No, all was not worthless. It was Germany's leaders that had led the country astray, had committed these crimes in the name of its people, behind their backs, in secret. But Germany was much more than the last ten years, and Hanna's patriotism was based on more than the shouted speeches of a jumped-up army corporal. The Americans thought the images would be the final push to make Hanna turn her back on Germany; they were wrong, they had the opposite effect. Hanna was fired up; she would not see her country destroyed because of the crimes of a few. She would help to restore the dignity and honour of Germany. She would stay and she would fight for it. In that instant all thoughts of suicide were gone.

When Hanna paid her respects at von Greim's grave it was with a very different concept of the future than she had previously contemplated. She had thought she would be joining him soon; instead she was now going to live and prove Germany's worth. Hanna now had a firm answer for the Americans: 'I am the German test pilot Hanna Reitsch. I will always remain a German, especially in this time of her misery.' She has been criticised for this attitude. Perhaps she should have sold out to the Americans like some of her friends – it would at least have earned her more sympathy. But Hanna was not after pity:

As a German and one who was happy to live under Hitler's rule when our country had never had it so good before, how could I suddenly point a jeering finger against it at this time when fortune was against it, with my eye on a fat American carrot? I may appear in some eyes to be a hopeless idealist. But dishonest and a hypocrite – never!

Was some of that statement aimed rather pointedly at a certain von Braun? Hanna might have been foolish, but her final decision to stay in Germany through the hard times ahead deserves respect.

Hanna's future now very much depended on which of the Allies finally took her prisoner. There was quite a bit of delay and Hanna was still in Kitzbühl when news came that the French were going to take control of that area. Uncertain what the French would do with German prisoners – after all, they had been occupied for several years and had lost much of their Jewish population to Hitler's fury – Hanna and others were evacuated by the Americans to another zone under their control. Hanna arrived at Innsbruck, but her heart was drifting away to Salzburg again. She wanted to see the graves of her family and of von Greim once more. She was about to board a train to make the journey when she was accosted and politely 'arrested' by an American intelligence officer. Hanna found herself officially in the hands of the Americans. There is a slight confusion in Hanna's autobiography concerning the timing of her arrest. Hanna refers to being transferred from Kitzbühl by the Americans, but according to her biography by Judy Lomax she was already in Innsbruck. However she came to be in US custody, her story had now taken an interesting turn.

'[Hanna] concerns [herself] with the Nazi and German interpretation of "honor,"' ran the US interrogation report on Hanna after she was first taken into custody:

Reitsch herself, in answering queries, carefully weighs the 'honor' aspects of every remark and then gives her answers carefully but truthfully. The use of the word amounts practically to a fetish complex with the source and is almost an incongruous embodiment of her entire philosophy. Her constant repetition of the word is in no manner as obvious to her as it is to the interrogator, nor is the meaning the same, nor does she recognize the incongruous use she makes of the word.

Looking at Hanna with British or American eyes is always problematic for culturally her outlook on life was so different from that of the Western Allies. Her interrogators found her honest, but driven by a burning desire to maintain her 'honour' at all costs. The old military culture of Germany had instilled in its people a strong attitude of obedience, respect for rank and the need to serve superiors even when wrong. Neither Britain nor the US had similar attitudes that they could reflect on to understand the German philosophy. For much of her life Hanna was persecuted because she stuck to this old code of honour, because she did not conform to the ways of Britain and America. She never denied she had served Hitler, nor laced her later memoirs with anecdotes of moral outrage conjured up in the quiet space of hindsight. Hanna's very honesty, which she equated with her own concept of honour, condemned her.

Hanna's views on honour were no more complicated than when she tried to explain to the Americans why she asked to remain in the bunker. The US interrogation report states:

> [von Greim and Hanna] begged to be allowed to remain in the bunker, and with their own lives atone for the great wrong that Göring had perpetrated against the Führer, against the German people, and against the Luftwaffe itself. To save the 'honor' of the flyers who had died, to re-establish the 'honor' of the Luftwaffe that Göring had destroyed, and to guarantee the 'honor' of their land in the eyes of the world, they begged to remain.

This allows us to make better sense of Hanna's desire to remain in the bunker. In a heightened moment of emotion she felt that the Luftwaffe, that body of flyers to which she felt so akin and honour-bound, would be destroyed by Göring's actions. She wanted to atone for him, not so much for the Führer's benefit, though that played a part, but for the benefit of posterity. To prove that not all Germans were traitors. Such actions fit perfectly with Hanna's character and nature. When it became plain that Hitler had given up and saw only defeat, Hanna was distressed for her country and her people:

> Reitsch sank to a chair in tears, not, she claims, over the certainty of her own end but because for the first time she knew that the Führer saw the

cause as lost. Through the sobs she said, 'Mein Führer, why do you stay? Why do you deprive Germany of your life?'

Hanna knew all too well that Germany was falling apart, that internal conflicts were causing its defeat as much as its over-reaching Führer. But at least with a figurehead such as Hitler it might struggle on and survive intact. Without him the people would give in; the soldiers, sailors and airmen would admit defeat. There would be surrender and then there would be the retribution of the Russians. Hanna could not see that Germany was doomed, even with Hitler alive.

As fascinating as Hanna's complex views were, the Americans wanted to know the truth about the men who had eluded them through death. Goebbels in particular caught their attention and they asked Hanna to describe him:

[Goebbels was] insanely incensed over Göring's treachery. He strode about his small, luxurious quarters like an animal, muttering vile accusations concerning the Luftwaffe leader … 'That swine,' Goebbels said, 'who has always set himself up as the Führer's greatest support now does not have the courage to stand beside him …' All this, as Hanna saw it, was in the best theatrical manner, with much hand waving and fine gestures, made even more grotesque by the jerky up-and-down hobbling as he strode about the room. When he wasn't railing about Göring he spoke to the world about the example those in the bunker were setting for history. As on a platform and gripping a chair-back like a rostrum he said: 'We are teaching the world how men die for their honour' … [Hanna] claims too, that after listening to these tirades she and von Greim often asked each other, with a sad, head-shaking attitude, 'Are these the people who ruled our country?'

Hanna had an even lower opinion of Eva Braun, who seemed to encapsulate the worst of womanhood:

Most of [Eva's] time was occupied in finger nail polishing, changing of clothes for each hour of the day, and all the other little feminine tasks of grooming, combing and polishing … Her constant remark was, 'Poor, poor Adolf, deserted by everyone, betrayed by all' … She was simply convinced that whatever followed the Third Reich would not be fit to live in for a true German. Often she expressed sorrow for those people who were unable to destroy themselves as they would forever be forced to live without 'honor' and reduced instead to living as human beings without souls. Reitsch emphasises that Braun was apparently of rather shallow mentality, but she also agrees that she was a very beautiful woman.

Surprisingly, Hanna did not believe that Hitler had married Eva Braun before their suicide. Admittedly, the ceremony was not traditional and was probably only legal under Nazi law, but it did indeed happen. As for Hitler himself:

It is apparent from Reitsch's conversation that she held the Fuhrer in high esteem. It is probably also true when she says that her 'good' opinion suffered considerably during the closing stages of the War. She is emphatic when she describes the apparent mismanagement she observed and learned of in the bunker … Reitsch claims that Hitler the idealist died, and his country with him, because of the incompetence of Hitler the soldier and Hitler the statesman. She concludes, still with a faint touch of allegiance, that no one who knew him would deny his idealistically motivated intentions nor could they deny that he was simply infinitely incompetent to rule his country … She repeatedly remarked that never again must such a person be allowed to gain control of Germany or of any country. But strangely enough she does not appear to hold [Hitler] personally responsible for many of the wrongs and evils that she recognises completely and is quick to point out. She says rather, 'A great part of the fault lies with those who led him, lured him, criminally misdirected him, and informed him falsely. But that he himself selected the men who led him can never be forgiven.'

'Hitler ended his life as a criminal against the world,' but she is quick to add, 'he did not begin it that way. At first his thoughts were only of how to make Germany healthy again, how to give his people a life free from economic insufficiencies and social maladjustments. To do this he gambled much, with a stake that no man has the right to jeopardise – the lives of his people. This was the first great wrong, his first great failure …'

1 The Grunau Baby was one of the first gliders Hanna flew. It was Wolf Hirth's personal Grunau that she took on a misadventure into a storm cloud, narrowly escaping with her life. In later years she was presented with her own Grunau.

2 The early days of gliding required a great deal of manual effort on the part of the students, but it also generated camaraderie, unless you were a woman – as Hanna discovered. Gliding with male students such as these was fraught with difficulties. (Joost J. Bakker)

3 The Wasserkuppe became synonymous with competitive gliding during the 1920s and 1930s and Hanna longed to fly there. Her first attempt at the Rhön soaring competition held at the Wasserkuppe was a disaster – she failed even to take off. (Marco Kluber)

4 Hanna shakes hands with an officer at the Rhön soaring competition of 1936. Hanna was not renowned for doing well at the competition and never matched the great successes of her fellow gliders, such as Heini Dittmar and Peter Riedel, but she enjoyed the experience. (German Federal Archives)

5 Wolf Hirth was legendary among gliders. He had survived several crashes, though it was a road accident that cost him a leg. He was a father figure to Hanna and died doing what he loved best – gliding. (German Federal Archives)

6 The Olympics in Berlin were hugely controversial. The Americans had threatened to boycott them due to the Nazi Party's anti-Semitic stance. Hanna, having just come from flying displays at the Winter Olympics, managed to ignore the strong atmosphere of controversy in Berlin. (Josef Jindrich Sechtl)

7 The Olympics introduced Hanna to several people who would subsequently become friends or enemies, including Captain Eric Brown, then a boy visiting the stadium, who was first fascinated by Hanna, but turned against her during the war. (Fallschirmjager)

8 Hanna performed several displays, both at the Olympics and two years later, when flying the first helicopter either in or near to the Deutschlandhalle. In 1938 its interior was made to look like an African village and Hanna had to perform flying stunts inside twice a day, feeling unhappily like a circus performer. (German Federal Archives)

9 The Germans built the first viable helicopter in 1938 and though Hanna could not claim to be the very first test pilot for the machine, she was the first woman inside. In this image it is difficult to tell the gender of the pilot, but it is tempting to think it might be Hanna. She proved skilful at flying the awkward machine and even impressed Göring.

10 Ernst Udet first met Hanna in the 1930s and became very fond of her. She, in turn, respected and adored him. Udet, however, was unsuited to his rank in the Luftwaffe, and pressure from above and the political interference of Göring eventually destroyed him. Udet committed suicide the year after this picture was taken. (German Federal Archives)

11 Charles Lindbergh was one of Hanna's heroes and he witnessed her flying the helicopter. She was especially enamoured of him because Lindbergh was generous in his praise of Germany and was not entirely against Hitler or Göring. Lindbergh would later be viewed as a Nazi by the US press, but Hanna thought he was honest and charming. (Library of Congress)

12 There is still debate as to why Ernst vom Rath, a German diplomat in Paris, was assassinated. It may have been pure bad luck on his part. Whatever the cause, the result was the terrible Kristallnacht, witnessed by Hanna Reitsch, and her first indication that all was not well in Germany.

13 A synagogue is burned to the ground in Siegen. Hanna witnessed a similar scene while on a night out with staff of the DFS. She was upset to realise that most of her colleagues were revelling in the destruction. Hanna stood up for the Jews, but this is often forgotten.

14 The day after Kristallnacht the streets were littered with glass from the broken windows of Jewish shops. Observers look on in this scene while a Nazi flag is reflected in the background. Hanna was questioned over her support for the Jews in the aftermath of that night.

15 In the early days of the war Hanna became a heroine in her hometown of Hirschberg. Here she gives a Nazi salute to well-wishers greeting her on a visit home. Hirschberg celebrated Hanna in many ways, including giving her a glider. (German Federal Archives)

16 A great deal of misinformation has circulated about Hanna's relationship with Hitler. She only met him on a handful of occasions and not until the last days in the bunker was she really able to talk to him in any depth. She didn't really like him, but could not reconcile this feeling with her belief in him as a leader. (German Federal Archives)

17 Hanna is seen receiving her title of Flugkapitän, with Göring grinning inanely to himself in the background. Hanna was disappointed by her first meeting with the Führer – he picked his nose and talked poorly. She cried for several days after the meeting. (German Federal Archives)

18 Hanna's favourite plane to fly was the Dornier 17. She flew various Luftwaffe officers in just such a plane. Hans Baur, Hitler's pilot, also liked the Dornier. (German Federal Archives)

19 The Gigant was an enormous glider that pushed the limits of what gliding could achieve. In fact, it was too big and, as Hanna discovered, very heavy to handle. Ultimately, the Gigant proved ungainly and was fitted with its own engines to operate as a transport carrier.

20 This is a rare old still of the Me 163b or Komet, famous for both its great speed and manoeuvrability, and also the high death toll it took on its own pilots. It was long thought that no original images of the Komet had survived, but grainy images such as this have emerged relatively recently.

21 A beautiful Komet now resides at the United States Air Force Museum in America. Komets were found by the Americans, after Germany capitulated, in various states of build. Many had not flown. All built by slave labour, these surviving Komets are now to be found in aeronautical museums across the world. (USAF)

22 Handsome rocket scientist Wernher von Braun, the only man in this image in a dark suit, stands among various Luftwaffe officials in 1941. Despite his later denials, von Braun willingly worked on rockets for the Nazis. His various designs were usually constructed by slave labourers. (German Federal Archives)

23 Rockets, including the V1, were tested at Peenemünde. Hanna went there to test the Komet, and was present when the site was first bombed by the Allies and largely destroyed, forcing rocket tests to be moved elsewhere. (German Federal Archives)

24 Hanna had little good to say about Hermann Göring, who she believed had let down the Luftwaffe. She was dismayed when she had lunch with him to discover how ill informed he was about various new projects. His betrayal of Hitler sparked Hanna's daring flight to the Führerbunker. (German Federal Archives)

25 Perhaps understandably, many of the images of the Führerbunker show it after the fall of Berlin. Built next to the Reich Chancellery, it was connected to the Vorbunker and, via a tunnel, to the older bunkers under the Chancellery. This image shows one of the entrances and a nearby ventilation tower. (German Federal Archives)

26 Himmler sent Hanna chocolate and fruit juice after her crash in the Komet. Having always perceived him to be unkind, the gifts made Hanna reconsider and she paid him a visit after she had recovered. Himmler was not what she expected and denied the atrocities committed on the Jews. Hanna came to think he had been misrepresented, much to the shock of her friends. (German Federal Archives)

27 General Robert Ritter von Greim was a veteran of the First World War and the man who replaced Ernst Udet as a father figure to Hanna. It was because of von Greim that Hanna found herself in Hitler's bunker. Von Greim committed suicide in 1945. (German Federal Archives)

28 A view inside the bunker. The SS had attempted to burn the interior. The bunker rapidly filled with water and by the time the Russians entered and were able to take photographs there was already an inch of floodwater on the floor. The image shows the grimness of the bunker where Hanna thought she would die. (German Federal Archives)

29 Hanna formed a tentative friendship with Magda Goebbels, which made it hard to view her actions dispassionately after the war. Hanna had also become deeply attached to the Goebbels children. In the background of this image stands Magda's first son, Harald Quandt, who would cause problems for Hanna within the aviation community after the war. (German Federal Archives)

30 The ruins of the Führerbunker in 1947. At this time Hanna was still being interrogated by the Americans about the possibility the she had helped Hitler escape and controversy was rife over whether Hitler had actually survived the war. Hugh Trevor-Roper was working on his famous book, which would prove Hitler had perished and portray Hanna in an unflattering light. (German Federal Archives)

31 The unfortunate Joachim Küttner was a gliding friend of Hanna who discovered he had Jewish ancestors when the Third Reich came to power. Banished from gliding – much to Hanna's outrage – he found it necessary to leave Germany. Hanna helped him get work abroad and eventually he ended up working on the US space programme, ironically alongside another of Hanna's gliding friends – Wernher von Braun.

32 Hanna had few friends in Germany when she was asked to go to India as a special ambassador and promote gliding. She desperately wanted to meet Prime Minister Jawaharlal Nehru (pictured here on the left) and actually managed to take him up in her glider. She became very friendly with all the Nehru family.

33 When her father died, Indira Ghandi (*née* Nehru) took his place for several years, until her assassination. She often wrote to Hanna and Hanna sent presents to Indira's two sons, including model aircraft.

34 After Hitler, Hanna's relationship with the president of Ghana, Kwame Nkrumah, was her biggest mistake. Though he preached freedom for Africans, he was in fact a dictator. A military coup ousted Nkrumah from power while he was out of the country. Hanna visited him in exile. He is seen here before the coup, speaking with President John F. Kennedy.

35 Karl Ritter was a movie producer with strong ties to the Nazi Party. He made propaganda films and befriended Hanna when she starred in a Ufa production. Demonstrating Hanna's complete lack of common sense when it came to politics, she is here seen sitting with Ritter post-war, when her reputation was at its worst and many deemed her still a Nazi. (Michael Ritter)

Hanna cannot be defended for her blind faith in the Führer, nor for her apologies for him even after the full extent of the Nazis' crimes were known. Hanna had believed in Hitler and could not now accept that she had been so utterly wrong. To do so would not only render the last six years worthless, but impart blame upon her, as on all Germans, for obeying and supporting so evil a man. In this view she was not alone; many Germans found themselves thinking along the same lines.

Hanna would defend Hitler to the very end. After his death, she found herself in the same room as Himmler once more. Determined to learn the truth, she asked him if he had really betrayed Hitler and contacted the Allies behind his back. 'But, of course,' Himmler answered with his ever jovial smile. Stunned, Hanna accused him of high treason. 'High treason?' Himmler laughed. 'No! You'll see, history will weigh it differently. Hitler wanted to continue the fight. He was mad with his pride and his honour. He wanted to shed more German blood when there was none left to flow. Hitler was insane. It should have been stopped long ago.' What words from the commander of the Gestapo and SS! Hanna, still reeling from news of Hitler's death and the dread of capitulation, let her temper get the better of her. 'Insane? I came from him less than 36 hours ago. He died for the cause he believed in. He died bravely and filled with the honour you speak of, while you and Göring and the rest must now live as branded traitors and cowards.' 'I did as I did to save German blood, to rescue what was left of our country,' Himmler said. Hanna retorted, 'You speak of German blood, Herr Reichsführer? You speak of it now? You should have thought of it years ago, before you became identified with the useless shedding of so much of it!'

Despite her contradictions, the Americans felt Hanna was at least trying to help them and Germany, as well as slowly reconciling herself to the horrors of Nazism:

> She claims that the only reason she remained alive is for the sake of the truth; to tell the truth about Göring, 'the shallow showman', to tell the truth about Hitler, 'the criminal incompetent', and to tell the German people the truth about the dangers of the form of government that the Third Reich gave them. She believes that she is fulfilling much of this mission when she speaks to the interrogator. It is therefore felt that her remarks may be considered as her deepest efforts at sincerity and honesty.

At the moment she is undergoing a severe mental struggle in an effort to reconcile her conception of 'honor' with her denunciation of Göring, of Himmler and of Hitler himself … it appears she is striving to exert a progressively more democratic influence over her countrymen.

Hanna was at least trying to make amends for her misguided past.

She was to remain under Allied scrutiny for five years. During that time her US interrogators tried to decide if she might be any use in an intelligence operation codenamed 'Skylark', tracking wanted Germans using Hanna either consciously or unconsciously, through her Luftwaffe contacts. They were also concerned that Hanna might be aiding wanted Germans to escape the country. Whether through good fortune or common sense, Hanna did nothing while under close surveillance by the Americans to make them think she was actively working to aid Nazis. In 1948 a sting was orchestrated to try and catch Hanna out as she was associating with old friends suspected of being involved in an escape organisation. Hanna was approached at her home in Hamburg by a German working for the Americans. He claimed he had once been with the SS and, along with seventeen others, had escaped from an internment camp where many SS men were held. He asked if Hanna could help him escape Germany, or at least to reach the American zone (they were currently in Hamburg, which was in the British zone). Hanna sobbed at hearing his story, but she answered firmly that she could not help him.

Suspicions of Hanna were not unfounded. In March 1947 she enquired about two former friends who were being held for trial at Nuremburg, accused of conducting medical experiments on concentration camp inmates, and even gave evidence to help one of them. A month later she wrote to Field Marshal Kesselring's defence lawyer urging him to do everything in his power to prevent injustice as it might deeply affect the German people and build new hatred towards the Allies. Hanna's assumption that her missive would spur the defence lawyer into greater effort probably points to her sense of self-importance.

The most significant part of Hanna's intelligence was her knowledge of the last few days in the bunker. A great number of the key witnesses to Hitler's end had either committed suicide, been shot escaping or been captured by the Russians. The Russians had been first on the scene.

The SS had tried to burn the interior of the bunker, but without thinking an SS man had switched off the ventilation system – after all it was not needed now – and this had starved the fire before it could do any great damage. Water had then flooded in and the Russians waded through the strange subterranean lair picking up discarded documents and taking an avid interest in the blood-stained sofa where Hitler had shot himself. By the time the British and Americans arrived, the Russians were firmly in charge. They had captured several eyewitnesses, including Hans Baur and Heinz Linge, and were interrogating them in their own brutal fashion. Baur had seen the bodies burning. Linge had seen the corpses of Hitler and Eva being removed. Their testimony, repeated over and over, implied firmly that Hitler was dead. But far away in Moscow, Stalin was not impressed. Locked away in his stubborn paranoia he nursed the idea that Hitler had escaped his fate. Even when charred remains were discovered in the spot Hitler was said to have burned, Stalin remained unimpressed. Over the next few months the Russians would muddy the issue of Hitler's death or survival by producing endless scenarios and 'evidence' both for and against. More than once they issued photographs of 'Hitler's corpse' which were fakes and fuelled the conspiracy theory that Hitler had had a 'double' slain to confuse the Allies and enable him to escape.

If he had escaped, it would have been by plane. Any other method would have been virtually impossible in the last days of Berlin. There were two candidates for pilot of that plane: Hans Baur and Hanna Reitsch. The Americans questioned Hanna closely about the possibility that she flew Hitler out of Berlin and this led to one of the main myths concerning Hanna – that she was Hitler's pilot. Because of this erroneous conjecture, it became commonly assumed that she had often flown the Führer to various destinations. Hanna struggled to understand this assumption; to her it was perfectly plain that she had never flown Hitler. It only required a slight knowledge of the Führer to appreciate that she would never have been his pilot. Hitler only trusted a couple of pilots to fly him who he had known for over a decade (indeed, Hans Baur insisted he was the only pilot Hitler trusted). As long as Baur was in the bunker, Hitler would not have considered flying with anyone else.

Adolf Hitler had an overpowering fear of flying, not unnatural in the early days of aviation, when getting airborne was never 100 per cent safe. In 1920, during the Kapp Putsch (an attempted coup to overthrow the Weimar Republic led by Wolfgang Kapp and Walther von Lüttwitz), Hitler had flown with Ritter von Greim from Munich to Berlin. Critical business had pressed Hitler to travel at speed and to risk a flight in a military plane. The experience lingered with the future Führer; bundled into a biplane with open cockpits, flying through rough weather with limited visibility and buffeted about until he was sick, the journey had not enamoured him with air travel. Matters were not improved when von Greim made a forced landing in territory under the rebels' control. By the time Hitler arrived in Berlin the putsch had been crushed and he bitterly stormed that he would have been better off staying at home.

Several years later, in 1932, Hitler overcame his fear of flying just enough to accept the services of pilot Hans Baur. Baur was a flying veteran of the First World War and nearly 40 when he became Hitler's private pilot. Typically Aryan in his looks, he was a thick set, stocky man, with a receding hairline and a face and neck that seemed to merge into one bulky block on his shoulders. A party member and an honorary SS man, he was as tough as they came and very little fazed him. His loyalty to Hitler turned into friendship and the Führer was best man at his wedding to his second wife in 1936. Hitler liked Baur's practical, no-nonsense nature. Baur was not a sycophant and spoke plainly to the Führer. In many regards he could be viewed as a male equivalent of Hanna Reitsch, who also saw no reason to sugar coat facts for her leader. Or perhaps that is just the nature of pilots?

From 1932 Hitler flew with Baur on all but one occasion. In that instance Baur was in Moscow, having escorted Ribbentrop to the Russian capital. Hitler wanted to be in Berlin when Ribbentrop returned, so took a chance with another pilot. He hated the experience so much he later told Baur, 'I thought I was going to die on that return flight without you.' There is a suggestion that Hitler had a second regular pilot, but Baur is adamant in his memoirs that this was never the case. Even if it was, this second candidate was not Hanna.

Baur was in the bunker with Hitler throughout the last days of the Third Reich. There would have been no call for Hitler to leave with Hanna when his pet pilot was ready and waiting to leave at any moment. In fact, Baur remained in the bunker until the end; he glimpsed the cremation of his master before he made a desperate attempt to escape

Berlin, only to fall into the hands of the Russians. For ten years he was at their mercy, for much of the time being forced to tell and retell over and over the story of those last days in the bunker. Though Baur was certain Hitler was dead (he had spoken with those who had burned the body), the Russians were concerned that he still lived and tortured Baur to try and get him to recant and say that Hitler had escaped.

Ten years of Russian captivity did little to soften Baur's feelings towards the Allies but hardened his belief in and loyalty to the Führer. When he was finally repatriated in 1955 he set about writing his memoirs, giving a frank account of life as Hitler's pilot and, though not explicitly justifying the worst atrocities, firmly made it plain he was still a National Socialist. Ironically, Baur never received the same level of condemnation as Hanna, though his memoirs were in some regards far closer to Nazi propaganda than anything Hanna wrote. He presented Hitler as a very ordinary man, told how nice he could be and worked as hard to spin a good story out of the Nazi mess as Goebbels would have done. Yet Hanna was the one who was vilified, not the man who had spent most of the 1930s and 1940s piloting Hitler and regarded him as a friend who had been failed by history.

Hanna was potentially a good candidate for inspiring co-operation with the Allies in post-war Germany. She had never been a member of the Nazi Party and now honestly declared to her interrogators that so much of what Hitler had done was foolish and wrong. There were some who thought she could be very useful, but before they could implement her ideas Hanna was moved by CIC to a prison in Salzburg. This was a far cry from the cosy chats she had previously enjoyed with interrogators; her cell was small and sparse, her guards pushed her around and there was none of the friendliness she had previously known. Hanna could only be glad her parents were not alive to see her treated in this manner. In the long hours of loneliness she scratched on the walls of her cell with her nails some of the verses her beloved mother had composed and sent to her. It soon became clear that the Americans were still obsessed with the idea that Hanna had helped Hitler escape the bunker.

Eric Brown, now working for British intelligence, managed to get an interview with Hanna during this period. He had been briefed to ask her about technical matters concerning the Me 163. Hanna was in a dreadful state when he found her: 'She was an emotional wreck …

and poured out more than she intended.' Brown had grown resentful towards his one-time heroine over the course of the war; her brief association with Hitler was enough to confirm in his mind that she was a 'fanatical Nazi'. This is clearly inaccurate. Hanna never joined the Nazi Party, nor was she politically motivated during the war. She supported Hitler because he was the German leader and to act against him would have made her a traitor to Germany. It was that 'honour' again. Eric Brown was very bitter about the aviatrix he had admired all those years ago at the Olympics, and his opinion of her was therefore highly biased. In contrast, Hanna's American interrogators, who had made no prior judgements on her, were convinced that she was opposed to Nazism. Unfortunately, Eric Brown's opinion is often taken as gospel without an understanding of his deep resentment and disappointment. In later years, Hanna would avoid him and this only enhanced his bitterness. Meanwhile, another British agent, Hugh Trevor-Roper, was investigating the exact circumstances of Hitler's last days in the bunker in order to prove that he really had died. Political tensions, worsened by the Russians' games, were making it essential that rumours of Hitler's survival were laid to rest. Trevor-Roper tried to get access to Hanna as a key witness, but was prevented by the Americans and had to make do with the interrogation reports they had compiled. This was later to cause Hanna some consternation.

Hanna was once more invited to America. At a reunion with Wernher von Braun, orchestrated by the Americans, attempts were made to get her to leave Germany. Hanna was more resolved than ever to stay and try to help her beleaguered country. She refused the offer and was shuffled between prisons, finally arriving at Oberursel in November. Hanna was indignant, feeling that she was being treated like a top Nazi criminal just because she had refused to sell out to the Americans. She couldn't fathom why she was so resented simply for being a loyal German. She could not see how she could have behaved differently.

Hanna was eventually moved to more comfortable accommodations in a large house converted by the Americans into a holding centre for military and political leaders awaiting interrogation or trial. Hanna was the only woman there, surrounded by a constantly changing group of fifty or so high-ranking Nazi officials awaiting their fate. Some were destined to be executed, but others were more valuable as potential witnesses and informants. At last Hanna had a proper bedroom and people to talk with. She formed a close friendship with Schwerin von Krosigk, Hitler's finance minister, with whom she could hold lengthy, cathartic conversations. Krosigk told her that Hitler had suffered a personality change brought on by the dangerous attentions of his personal doctors. This brought Hanna great relief, making her believe that her loyalty had not been entirely misplaced – she could blame the doctors rather than Hitler for the catastrophic defeat of Germany. Another great comfort was learning that her brother Kurt was still alive. She was not the sole Reitsch to survive the war.

The Americans now had a very comprehensive account from Hanna of her last days in the bunker and her opinion of Hitler and Nazism. They thought they could use this to their advantage and arranged a press conference where Hanna would repeat the many criticisms she had made of Hitler and his policies. To have a German making such statements, particularly one who was a well-known part of the regime, would greatly aid the Allies' work within Germany. Things did not go to plan, however. Hanna was briefed before the conference by an obnoxious officer called Captain Cohn, who informed her that she must either denounce Hitler and become rich and famous, or defend him out of misplaced honour and loyalty and suffer for the rest of her life. Cohn was right about her options, but the way he presented them to Hanna ruffled her feathers. Infuriated at his bullying tactics, she stormed into the conference with her temper flared and the foolish obstinacy that always emerged when she was truly angry got the better of her. To 'get back' at Cohn she denied calling Hitler a criminal and said she had been willingly loyal to him and would be so again if she could go back in time. Cohn retrieved her after only a few questions, cursing her stupidity. Hanna was jubilant at her own defiance; as ever, she was completely blind to the wider consequences of her actions.

In the end her outburst didn't matter. The articles published about Hanna's experiences were based on her interrogation reports. When Hanna first saw the news pieces she was appalled. She denied having said much of what was written and was mortified that critics of Hitler would perceive her as more loyal than she really was, while supporters would consider her a traitor. Hanna had not expected the things she said during interrogation to be made public and it upset her deeply that her inner thoughts on the Nazi regime and her Führer were now available to everyone who read a newspaper. Hanna was always a private person and these reports seemed a violation of that privacy. Attempting to distance herself from such embarrassment, she convinced herself she had not said the things reported, or that she had been misunderstood. By this point, she had also lost her early good opinion of her captors. Her trust in them had been betrayed and she had been housed with fanatics prone to talking about the 'good old days'. As Hanna always tended to absorb other people's views rather than create her own, this influence had impacted on her memories of the last days of the war. Hanna would be even more furious when she saw what a young British writer had put in his bestselling book concerning her a few years later.

As Hanna Reitsch sat in the company of American interrogators, so the place that had come close to being her grave crumbled. The Führerbunker was never meant to be a permanent structure and with the diesel generators and pumping system shut down, it rapidly rotted in on itself. Groundwater seeped in, so by the time the Russians staged photo shoots in the bunker there was an inch of water on the floor. When Hugh Trevor-Roper visited the bunker as part of his research on Hitler's final days, he found himself:

> wading through the flooded passages and noisome, cell-like rooms ... overwhelmed by a sense of terrible irony. An all-powerful tyrant, whose bullying oratory had electrified vast crowds at mass rallies, had passed his last weeks hiding underground in this squalid burrow, ranting to a dwindling entourage. As he fingered sodden, disintegrating papers that the Russians had unaccountably left undisturbed, Hugh identified the megalomaniac architectural plans that Hitler and Goebbels had studied together while overhead the Russian shells rained down constantly on their ruined capital ...

By 1947 the observation towers and concrete exit bunker were in ruins. In 1949 an attempt was made to destroy the bunker completely, but its construction proved effective against explosives (Hitler would have been pleased!) and the demolition remained incomplete. Soil was heaped onto the remains and raked over, and for decades a mound remained to mark the last headquarters of Hitler. Finally, in the 1980s the site was reclaimed for the use of living Germans. The mound was destroyed, the holes in the ground filled in, the last remains of the observation towers removed and a road and apartment block built on top. Ironically, even the Führerbunker would outlast Hanna Reitsch. She was very ill when she was finally released from American custody. Her legs had become severely swollen and her lips always had a bluish tinge, suggesting poor circulation. It is likely that this was a consequence of her battle with scarlet fever; the damage to her heart was finally showing itself. Hanna was allowed a sort of freedom, while constantly watched by the Americans. Over the next several months her initial rapport with her early interrogators, and thus respect for the Allies, faltered and finally failed. The publication of Hugh Trevor-Roper's *The Last Days of Hitler* was the final straw.

British intelligence officer Huge Trevor-Roper was prowling the British sector of Germany in 1945 when he stumbled upon Dick White, the then chief of the British Counter-Intelligence Bureau. Over a lengthy drinking session the conversation drifted to Hitler's bunker. Dick White was adamant that without a detailed analysis of the last days of the Führer all manner of myths and lies would percolate about what had happened in April. 'No one has yet made any systematic study of the evidence, or even found any evidence, and we are going to have all kinds of difficulty unless something is done,' White told Trevor-Roper, his eyes almost popping from his head. 'Already the Germans are saying that the old boy's alive, and the journalists are encouraging them, and the Russians are accusing us of concealing Eva Braun.'

Trevor-Roper took the hint. He set out to write a definitive report on those final days in the bunker, interviewing those witnesses who were alive and accessible to the British, including Albert Speer, Hitler's former architect. Hanna Reitsch was not available to him in person, but he gained access to her American interrogation files. Over the next few weeks he drafted a report based on what he had learned and submitted it to Dick White and others in November 1945. White was pleased by the scope of the work, but he wanted to disseminate the real story of Hitler's death further than a few desks in MI5 – he felt it important that the British, American, German and Russian publics knew the truth as well. The latter would be difficult as for many years Russia refused to allow the sale of the book. (Stalin had decreed that Hitler was alive and no one argued with Stalin, even if he was wrong!) *The Last Days of Hitler* was published in 1947, not without some hesitancy from the head of the Secret Intelligence Service. It was widely acclaimed and a commercial success, though not everyone was happy. Maurice Bowra wrote to Evelyn Waugh, not without a hint of jealousy, 'Trevor-Roper is a fearful man, short-sighted, with dripping eyes, shows off all the time, sucks up to me, boasts, is far from poor owing to his awful book, on every page of which there is a howler.'

It was natural that Trevor-Roper's book would cause controversy; there were plenty of people who would criticise his findings and who adamantly believed that Hitler lived. The Jesuits were not impressed with comments made in the first edition that Goebbels was once the prize-pupil of a Jesuit seminary and comparisons of his propaganda methods to Jesuit teaching. This was one of the few instances of Trevor-Roper failing to back up his evidence and making a blunder. He corrected it in later editions, remarking, 'The Jesuits still furiously rumble in dark, and hitherto unknown, organs issuing from Dublin and the less rational quarters of Liverpool. The noise of their anathemas reaches me not unpleasantly through the Press-cutting Agencies.'

The Jesuits had a general complaint, but Hanna's was a direct one. Trevor-Roper had used the statements she had made to the Americans to flesh out her arrival in the bunker with von Greim, painting a vivid picture of a sycophantic young woman begging to die alongside her master. Hanna was furious; not least because she now claimed that some of the things said about Hitler, in her own testimony, were inaccurate and wrong. She had not said such things, she complained, even though they were in black and white in her interrogation file. Heartbroken and embarrassed to see her own words of the Führer now repeated nationally and internationally, she protested to Trevor-Roper, demanding he make changes and threatening legal action if he didn't. Trevor-Roper conceded slightly, toning down his paragraphs on Hanna, though explaining it was all based on her own evidence in the American interrogation reports. Hanna was still mortified. She had publically denigrated her own hero. Her sense of honour and fear of what others would think mingled with her shame. The interrogation reports, in her mind, had been for the Americans alone. She had never thought they would be used in such a manner and to undermine the man she had served so loyally.

She felt increasingly persecuted and slandered, treated like a criminal or portrayed as a sycophantic Nazi. Poor naïve Hanna still failed to understand the mind games of politics, or how her honesty about her thoughts, feelings and actions during the war might be used against her. A cannier person would have held their tongue or even accepted the American offer. Hanna didn't and her life was a misery. There were all sorts of rumours flying about her – she was allegedly driving huge American cars, she was sleeping with American officers, and she had had affairs with nearly every high-ranked Nazi – all malicious and hurtful. Hanna felt very alone. Throughout her life she had made few close friendships, instead relying on her family for emotional support. Without them, she had no one to turn to and her mind kept wandering to the suicide capsule she still had in her possession.

A Catholic priest saved her. A friend of the Heuberger family, Father Freidel Volkmar, found Hanna in tears one day and extracted a convoluted confession. 'You must stick it out,' he persuaded her. 'Walk through the streets with your head high, even when other people are pointing their finger at you. With God you are stronger than all of them together.' Volkmar became Hanna's new father figure and with his support she was able to survive the onslaught of rumours and half-truths against her. He was a much-needed ally when Hanna faced her denazification hearing. Volkmar contacted her old friends and requested favourable letters that could be read out at the hearing. One came from Joachim Küttner; as a half-Jew who had been persecuted by the Nazis, his testimony on Hanna's behalf was very significant.

Volkmar also put her in touch with Lotte Schiffler, a Catholic who was working to rehabilitate refugees and who, during the war, had been part of the resistance against Hitler. Schiffler wondered how she would get on with the woman people had called Hitler's heroine, they clearly had very different views and had worked against each other in the war. Hanna, however, surprised her. 'There was a tiny girl, small, dainty, with clear searching eyes. I felt immediately protective. She had suffered so much. I was determined that nothing more must be allowed to happen to that child!' Hanna was 35! But her size and strange innocence often made her seem younger and inspired protective feelings in others. A similar change of opinion occurred when Hanna was introduced to Yvonne Pagniez, a member of the French Resistance who had spent time in, and escaped from, the notorious Ravensbrück concentration camp. Pagniez had, naturally, heard of Hanna and expected to meet an ardent, arrogant Nazi. 'My astonishment was boundless when I saw before me not the Valkyrie I had imagined, but a tiny person who looked so modest, whose body seemed so frail, and who smiled hesitantly at me as she wiped away her tears.' They became friends.

Hanna was locked into a depression brought on by the trauma and tragedy of the last few years. Her health was not at its best and Schiffler felt a project might ease some of her mental anguish. She suggested Hanna write an autobiography. Entranced by the idea, which would offer the opportunity to counteract the lies circulating about her, Hanna went into seclusion to work on the book. She showed the first draft to her old gliding friend Mathias Wieman. He told her it was too personal and only people who knew her would be able to understand the idealism she expressed in her text. She would have to rewrite it. Hanna changed her style and spoke into a microphone rather than write down her words, allowing Schiffler to do the typing.

Her first book, *Flying is my Life*, was published in 1951. Its reception was mixed. Five bookshops in Frankfurt initially stocked the book and then withdrew it because of anonymous threatening letters. Hanna, illogically, blamed the Americans, as she blamed them for all that had gone wrong in her life since 1945. Despite problems, the book sold well enough to earn Hanna some money. She was in financial difficulties now her test pilot days were over and the book helped to tide her over. Her life was now in tatters; there was no more flying in Germany so she devoted her time to helping others, volunteering for charities that watched over refugees. It was exhausting work and provided an outlet for Hanna's energy, but she still dreamed of flying and she couldn't quite give up the hope that one day she might be up in the sky once again.

11

ADRIFT IN AFRICA

As the 1940s turned into the 1950s Hanna hoped to leave behind the sinister shadow of Nazism and Hitler. The last five years had been bitter and full of disappointment. Hanna was haunted by American agents determined to catch her out for the slightest transgression. Worse, however, was the condemnation of her fellow Germans. It seemed the wider world found it easier to forgive her than did her neighbours.

In 1951 Hanna flew publically again. The Allies had remembered the gliding loophole the Germans had exploited after the First World War, and after 1945 had slammed down restrictions on so much as making a model aeroplane to try and combat the German desire to fly. It hadn't worked, and there were rumours in 1949 that Hanna, among others, had competed in gliding at the Wasserkuppe. Anticipating the inevitable, the Allies relaxed their rules so that in the second year of the 1950s Hanna was not only able to swoop through the skies without secrecy, but could lecture on the subject of gliding. Hanna was an enthusiastic speaker, her arms told the story for her as she waved them about, demonstrating each word with a flick of her hands, a sweep of the arm. She conjured with the air. Some were not impressed. 'Hear Hanna once and you've heard it all!' was a spiteful comment circulated by some, who did not know the effort and careful preparation Hanna put into each talk. It has to be said that Hanna sometimes came across as boastful, egotistical and just a little prone to exaggeration.

Wolf Hirth was also busy. He had set up a business making gliders just before the war. During the conflict he had made parts for some of the fighters and bombers. Post-war he survived by turning his factories to making furniture, but it was wholly unsatisfying to an aviator. In 1951 the first legitimate gliding contest at the Wasserkuppe was held. Hanna shared a caravan with Wolf Hirth and his wife. Shortly after, the German Aero Club was reinstated with Hirth as its president. Germany was flying again; Hirth resumed his business making training gliders, and Hanna took to the air in the first post-war Focke-Wulf glider. Before the year was out, the Americans estimated that there were 750 gliding clubs in West Germany.

Hanna could not have been happier. She finally felt she was putting Hitler behind her when she flew in a contest in Madrid in 1952 and won a bronze medal. Her elation was short lived. The German press, rather than praising her success, printed a picture of her with Otto Skorzeny (of Mussolini rescue fame), who was known to be living in Madrid, and implied that she had gone to Spain simply to make contact with a fellow Nazi. If Hanna thought she could redeem herself in German eyes by flying successes she was mistaken. In 1954 an international gliding competition was to be held in Derbyshire, England. Hanna was part of a West German team set to attend. Then, on the Saturday before the competition, the German Aero Club was instructed by the government in Bonn to withdraw her. The British press had linked Hanna's name with Hitler and the West German embassy in London had grown panicked. Hanna had no option but to leave the team. Her teammates offered to stand by her, but the authorities had other ideas and it was decided that it was in the best interests of international relations for them to attend without her. In Britain the press reported that Hanna had withdrawn for 'personal reasons', a complete lie and Hanna seethed with righteous indignation. Never one to let a wrong go by unmentioned, she wasted no time in finding a *Daily Mail* reporter who would record the true story of her discharge from the team. For once Hanna's fury attracted support in the German newspapers, but it alienated other gliders, who felt she should have held her tongue. Heinz Kensche wrote to her angrily: 'Could you not for once have put yourself in the background and have kept quiet for the sake of gliding and of your colleagues?'

Hanna found it impossible to forget the snub. When she competed at the next International in France in 1956 she was awkward around the British and defensive about what she said. Hanna had always believed gliding should rise above politics. She had failed to appreciate human nature yet again. In 1958 matters came to a head with the International being held in Poland. Hanna had mixed feelings concerning the competition; Silesia was now officially part of Poland, her old hometown of Hirschberg had been renamed. There was something uncomfortable about returning after more than a decade to the place she had first learned to fly. Hanna agreed to go, but as a spectator, ceding her place on the team to a glider named Dr Ernst Frowein, who had repeatedly just missed earning a place. The gesture, which Hanna perceived as one of generosity, was fraught with difficulties. First, the rules of the Aero Club stated a person could only concede their seat to the next pilot below them on the list, which was not Frowein. Second, Frowein was not a well-liked individual and his performance in a glider could be erratic at best. From the team's perspective he was not likely to win or to represent Germany well. Hanna, as usual, was oblivious to these controversies when she made her decision. After weeks of arguments, Frowein declared he would not accept the place anyway and Hanna was officially reinstated – she would be gliding in Poland.

But now the Polish authorities refused her a visa without explanation. Aggrieved, Hanna turned to the new president of the Aero Club, Harald Quandt, son of Magda Goebbels and stepson of the notorious Dr Goebbels. Poland had refused the visa two days before the West German team were due to leave. An emergency meeting of the remaining gliders generated support for Hanna, but Quandt persuaded them all to continue to Poland and lodge a protest with the Polish Aero Club and the FAI (the World Air Sports Federation). Hanna returned to Berlin with one ray of hope; she was convinced that if the protest failed and her visa was not granted, her teammates would withdraw from the competition in support. She was sorely mistaken. No visa came and Quandt had her replaced. The team flew as planned, Quandt arguing that politics and sport should not mix. In short, Hanna was not that important to worry about; gliding was what really mattered. Hanna felt deeply betrayed. Had she not flown out the last letters of Quandt's mother and stepfather in those final dark days of war? That one of the West German team became World Champion only made her more bitter – what was success when gained at the expense of team loyalty?

The furore grew; Hanna wanted an apology from the Aero Club, the club refused but was happy for Hanna to remain a member. The Alte Adler, an association of veteran pilots, joined the fray on Hanna's side and found that the Aero Club had acted improperly and should make a public apology. Similarly, the head of the International Gliding Commission found that Hanna had been unfairly penalised. The Aero Club stuck to its guns and refused to make even a gesture of apology. Slowly it became plain that it would not back down. Hanna's supporters realised they were not going to win and quietly suggested she let the matter drop. Hanna could not, her honour would not allow it and her stubbornness and pride – once such useful commodities in test flying – now locked her into a losing battle. She severed connections with the Aero Club, effectively meaning she could not fly in any competition in West Germany. Hanna had once refused the Americans because she would only fly in Germany, where she had honour. Now she did not even have that. What had she gained from refusing to flee to America with the rest? Wernher von Braun was making a name for himself in the US space programme. She could surely have done the same within US gliding. Instead, she had stayed in Germany – for what? She was an embarrassment, a reminder of how far Germany had fallen. No achievement would wipe that stain from her. Hanna realised that Germany was no longer her home, she would have to move on. The question that remained was, where to?

The offer to go to India as an ambassador for West Germany was both unexpected and ironic considering the pains to which the government had gone to avoid Hanna going to England as a representative of her country. Eight years earlier India had become a republic; its first president, Rajendra Prasad, took office on 26 January, the same day the new constitution came into force. Britain had relinquished control of its Indian colonies in the late forties, enabling Jawaharlal Nehru to become the first prime minister of India as part of an interim government in 1947. In 1958 Nehru was serving as minister of finance, his daughter Indira Gandhi (she married Feroze Gandhi, no relation to Mahatma Gandhi) was serving as Chief of Staff in the government, a role in itself remarkable for a woman at that time. Hanna desperately wanted to meet them both, but was informed that it was impossible.

Still, the chance to travel again and be of some use was welcome. India had several gliding clubs by the 1950s, including one at Delhi. Unfortunately, a jet fighter had crashed into the hangar at Delhi and destroyed all the club's gliders. The West German diplomat Georg

Steltzer suggested his country donate a replacement glider to generate goodwill. India was an up-and-coming country, with great potential and Germany could use all the links and support it could get. It was decided to send the glider, along with an ambassador – Hanna had served such purposes well prior to the war and she was a known name, as well as being a woman, which might appeal to certain elements in India. Hanna accepted the offer gladly enough and found herself in India in April 1959. India is a busy, vibrant country. Hanna was overwhelmed by the noise and colour. The heat was oppressive, but the joyous welcome she received overcame all else and she was suddenly happy. She hopped from aerobatic gliding displays to cocktail parties with ease, and talked to as many people as would listen. It was like the old days once more, and at least all Hanna had to worry about was flying. Originally invited for two weeks, Hanna stayed for two months.

One aspect of Hanna's life that had floundered since the death of her mother was her spirituality. Always a slightly superficial Christian, the loss of her mother's guidance had caused her to drift. A gulf had opened up within her that she hardly knew how to fill. Now she was attracted to the various forms of Eastern religion, particularly medita-tion. It seemed to Hanna that this might help combat her anxiety and emptiness. She went on a pilgrimage to Pondicherry, where an 80-year-old Frenchwoman held court as 'Mother' of an Ashram community. Her followers were a wide collection of nationalities who scorned worldly wealth and placed great value, instead, in meditation. Despite this the Ashram could boast schools, a university, a laboratory, sports field, tennis court and swimming pool! Hanna met the aged Mother and gained great comfort from her words: 'I recognise you,' said the Mother. 'You don't only fly aeroplanes, your soul flies higher than any aeroplane. We shall see each other again and shall meet in another world.'

Hanna could not have hoped for a better confirmation of her own thoughts on flying. She left uplifted, and more exciting news was soon on its way. Jawaharlal Nehru wanted her to take him gliding! Nehru was one of the most famous political figures of the period, in his late sixties and only five years off his own death from a stroke and heart attack, he was at his height in 1958–59. Some have argued that had Nehru retired in 1958 he would not just be remembered as India's best prime minis-ter but as one of the great statesmen of the modern world. This quiet, sage-looking man with a sad smile had been working for Indian independence from 1912. Educated in England, he had an insight into the powers which held India as a colony and was a staunch supporter of Gandhi. He spent much of his daughter's childhood in prison for his protests, where he read books by Karl Marx, though he was wise enough to see the shortcomings of Marxism.

The various troubles of India after it became independent had told on Nehru and aged him considerably, stripping his flesh from his bones and making him look two decades older than he really was. He was constantly under guard and had survived three assassination attempts (and would survive a fourth in 1961), but his government was taking no chances and the glider Hanna intended to use was put under twenty-four-hour watch to ensure it was not tampered with. To put Nehru, or rather his bodyguards, at ease, Hanna proposed taking Georg Steltzer for a flight before she flew the prime minister.

Gliding appealed to Nehru, who believed in people soaring above their petty problems. It was also a chance to escape the constant pressures and anxieties that afflicted him on the ground. He stayed up in the air with Hanna for two hours, enjoying the feeling of complete freedom. The next day Hanna was invited to lunch with Nehru and Indira Gandhi. Hanna could hardly believe her luck. She accepted the invitation excitedly and, though she struggled to eat food with her fingers like her hosts, she found it easy to fall into conversation with them. Indira had also been educated in England, so the talk could be held in English, which Hanna spoke almost fluently. Nehru was particularly curious about the rumour that Hanna had been Hitler's mistress. Once again the shadow of the former dictator loomed over her, but Hanna did not mind recounting her time in the bunker. At least with this audience she could speak openly and would not be automatically condemned. In fact, Nehru liked her enough that he insisted she move into the prime minister's house for her last few days in India. This was the first time a German had been his personal guest since the war.

Hanna met Nehru's grandsons Rajiv aged 15 and Sanjay aged 13, who were enthusiastic, as only young boys can be, over all things to do with flying. They showed Hanna their model aeroplanes and escorted her around Delhi. At her final lecture three generations of the Nehru family – Nehru, Indira, and Rajiv and Sanjay – were all in attendance.

Hanna's confidence could not have been boosted higher. She returned to Germany absolutely ecstatic, much of her old faith in herself restored. She remained in contact with the various members of the Nehru family over the next few years. She was saddened by Nehru's death, but was pleased to hear of the progress of Rajiv and Sanjay. She had always felt it important to express her concerns about communism to the prime minister and to advise him time and again to avoid it, which makes a later decision in her life all the more odd.

Back in West Germany her feud with the Aero Club had not ended. There had been talk while she was away that she was suffering from religious mania, or a mental breakdown. Hanna was hurt by the suggestions. She had indeed brought back spiritual ideas from India, largely meditation and yoga, but these by no means implied she was mentally unstable. Hanna had no prospects of flying in Germany, so she travelled further afield. She was welcomed in Finland, where so many years before she had encouraged gliding, and six months later, at the suggestion of Wernher von Braun, she visited America and was received at the White House by President Kennedy. She also met the 'Whirly Girls', an international association of women helicopter pilots founded in 1955. Hanna discovered she had the honour of being Whirly Girl No 1 because she had been the first woman to fly a helicopter. For these women Hanna was a pioneer and there was no talk of her later, unfortunate, associations.

Not all was forgotten, however. Hanna was invited to give a talk at the space centre where von Braun and another old friend, Joachim Küttner, were working on US space rockets. She was present at the launch of the second Saturn rocket – a monstrous, roaring thing that made the rockets Hanna had once flown seem impossibly small – before giving a lecture about her time in India. She was perturbed to find a swastika draped over the reading desk. It was hastily removed and it was the only indication that someone was unhappy about her presence.

America was restored in Hanna's opinion. She left with a feeling of warmth and friendliness. At home again, she was still feuding with the Aero Club, but her contributions to aviation were finally accepted by some of the German aviation community and she was presented with a glider all of her own. This meant more than medals or titles. The glider meant Hanna could fly whenever she wanted without having to rely on the generosity of friends loaning their planes to her.

The problem of Hanna's public reception in Germany remained, however. She was unpopular; it was as simple as that. At an aviation reception she was completely ignored by all except Peter Riedel, whom she had not seen in years. Riedel had defected to the US and was also very unpopular in Germany. He too was ignored by the rest of the party-goers. Despondent, the neglected pair left together. Riedel accepted his ostracism as the price he paid for leaving Germany. Hanna, however, could not bear it. Being shunned ate into her and every time she went abroad and felt restored the return to Germany crushed her again. An offer to go to Ghana seemed the perfect antidote to the depression that had once again settled on Hanna. She was personally invited by President Kwame Nkrumah of whom she knew nothing except that people were calling him a dictator. All she knew about Ghana was that it was once under British control and known as the Gold Coast, and a part of it had been a German colony. Hanna was swayed by the prospect of opportunity in Africa and was encouraged by the German government, who wanted to establish good relations with Ghana. The move would prove politically dangerous for Hanna, not least because she was now dealing direct with a communist power – the same ideology she had begged Nehru to avoid at all costs.

Kwame Nkrumah had started as an idealist and, at first, had seemed a promising prospect for establishing an independent Ghana. Talk of independence had been circulating for years and had spawned the UGCC (United Gold Coast Convention), which was exploring options for Ghana to gain its freedom from British rule. In 1947 Nkrumah was asked to become general secretary to the UGCC. He promoted civil disobedience and strikes to make the voice of the people heard. The British had made a tentative suggestion to offer a constitution under which those with sufficient wages and property could vote. Nkrumah was appalled: independence meant *all* the people could vote, not just the rich, who were often white and favoured the British. A combination of increased resistance and international protest concluded the matter with the British deciding to leave. A British organised election saw Nkrumah's party, the CPP (Convention People's Party), gain power even though its leader was in prison. When Nkrumah was released he was instructed to form a government and in 1952 the constitution was amended to include the role of prime minister – Nkrumah himself.

Initially Nkrumah looked like he had promise. Admittedly he had to learn to govern 'on the job', as well as to unify the four territories of the Gold Coast and gain full independence from Britain, which retained a tentative hold. In 1957 Nkrumah declared Ghana independent and was proclaimed by some as the 'redeemer'. In 1960 he announced that Ghana would become a republic with a new constitution and in April of that year he was declared president. In those early years of Nkrumah's rule, forestry, fishing and cattle breeding expanded, cocoa (Ghana's main export) production doubled and the construction of a dam provided hydro-electricity for the nearby towns as well as the new aluminium plant. Government funding went into building schools and roads, while free health care and education was introduced. With all this promise of progress it is not surprising that Nkrumah paid a visit to US president Kennedy in 1961; a photograph from the time shows them laughing together.

The dark side of Nkrumah's power was well concealed, at least at first. Nkrumah believed in socialism and Pan-Africanism (the unity of Africans around the globe to create solidarity). He very rapidly began to conceive of this as a religion, not just an ideology. In 1961, while he was building roads and schools, he was also building the Kwame Nkrumah Ideology Institute, where Ghanaian civil servants were trained in his personal beliefs and taught to promote Pan-Africanism. Before long this brainwashing moved into the colleges, where all students were expected to attend a two-week 'ideological orientation' at the institute: 'trainees should be made to realize the party's ideology is religion, and should be practised faithfully and fervently,' stated Nkrumah.

Further warning signs were everywhere. In 1954 there had been a cocoa boom and the price had soared. Cocoa farmers expected to benefit, but Nkrumah increased levies on the farmers so that the money went to him. He used it to fund various government projects, but in the process alienated a large chunk of his former supporters. Paranoia now seeped into the Nkrumah regime. There had been a gold miners' strike in 1955, so Nkrumah made strikes illegal, which was ironic since Nkrumah had protested against the British banning strikes! He wanted industrial progress and so opposed industrial democracy. He began to fear his opponents, so created a new law that anyone could be arrested, detained and charged with treason without trial. Prisoners thus detained had only one option – a direct appeal to Nkrumah, or else they languished in jail. When railway workers went on strike in 1961 he had the strike leaders and opposition politicians arrested. The good of the nation, he told his outraged opponents, superseded the good of the individual workers, including decent pay.

When Hanna arrived in Ghana there was already a great backlash against Nkrumah, not least from the British press, who were reporting on his authoritarian behaviour – not without a little glee. One of Nkrumah's closest supporters at the time was the journalist Kofi Batsa, who defended his president in his book *The Spark* (1985):

> The British press had always attempted to paint a picture of Nkrumah as a dangerous and militant communist revolutionary. [The British] went out of their way to associate the overwhelmingly exciting atmosphere of nationalism and patriotism with communism … if my hero Kwame Nkrumah was responsible for importing communism into the Gold Coast, then communism, I thought, must be a good thing.

As usual, Hanna was oblivious to the political crisis surrounding her new saviour. Her first meeting with Nkrumah filled her with hope. He was elegantly dressed, well mannered and spoke optimistically about teaching his people to glide. When Hanna suggested gliding was an ideal way to 'train the character' of young Ghanaians (or rather to mould them into loyal followers like pre-war Germans), Nkrumah could not have been more enthusiastic. His idealism, however, had blinded him to the practical situation.

What remained of Ghana's only gliding club, established in 1957 largely for the British and European residents as the local Africans showed no interest, was a small airfield serving as pasture most of the time for the local villagers' cattle. Rent for the site was paid in gin to the chiefs and the cattle only caused a problem on weekends when the few remaining flying members wanted to go up. To get airborne one relied on an old length of fence wire and the struggling engine of a Chevrolet which acted as tow. It was not particularly promising. Hanna spent some time working on proposals for the establishment of a true gliding school and submitted these to Nkrumah before returning to Germany. Promises were made to begin building work, including proper hangars. The diplomats in West Germany were pleased with Hanna's work: they were still eyeing up the potential of good relations with the African president. To further matters they invited Ghana to send a group of young men to Germany to gain experience of flying and mechanics in the heart-. land of gliding, the hope being they would return to Africa and share their knowledge.

Hanna met the new arrivals and was disheartened to discover they were all young and inexperienced. Nevertheless, she was able to train them in gliding and basic mechanics, but it was out of the question to expect these young men to train others successfully. West Germany offered to send two assistants with Hanna when she returned to Ghana. Again Hanna faced disappointment when she arrived in Africa. Very little had been done to the airfield except to partially build a new club house for the British. It was hopeless. Hanna went to Nkrumah and demanded something be done. He agreed and Hanna was to supervise the work. What she failed to appreciate was the cost required to establish an airfield. She was asking for vast sums of money beyond the means of a new country, particularly as they would be better used on practical projects rather than an exercise in gliding whose value was debatable. The British flyers, who felt they had a better grasp of internal politics and funding than Hanna (a reasonable assessment), argued over her expenditure. Hanna flew at their representatives with predictable fury – Nkrumah wanted a top-class training school and Nkrumah was going to get it! She got her wish, at the expense of friendship with the British flyers, thereby further demoting herself in general British opinion.

Weeks turned into months; the buildings grew, but enthusiasm for gliding among the native population did not. Young Ghanaians were recruited for training but failed to see the point; they resented being asked to work during the heat of the day and were so uninterested that being grounded for a misdemeanour was deemed a privilege rather than a punishment. Hanna caused further antagonism by fencing off the airfield and preventing the grazing of the cattle. When she cut down a tree her students were horrified – it was sacred and only a gory ritual could 'heal' the wound in the land and in local goodwill.

From a personal perspective, Hanna's reputation was in serious danger. She had again aligned herself with a man many considered a dictator. Hanna failed to see this, but other Germans were more aware of the unpleasant side of Nkrumah's regime. As international opinion slowly turned against him, so Germany wanted less to do with the Ghanaian president. During her time in Ghana Hanna saw three West German diplomats come and go; none of them she particularly liked and at least two of them held the opinion that Hanna was representing the old, Nazi Germany in her activities, even if unconsciously. Hanna's dogmatic attitude towards the school, largely based on her deep desire to fly and promote gliding there now that she was scorned in Germany, brought her into conflict with more and more people. Some felt she was trying to raise a neo-Nazi culture through the school, pointing out how her youthful flyers bore echoes of the Hitler Youth. It was not Hanna's fault that her first volunteers had been chosen from the ranks of the Young Pioneers, a political youth movement, but it did have unfortunate con-notations. Worse was that Hanna could see no wrong in Nkrumah and had an over-inflated sense of her own importance in his party. She did a good job of upsetting both those who supported Nkrumah and those who were against him, but then Hanna had invariably been better at making enemies than friends.

Why did Hanna set herself up to fail in such a way? Bitterness played a part: bitterness with Germany, with the Aero Club, with a world that would not forgive her. She was angry and to console herself focused on the gliding school to the point where it became the all-absorbing focus of her life. Nothing, therefore, could be allowed to destroy it. Her loyalty to Nkrumah was misplaced, but it came from desperation. He was a lifeline, he provided her with a way of making her name in gliding, an escape from the shame and guilt laid upon her in Germany. She needed him to succeed, because if he didn't, what was left for her?

Hanna remained hopeful. By 1965 the school was showing some promise. Well-trained Ghanaian instructors proved the gliding school could work and though she had had to relinquish some of her grander schemes for the club, it was mostly built and ready for use. After a brief stay in Germany over Christmas Hanna returned to Ghana in 1966, oblivious to the disaster about to befall Nkrumah. 'The word "coup" should not be used to describe what took place in Ghana on 24 February 1966. On that day, Ghana was captured by traitors among the army and police who were inspired and helped by neo-colonialists and certain reactionary elements among our own population,' wrote Nkrumah bit-terly in the years after he was deposed.

Nkrumah was on his way to Hanoi to see President Ho Chi Minh, armed with proposals for ending the war in Vietnam, when news reached him that his country had been seized in a military coup. He was in Peking when the Chinese ambassador approached him: 'Mr President, I have bad news. There has been a coup d'etat in Ghana.' Nkrumah was so stunned he didn't believe his ears: 'What did you say?' 'A coup d'etat in Ghana.' 'Impossible,' declared Nkrumah. But it was very possible. Ghana was no longer under his control, and Hanna was no longer welcome. It would not be long before her gliding school was shut down. Nkrumah fumed: 'The school, recognised as among the best in the world, was providing valuable initial flying training for members of the Young Pioneers, Army and Air Force Cadets, and for trainees from other African countries.' Nkrumah was rather optimistic in his assessment of the school. In any case, the new power in Ghana felt no need to continue to indulge Hanna and her gliding.

Hanna left Ghana as soon as she could and went to Guinea. Nkrumah had fled there himself shortly after the coup. He had made attempts to restore himself to power in Ghana, giving broadcasts to his people from the safety of Guinea. The new government made it a criminal offence to listen to any of Nkrumah's speeches and ultimately he gave up on the broadcasts, realising they served little purpose. His people knew where he was, anyway. He would focus on writing about his struggle and use that as a weapon.

When Hanna arrived she was travelling incognito with her hair dyed as a disguise. She came to offer her support to Nkrumah and to give him her own eyewitness account of the coup. She warned him about returning too soon for there had been great scenes of celebration and general chaos after the power change – not comforting words for a deposed president. '[Her] lurid, superficial descriptions were tactless. She seemed to imply that because she had seen some people applauding the soldiers in Accra that the Ghanaian people as a whole had turned against Nkrumah,' June Milne, Nkrumah's research assistant and publisher, wrote angrily.

Hanna did not stay long in Guinea and though she left with assurances she would come to Nkrumah's aid if ever he needed it, she never visited nor saw him again.

12

LOST AND ALONE

Hanna was now 54, not so very old, but the toils of war, illness and test flying had aged her. She was also beginning to feel very alone. Wolf Hirth had died in an air crash in 1959, and a year later Heini Dittmar had joined him. Peter Riedel was living in America and so many others had not survived the war. Hanna wondered what was left for her. Her last energies had been thrown into the abortive Ghanaian gliding school, which was now a lost dream. She had a small flat in Frankfurt, but she was not entirely happy there. When she could, she sneaked away to fly. She had her own glider now and in the air at least she felt free. Maybe sometimes she dreamed of ending her days this way, crashing to the ground like Hirth and Dittmar. In 1970 she flew over the Austrian Alps, setting a women's alpine gliding record, which was an unexpected bonus, since she flew these days purely for pleasure.

The German public still viewed her with suspicion, though time had dimmed some of the controversy and there were some who now celebrated her, albeit tentatively, as a pioneer of women's flying. Others still criticised her for her poor political choices. Her time with Nkrumah had not improved this; some felt Hanna was not happy unless serving a dictator. So many years ago Hanna had refused to leave her Germany, believing she could serve a purpose reinvigorating it. Now she realised that was a vain hope. No one wanted Hitler's heroine telling them how wrong the Nazi regime was, it was hypocritical and it drew resentment. Finding Germany harder and harder to live in, Hanna made the decision to spend part of her time in Austria, where at least she felt free from the resentful stares of her contemporaries.

That same year Hanna attended the Golden Jubilee of the Wasserkuppe. She had not flown at the competition since falling out with the Aero Club, but she would not miss this grand occasion for the world. Guest of honour at the event was US astronaut and keen amateur glider pilot Neil Armstrong. When Hanna had visited America in the 1960s, Armstrong had been in the audience at one of her lectures; now he was an American hero and the first man to set foot on the moon. Hanna dined with Armstrong and her fellow Germans and discussed the tiny museum that had been arranged to celebrate the Wasserkuppe. They all agreed it was rather poor and before long Hanna and a friend were discussing building a bigger one. From then on it was a matter of funding.

Hanna suggested a glider mail flight – in the early days of aviation airmail had been a popular novelty and people paid large sums to have a postcard delivered by air. Fifty years on traditional airmail would not raise any interest, but the idea of using gliders to deliver special commemorative postcards was another matter. A stamp company agreed to support the venture and pay 5 marks each for 2,000 postcards, as long as Hanna signed them all. It seemed an agreeable arrangement until Hanna discovered how long it took to write 2,000 signatures. 'I never want to write my own name again,' she grumbled afterwards. She also passed around a hat at her lectures and donated money from the sale of signed copies of her book. The funds gradually grew, but it would be years, long after Hanna's death, before the gliding museum was finally opened in 1987.

In 1971 Hanna took part in a helicopter competition; this breached her personal ban on flying in German competitions since her split from the Aero Club, but her justification was that a helicopter was not a plane. Only six women entered the competition and Hanna came first in the women's class. There was also a helicopter slalom and Hanna went over and over the course in her mind while her fellow competitors went to lunch, practising how she would bend her knees and move her arms. This mental exercise paid off as she came second. She was placed sixth in the overall competition. In 1972 Hanna travelled to American at the invitation of the SETP (Society of Experimental Test Pilots), who wanted to make her an honorary member. She had been invited the year before, but it clashed with the helicopter competitions so she could not go. The invitation was prestigious since women had never been asked to become members of the society before 1971. To her delight,

Hanna was also awarded Pilot of the Year in Arizona. She beamed with pleasure and fought back tears. The SETP award dinner was held at the Beverley Hilton in Beverley Hills, California and Hanna was sat beside Barron Hilton, owner of the hotel chain. She could hardly believe that in such prestigious company and surrounded by 2,000 other aviators she was deemed the star attraction. Barron Hilton later wanted to name a flying competition after Hanna – the Hanna Reitsch Cup – though it never happened.

Hanna was once more walking on air when she returned to Austria, and, once again, no sooner was she home than her positivity was shattered. A new film had just come out starring Alec Guinness as Hitler and portraying the final days in the bunker. Said to be based on Hugh Trevor-Roper's book, as usual in the movies the director and scriptwriter had used artistic licence to make the film more enticing to an audience. Naturally Hanna was featured in her typical role of Nazi dreamer, based far more on post-war interpretations of her time in the bunker than actual fact. Most eyewitness accounts of Hanna's appearance in Hitler's underground lair back up her own contention that she rarely saw Hitler and spent most of her time with von Greim or the Goebbels children. Nor do these accounts portray her as a sycophantic ninny intent on sacrificing herself on the altar of Nazism. Hanna had not been consulted before the film was made and she complained bitterly afterwards. But by now she had complained so often that few were listening.

In fact, Hanna's obsession with criticism often made her complain about trivial or silly things. Worse was her criticism of the collective guilt still being thrust on Germany when other countries had, in her eyes, committed equally heinous crimes. Why was Germany still being punished thirty years on? Why were war criminals still being held in prison? Hanna's ranting, which was as much driven by irritation at her own constant defamation as moral outrage, hardly improved her standing with the British. Only in America was she appreciated for her role as a pioneer female pilot. In 1975 SETP invited her again, to give a talk to an audience of 2,000 about her experiences with the Me 163 and manned V1 flying bomb.

Flying honours did not eliminate the isolation and anxiety Hanna felt whenever she was in Germany. Frankfurt had become a city of unrest. Her flat was in an area where some of the worst violence took place. The police instructed her that they could not guarantee her safety on the streets and advised she take taxis rather than walk. Frankfurt was in serious need of redevelopment, but when speculators bought up old houses to demolish them and build high-rise flats there was a spate of riots. Protestors squatted in the houses either side of Hanna's flat.

Anxiety became an overwhelming part of Hanna's life. After an attempted break-in at her flat she took to carrying a small pistol in her handbag. The continued violence and fear was too much and in 1973 she was fortunate to find another flat in a better part of the city. She could never have afforded it had not the landlord been a fan of her achievements. The day Hanna moved a car was overturned outside her old flat and set on fire. Hanna had to wonder what had happened to Germany. She decorated her new flat with black and white pictures of the Alps and gliders, family photos, a watercolour painting by Otto Fuchs while in Libya and portraits of von Greim and the priest Volkmar, who had recently died and left Hanna even more bereft. Flying trophies, wall hangings and mementoes from her various travels abroad helped to make her at home. The big windows of the flat overlooked a tree-filled garden and a church clock tower. When she felt lonely Hanna could feed the birds on her balcony. She set to work on her next book, another autobiography that aimed to debunk many of the myths that had grown up around her. She called it *Ups and Downs*, which was appropriate as the last decades of her life had proceeded very much in that fashion, as had her moods. Hanna swung from enthusiasm to depression far more easily these days than when younger; in some regards she now mirrored her father at the same stage in his life. She threw herself into as many activities as possible to dispel the mental gloom and still flew whenever she could, but for every glory there always seemed to be somebody ready to throw back at her those dark days of 1945. Emy had shown considerable foresight when she worried about her daughter receiving two Iron Crosses and Nazi accolades; she had recognised the predicament her daughter might face one day. Unfortunately, she was not around to help.

Controversy dogged Hanna. In 1978 she and Hans Baur attended a public tribute to German pioneering pilot Hermann Köhl, a known anti-Nazi who had been banned from public speaking by Göring in 1934. Köhl had died in 1938, making the event the fortieth anniversary of his death and a big gathering was expected. That Hanna and Baur were invited as VIPs was a bad oversight – former followers of Hitler attending a tribute to an anti-Nazi was obviously going to produce bad press. Hanna, as usual, picked up most of the flak.

Meanwhile, she was trying to promote women in gliding. Women had never been prominent in the sport, but in recent years there seemed to be even fewer. Hanna often found herself with only a handful of female pilots at competitions. She aimed to reinvigorate the sport among women and the only way she knew of doing this was to prove herself as a female pilot. Hanna took to the air and was once more breaking records: in 1978 she set a new women's world record flying over the Alps for ten hours. The feud with the Aero Club also at last came to an end after its new president wrote to Hanna to congratulate her. Hanna decided it was time to put the past behind her.

As usual, the past had other ideas. Hanna was invited to give a lecture at Bremen, a city with a strong communist element, particularly among students at the university. Typically oblivious, Hanna could not understand why they might object to a lecture by her on gliding. The organiser of the lecture feared protests, but after weeks of negotiations it was agreed that the lecture would go ahead. The 8 November 1978 was booked. No one appeared to remember the significance of that date. Forty years ago that night the horrors of Kristallnacht had been about to erupt. Though Hanna had not been involved and, indeed, had protested against the violence, her name remained blackened by her later association with Hitler, and many felt it was in poor taste that she should give a lecture the day before such a poignant anniversary. Even the mayor of Bremen was aghast at the audacity of the event. What Hanna did not know was that the organiser behind the lecture was a hard-core nationalist, part of a movement closely associated with fascism. The organisation she was due to speak to was the Stahlhelm Youth, which many considered a barely disguised reinvention of the Hitler Youth. The reaction against the lecture was therefore quite natural.

For once Hanna realised the danger in time. She cancelled her appearance at almost the same time as the organiser was doing the same. The public was not so easily mollified. The usual statements about Hanna began to circulate, adding to her negative press but representing her as more of a Nazi than she ever really was. Hanna once again went into action, accusing people of slander and demanding a public apology.

The event had tarnished her reputation. She had hoped to sell copies of her book, and now she wondered if shops would begin to remove it from their shelves. She retreated to Salzburg mournful, confused as to why everything she did turned out so badly. By her parents' grave she asked herself where it had all gone so wrong.

The torment continued. In 1979 Hanna was accused of anti-Semitism in her writing. She took the accuser, and the evangelical church he represented, to court for slander and won her case. But the press coverage raked up old dirt again. Hanna wanted a public apology. It was refused and a new feud looked likely to begin. Again her friends begged her to drop the matter and again Hanna refused because it went against her honour. The constant antagonism drove Hanna into a depression. She brushed it off briefly for a trip to America, where she stayed several weeks in Pennsylvania, writing another book and flying. She even attempted, and succeeded, to set a new world record. Unfortunately, it was claimed that her flight had not been correctly monitored or recorded. The controversy descended into another war of words that would last months.

Back in Frankfurt Hanna was feeling unwell. The strain of all these arguments and her hectic schedule were becoming too much. Suddenly she dreaded public speaking, but could not renege on the promises she had made. On 22 August Hanna told a friend over the phone that she was having pains in her chest. The next day Joachim Küttner rang to ask if she would like to meet him at the airport, as she had so often done in the past. 'I really have a problem – I need you – I need your help,' Hanna said over the phone. 'But I don't think I can come – you come here.' Küttner failed to realise the seriousness of the situation. He only had limited time and said he would call on Hanna another time. After all, it was not unknown for Hanna to react dramatically to the most mundane of problems. Her request for help was probably nothing. That night Hanna dined with a guest who thought she looked exhausted and worn out. A thought ran through his head: 'My God, how long can she keep this up?'

His answer came all too soon. The following morning Hanna was found dead in her bed. A doctor declared that she had had a massive heart attack, but rumours began almost at once that Hanna had taken her own life. Where was the suicide pill? It was never found, but it is highly unlikely that it would have killed Hanna if she had used it. After more than thirty years the cyanide would have degraded. Some Nazis who had used capsules in 1945, which had been issued five or six years earlier, discovered to their horror that the poison was no longer lethal. Instead, they suffered a torturous few hours, emerging from the experience very much alive. There is little reason to suppose Hanna killed herself. She had been depressed and felt tired, but she also had plans and was still determined to do something for Germany. That her heart ultimately gave out is hardly surprising: after her close encounter with scarlet fever it had always been weak and the strain of travel, flying and very public arguments would not have helped. That she told a friend a day before her death that she was suffering chest pains is the most convincing evidence that it was a heart attack that killed her. Hanna was neither a liar nor cunning enough to attempt misdirection.

In any case, Hanna did not perceive suicide as something to hide. It could be a last gesture of honour. Had she indeed contemplated it, Hanna would surely have left a note and ensured all knew what she was about. It is hardly conceivable that such a talkative person would miss one final opportunity to speak to the world. Hanna died a natural death. That this has spawned one more myth concerning her should hardly be surprising.

'If flying, like a glass-bottomed bucket, can give you that vision, that seeing eye, which peers down to the still world below the choppy waves – it will always remain magic,' wrote Anne Morrow Lindbergh of the mystical aspect of her experience of flight. Her words could echo the way Hanna Reitsch felt about flying. It was that pull, that mystical experience that had locked her to a dangerous regime. Hanna has to be viewed through her flying to understand her, but one cannot ignore the poor decisions she made in life, her support for Nazism and her association with some of the worst examples of the regime.

How could Hanna be blind to all that was around her? Historians continue to argue about the level of knowledge ordinary Germans had of the criminal activities of their superiors. Many have argued that ignorance was rife, but in *Soldaten*, an historical and psychological analysis of German soldiers through their interrogation records, Sönke Neitzel and Harald Welzer argue that knowledge of the atrocities was wider than first thought. Nearly all the soldiers had heard stories; some believed them, some did not. Many were worried that Germany's reputation after the war would be tarnished by the actions of the few. Many denied having anything to do with the execution of 'undesirables', though the evidence indicates the Wehrmacht was heavily involved with transport and executions. Even more surprising was the number of soldiers who had witnessed something personally that either later troubled them or made them think the rumours they had heard about mass murder were true.

These were soldiers, directly involved in fighting and naturally caught up in the execution of grisly tasks, but Neitzel and Welzer have also shown that at the civilian level many people knew that things were wrong in the Reich and simply chose to ignore them. A classic example is given by Mary Fulbrook in her book *A Small Town near Auschwitz*. She learned that a friend of her family (Fulbrook's mother was originally from Germany) was once the principal civilian administrator of the town of Bedzin, Poland – part of Polish Silesia and just over three hours away from Hanna's hometown. Udo Klausa had claimed he was a decent man, had not participated in any crimes during the war and had had no knowledge of the gradual eradication of Jews from his town. In fact, he had happily massaged dates to prove that he was never around when the worst atrocities occurred. Fulbrook proved that Klausa had been an integral part of the governing system of Bedzin and *had* to have known what was happening to the Jews under his jurisdiction. He was helping the Nazis in a very mundane way by signing forms and ignoring the consequences. Neitzel and Welzer argue that this holds true for every civil servant who worked under the Nazi regime, continuing with their duties without questioning them. A concentration camp does not function without an administrative system; atrocities cannot be limited to the person who fired the bullet. The blame resonates out further and further, down through the system to the man who signed the form for the camp to be built, to the clerk who typed it up and filed it. Even to the civilians who looked on and did nothing.

Hanna may not have been an anti-Semite, but she was aware of anti-Semitism around her and continued to work for a regime that endorsed heinous crimes. Worse, she defended the leader of that regime, the man who demanded Jewish blood. What we must do is observe Hanna's blind devotion to Hitler within context; first she had been raised in a cultural environment where 'true' Germans were constantly distinguished as superior to other races, including the Jews. Her mother often ranted about how foreign influence had wrecked Germany and her accusations fell on Jews as much as anyone else. Such laying of blame is not uncommon, even today, and probably Frau Reitsch meant very little by it, certainly not condoning mass slaughter. But the effect on a young mind of a combination of denigration of other races and the constant uplifting of German blood (and Hanna in particular) cannot be ignored. Hanna was always easily led; she rarely held opinions that were solely her own and she was superficial in her judgement of others. It was easy enough for such a person to become accustomed to accepting her superiors' lies over the unpleasant truths others presented to her. Part is due to idolisation, part is due to the horror and fear of what might lie beyond acknowledging the truth. It does not make a person less culpable, but it does make them very human. We all cherry-pick the truth as we see fit, so we can continue to exist in our own world as contentedly as possible. We support a political party and ignore its failings, or at least brush over them. Some take this to extremes and will not admit that the party they support can do anything wrong. Today these wrongs are poor economic decisions, sex scandals and dubious monetary dealings, but the principle is the same. Ordinary, good people prefer loyalty to a party over deeply questioning their political choices. For many it is very simply the easiest option. And we mustn't forget that for many it is too embarrassing, too shameful, to ever admit publically that they were wrong, even if they accept it privately.

So what makes a Nazi? British pilot Eric Brown, who met (and once idolised) Hanna, stated she had to be a Nazi because she defended Hitler. That is a very simplistic, black-and-white statement. Nazism had far more shades of grey. Even the British POW system recognised that there were ardent Nazis (coded black), non-Nazis (white) and those who were somewhere in the middle (grey). The 'greys' made up the vast majority of POWs. Nazism meant different things to different people. For Udo Klausa it was a means to an end. He was an early Nazi, signing up with the party when he realised the power of the movement. He believed, quite rightly, that if he did not join it would hamper his chances of a career in civil administration. Other people joined out of ignorance, or because they liked one policy the NSDAP was promoting. Few joined because they wanted the annihilation of the Jews, and even those who did would not necessarily have agreed with the mass execution the Nazis employed.

Hanna was never a member of the Nazi Party, but she did believe in Hitler in her naïve, lost way. She was deceived by his charisma and led by the fact that he had helped her achieve her dream of flying. She was not a sycophant as some films have portrayed her; she would stand up to Hitler and tell him he was wrong if she saw fit, but she did hero-worship him. Like many Germans, she maintained the belief that Hitler knew nothing about the destruction of the Jews – it was all the fault of his treacherous subordinates, Himmler and Göring, who had betrayed him. Hanna thought of Hitler as she did herself; a naïve visionary who had been betrayed by his own government. She had never liked Himmler and it was easy to blame him for Hitler's, and Germany's, fall, much as her mother had found it easy to blame the Jews and foreign influence for the problems Germany faced between the wars.

Does that make Hanna a Nazi? It depends greatly on one's definition of Nazism. She never killed anyone, nor supported the eradication policies, but she did turn a blind eye to the worst excesses of her government. She did train people to fly – ultimately many of her students entered the Luftwaffe – and she considered the options of suicide missions to cripple Britain. But equally there were many who did similar things during the Second World War who slipped back into normal life afterwards without a hint of Nazism clinging to them. Hanna did not really believe in the National Socialist Party and its ideology – that is plain – but she did believe in Hitler. Ultimately, what she really wanted was a chance to fly, and the war provided that. In a sense she was no different to some of the women who flew planes for the British ATA (Air Transport Auxiliary) during the war and later said they were disappointed when the war ended as it meant the end of their flying careers. Hanna was wrong in her choices, she was wrong in her belief in Hitler, but that does not make her a Nazi or worthy of the extreme demonisation she has suffered, especially in comparison with some of her fellow Second World War survivors.

Mary Fulbrook remarks on the difficulty of assessing a person's beliefs or criminal culpability at such a distance of time:

Any attempt now to evaluate the acts of a former Nazi – in whatever sense – is complicated by the need to draw lines with respect to degrees of both reprehensibility and responsibility. To err in one direction may mean to concede legitimacy to essentially Nazi arguments, while to lean unduly to the other, expressing moral outrage about any kind of complicity … may be to gloss over real distinctions in degrees of relative responsibility and the historically uneven distribution of the undoubted overall burden of guilt.

Reading the US interrogation reports on Hanna, it seems that there was a feeling among her interviewers that she was generally appalled at the outcome of National Socialism. Again this has to be accepted warily as many former Nazis made emotive and convincing statements of their horror of the system after the war. There were plenty who claimed they had not really known what was happening. Hanna, however, seems to have genuinely felt betrayed by her leaders and shocked at the cruelty of the crimes they had committed.

In comparison with many contemporaries, Hanna has been treated unfairly. In some regards she had an integrity and sense of honour that betrayed her time and again. She would not deny what she had done, nor what she had thought or felt during the war simply to appease post-war audiences. Others reshaped themselves to fit into a new world; Wernher von Braun, for example, the blue-eyed boy of the Nazi rocket industry, had made himself useful to the Americans and so had avoided being tarred with the brush of war crimes. Yet he *had* worked on the V2 and other rocket-propelled weapons and, certainly in the early days of the war, was willing enough to do so. An enthusiast for rockets, the Nazi regime allowed him the freedom to tinker with designs and test engine after engine. A clever man such as von Braun could hardly have been unaware that this was a military operation, and that eventually the rocket would be viewed in the light of how it could win a war. As the years passed this only became more obvious – not to mention the slave labour used to build the rockets. Von Braun carefully avoided all mention of this. Then there are his actions with test pilot Erich Warsitz: despite having no reliable prototype rocket, he was prepared to send up a man, to his very likely death, to test a rocket engine in flight. Pressure from above is one thing, ethics is clearly another. Post-war, Wernher von Braun worked for NASA and was eventually integral to the historic moon landing. He quickly put any associations of complicity with the Nazis behind him. In 1964 he remarked that 'Having experienced the tragic misuse of power and the gradual destruction of personal freedom in a totalitarian regime, I consider it a blessing and privilege to pursue the peaceful exploration of space in the service of a truly free country and in the interest of all mankind.'

Von Braun became an American hero, not least by suggesting his actions during the war had all been due to Nazi dominance – in his words, he had not been free to do anything else. His hands were tied – he *had* to build rockets of death. We can judge this denial and justification as we wish; would it have gone down so well had von Braun not been so useful to the Americans? Hanna was of no real use to anyone, so she was not worth protecting from the post-war slings and arrows flying at all involved in Hitler's regime. Her life had intertwined repeatedly with von Braun's, but she was the one, not the man who created the V2 bomb, who became a villain.

At the end of the day, Hanna was a complex human being who made mistakes and paid for them heavily. Her story is one of triumph through adversity, of bravery and determination, as well as defeat and despondency. Hanna may have failed herself, but her legacy in the world of women's aviation cannot be denied. She was a pioneer and a dreamer. She wanted the world to fly and to enjoy the spiritual experience of being airborne that she so enjoyed. Unfortunately, she did not understand that not everyone was attracted to flying for peaceful reasons. Hanna Reitsch will always be a name that sparks controversy as well as adulation. To some extent this is the price of fame – after all, if not for Hitler's influence would we still be talking so much about a German test pilot whose halcyon days were seventy years ago, even a female one?

APPENDIX 1

LETTER FROM DR JOSEPH GOEBBELS

To Harald Quandt, 28 April 1945, as remembered by Hanna Reitsch; written in the Führer's bunker

My Dear Harald,

We are now confined to the Führer's bunker in the Reich Chancellery and are fighting for our lives and our honour. God alone knows what the outcome of this battle will be. I know, however, that we shall only come out of it, dead or alive, with honour and glory. I hardly think that we shall see each other again. Probably, therefore, these are the last lines you will ever receive from me. I expect from you that, should you survive this war, you will do nothing but honour your mother and me. It is not essential that we remain alive in order to continue to influence our people. You may well be the only one able to continue our family tradition. Always act in such a way that we need not be ashamed of it.

Germany will survive this fearful war but only if examples are set to our people enabling them to stand on their feet again. We wish to set such an example. You may be proud of having such a mother as yours. Yesterday the Führer gave her the Golden Party Badge which he has worn on his tunic for years and she deserved it. You should have only one duty in future: to show yourself worthy of the supreme sacrifice which we are ready and determined to make. I know that you will do it. Do not let yourself be disconcerted by the worldwide clamour which will now begin. One day the lies will crumble away of themselves and truth will triumph once more. That will be the moment when we shall tower over all, clean and spotless, as we have always striven to be and believed ourselves to be.

Farewell, my dear Harald. Whether we shall ever see each other again is in the lap of the gods. If we do not, may you always be proud of having belonged to a family which, even in misfortune, remained loyal to the very end to the Führer and his pure sacred cause.

APPENDIX 2

LETTER FROM MAGDA GOEBBELS

To Harald Quandt, 28 April 1945, as remembered by Hanna Reitsch; written in the Führer's bunker

My beloved Son,

We have now been here, in the Führer's bunker, for six days – Papa, your six little brothers and sisters and I – in order to bring our National-Socialist existence to the only possible and honourable conclusion. I do not know whether you will receive this letter. Perhaps there is still one human soul who will make it possible for me to send you my last greetings. You should know that I have remained here against Papa's will, that only last Sunday the Führer wanted to help me escape from here. You know your mother – we are of the same blood, so I did not have to reflect for a moment. Our splendid concept is perishing and with it goes everything beautiful, admirable, noble and good that I have known in my life. The world which will succeed the Führer and National Socialism is not worth living in and for this reason I have brought the children here too. They are too good for the life that will come after us and a gracious God will understand me if I myself give them release from it. You will go on living and I have one single request to make of you: never forget that you are a German, never do anything dishonourable and ensure that by your life our death is not in vain.

The children are wonderful. They make do in these very primitive conditions without any help. No matter whether they sleep on the floor, whether they can wash or not, whether they have anything to eat and so forth – never a word of complaint or a tear. Shell-bursts are shaking the bunker. The grown-ups protect the little ones, whose presence here is to this extent a blessing that from time to time they can get a smile from the Führer.

Yesterday evening the Führer took off his Golden Party Badge and pinned it on me. I am happy and proud. God grant that I retain the strength to do the last and most difficult thing. We have only one aim in life now – to remain loyal to the Führer unto death; that we should be able to end our life together with him is a gift of fate for which we would never have dared hope.

Harald, my dear – I give you the best that life has taught me: be true – true to yourself, true to mankind, true to your country – in every respect whatsoever.

[*new sheet*]

It is hard to start a fresh sheet. Who knows whether I shall complete it but I wanted to give you so much love, so much strength and take from you all sorrow at our loss. Be proud of us and try to remember us with pride and pleasure. Everyone must die one day and is it not better to live a fine, honourable, brave but short life than drag out a long life of humiliation?

The letter must go – Hanna Reitsch is taking it. She is flying out once more. I embrace you with my warmest, most heartfelt and most maternal love.

My beloved son
Live for Germany!
Your Mother

APPENDIX 3

SELECTED WORLD RECORDS AND AWARDS EARNED BY HANNA REITSCH

1932 Women's Gliding Endurance Record (5.5 hours' gliding time)
1936 Women's Gliding Distance Record (305km)
1937 First woman to cross the Alps (accidentally)
1937 Given rank of flugkapitän, first woman to receive such a promotion
1937 World Distance Record in a helicopter (109km)
1938 First person to fly a helicopter inside an enclosed space (debatable which of the two helicopter pilots present earned this)
1939 Women's World Record in gliding (for point-to-point flying)
1943 First woman to fly a rocket plane (Messerschmitt 163b)
1943 Awarded the Iron Cross, First Class
1955 German Gliding Champion
1956 German Gliding Distance Record (370km)
1957 German Gliding Altitude Record (6,848m)
1970 Earned the Diamond Badge (FAI)
1971 First in Women's Class at the World Helicopter Championship
1972 Made an honorary member of the Society of Experimental Test Pilots (America)
1972 Won Pilot of the Year (Arizona, US)
1978 Women's World Record for flying over the Alps (10 hours)

BIBLIOGRAPHY

Batsa, Kofi, *The Spark: From Kwame Nkrumah to Limann* (London: Rex Collings, 1985).

Baur, Lt. Gen. Hans, *I Was Hitler's Pilot: The Memoirs of Hans Baur* (Barnsley: Frontline Books, 2013) (English translation first published 1958).

Carruthers, Bob, *Voices from the Luftwaffe* (Barnsley: Pen and Sword Aviation, 2012).

Clark, Christopher, *Iron Kingdom: The Rise and Downfall of Prussia 1600–1947* (London: Penguin, 2006).

Dank, Milton, *The Glider Gang* (London: Cassell, 1977).

Davenport-Hines, Richard (ed.), *Letters from Oxford: Hugh Trevor-Roper to Bernard Berenson* (London: Phoenix, 2007).

Fest, Joachim, *Inside Hitler's Bunker: The Last Days of the Third Reich* (London: Macmillan, 2004).

Fulbrook, Mary, *A Small Town near Auschwitz: Ordinary Nazis and the Holocaust* (Oxford: Oxford University Press, 2012).

Hargreaves, Richard, *Hitler's Final Fortress: Breslau 1945* (Barnsley: Pen and Sword, 2011).

Herwig, Dieter & Rode, Heinz, *Luftwaffe Secret Projects: Ground Attack and Special Purpose Aircraft* (Hinckley: Midland Publishing, 2003).

Hilton, Christopher, *Hitler's Olympics: The 1936 Berlin Olympic Games* (Stroud: Sutton, 2006).

Junge, Traudl, *Until the Final Hour: Hitler's Last Secretary* (London: Weidenfeld and Nicolson, 2003).

Killen, John, *The Luftwaffe: A History* (Barnsley: Pen and Sword, 2003).

Linge, Heinz, *With Hitler to the End: The Memoirs of Adolf Hitler's Valet* (London: Frontline Books, 2013).

Lomax, Judy, *Flying for the Fatherland: The Century's Greatest Pilot* (New York: Bantam, 1988).

McNab, Chris, *The Fall of Eben Emael – Belgium 1940* (Oxford: Osprey, 2013).

Milne, June, *Kwame Nkrumah: A Biography* (London: Panaf, 1999).

Neitzel, Sönke & Welzer, Harald, *Soldaten: On Fighting, Killing and Dying. The Secret Second World War Tapes of German POWs* (London: Simon & Schuster, 2012).

Nkrumah, Kwame, *Dark Days in Ghana* (London: Panaf, 1968).

Reitsch, Hanna, *The Sky My Kingdom: Memoirs of the Famous German World War II Test Pilot* (London: Greenhill Books, 2009).

Sisman, Adam, *Hugh Trevor-Roper: The Biography* (London: Weidenfeld and Nicolson, 2010).

Spick, Mike, *Aces of the Reich: The Making of a Luftwaffe Fighter Pilot* (London: Greenhill Books, 2006).

Spick, Mike, *Luftwaffe Fighter Aces* (London: Greenhill Books, 1996).

Taylor, Blaine, *Hitler's Headquarters: From Beer Hall to Bunker 1920–1945* (Washington, DC: Potomac Books, 2007).

Trevor-Roper, Hugh (ed.), *The Goebbels Diaries* (London: Book Club Associates, 1978).

Trevor-Roper, Hugh, *The Last Days of Hitler* fifth edition (London: Macmillan, 1978).

Vaizey, Hester, *Surviving Hitler's War: Family Life in Germany 1939–48* (Basingstoke: Palgrave Macmillan, 2010).

Walters, Helen B., *Wernher von Braun: Rocket Engineer* (London: Macmillan, 1964).

Ward, Bob, *From Nazis to Nasa: The Life of Wernher von Braun* (Stroud: Sutton, 2006).

Warsitz, Lutz, *The First Jet Pilot: The Story of German Test Pilot Erich Warsitz* (Barnsley: Pen and Sword, 2008).

Winters, Kathleen C., *Anne Morrow Lindbergh: First Lady of the Air* (Basingstoke: Palgrave Macmillan, 2006).

Yenne, Bill, *The White Rose of Stalingrad: The Real-Life Adventure of Lidiya Vladimirovna Litvyak, the Highest Scoring Female Air Ace of All Time* (Oxford: Osprey Publishing, 2013).

INDEX

If you enjoyed this book, you may also be interested in...

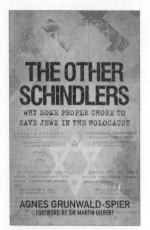

The Other Schindlers

AGNES GRUNWALD-SPIER

In the midst of Hitler's extermination of the Jews, courage and humanity could still overcome evil. While 6 million Jews were murdered by the Nazi regime, some were saved through the actions of non-Jews whose consciences would not allow them to pass by on the other side. As a baby, the author was saved from the horrors of Auschwitz by an unknown official, and is now a trustee of the Holocaust Memorial Day Trust. She has collected together the stories of individuals who rescued Jews, which provide a new insight into why these people were prepared to risk so much for their fellow men and women. This is an ultimately uplifting account of how some good deeds really do shine in a weary world.

978 0 7524 5967 7

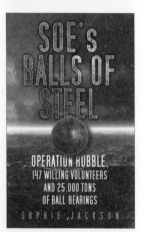

SOE's Balls of Steel

SOPHIE JACKSON

In 1940 the Nazis hoped to cripple the British war effort by blockading Swedish cargo ships containing ball bearings, steel and tools vital for making arms and equipment. In desperation, the newly formed SOE was asked to rescue these badly needed supplies. It was a dangerous mission and the 147 men involved knew there was a high chance they would not come home. It was a success that was never repeated. Making use of newly released files from the National Archives, Sophie Jackson tells the story of a forgotten adventure that saved Britain and her troops from certain defeat, all because of brave men willing to sacrifice their lives for millions of small balls of steel.

978 0 7524 8756 4

Nazi Princess

JIM WILSON

Stephanie von Hohenlohe lived a controversial life. After marriage to a prince of the Austro-Hungarian Empire, she became a close confidante of Hitler, Göring, Himmler and von Ribbentrop. After arriving in London in 1932, she moved in exclusive circles. Most notoriously, she was paid a retainer of £5,000 per year by Lord Rothermere, owner of the *Daily Mail* and open supporter of the Nazi regime. In 1939 she fled to the USA; a memo to President Roosevelt described her as a spy 'more dangerous than ten thousand men'. Here Jim Wilson uses recently declassified MI5 files and FBI memos to examine what motivated both Stephanie and Rothermere, shedding light on the murky goings-on behind the scenes in Britain, Germany and the USA before and during the Second World War.

978 0 7524 6114 4

Visit our website and discover thousands of other History Press books.

www.thehistorypress.co.uk